Low Maintenance Gardening

The TIME LIFE
Complete ☀ Gardener

Low Maintenance
Gardening

By the Editors of Time-Life Books
ALEXANDRIA, VIRGINIA

The Consultants

Jeff Cox is the author of numerous books on gardening, including *The Perennial Garden* (1985), *How to Grow Vegetables Organically* (1988), *Landscaping with Nature* (1990), and *Creating a Garden for the Senses* (1993), which won the 1994 Garden Writers' Association of America Annual Award for Writing. He has been managing editor of *Organic Gardening* and has written columns for the magazine for the past 25 years. Cox also writes "The Kitchen Gardener," a column in the *San Francisco Chronicle,* and is host of the PBS television series *Your Organic Garden.* He consults in the areas of horticulture, landscape design, and winemaking.

Robert S. Hebb is a horticultural consultant, garden designer, and frequent lecturer on gardening. He received a diploma of horticulture from the Royal Botanic Gardens in Kew, then became assistant horticulturist for the Arnold Arboretum of Harvard University, where he wrote the pioneering book *Low Maintenance Perennials*. Hebb has been director of horticulture for the Mary Flagler Cary Arboretum of the New York Botanical Garden and executive director of the Lewis Ginter Botanical Garden in Richmond, Virginia. The recipient of the Massachusetts Horticultural Society Silver Medal for leadership in American horticulture, Hebb is the author of numerous works on low-maintenance gardening and oversees several estate gardens in the Richmond area.

Time-Life Books is a division of **TIME LIFE INC.**

PRESIDENT and CEO: John M. Fahey Jr.
EDITOR-IN-CHIEF: John L. Papanek

TIME-LIFE BOOKS

Managing Editor: Roberta Conlan

Director of Design: Michael Hentges
Director of Editorial Operations: Ellen Robling
Director of Photography and Research:
John Conrad Weiser
Senior Editors: Russell B. Adams Jr., Dale M. Brown,
Janet Cave, Lee Hassig, Robert Somerville,
Henry Woodhead
Special Projects Editor: Rita Thievon Mullin
Director of Technology: Eileen Bradley
Library: Louise D. Forstall

PRESIDENT: John D. Hall

Vice President, Director of Marketing:
Nancy K. Jones
Vice President, Director of New Product Development:
Neil Kagan
Vice President, Book Production: Marjann Caldwell
Production Manager: Marlene Zack
Quality Assurance Manager: James King

THE TIME-LIFE COMPLETE GARDENER

Editorial Staff for *Low Maintenance Gardening*

SERIES EDITOR: Janet Cave
Deputy Editors: Sarah Brash, Jane Jordan
Administrative Editor: Roxie France-Nuriddin
Art Directors: Cindy Morgan-Jaffe (principal), Alan Pitts
Picture Editor: Jane A. Martin
Text Editors: Sarah Brash (principal), Darcie Conner
Johnston, Paul Mathless
Associate Editors/Research-Writing: Sharon Kurtz,
Katya Sharpe, Robert Speziale
Technical Assistant: Sue Pratt
Senior Copyeditor: Anne Farr
Picture Coordinator: David Herod
Editorial Assistant: Donna Fountain
Special Contributors: Jennifer Clark (picture research);
Jamie R. Holland, Marianna Tait-Durbin, André Viette,
Cheryl Weber (research-writing); Marfé Ferguson-
Delano, Rita Pelczar (writing); Marge duMond (edit-
ing); John Drummond (design); Lina B. Burton (index)

Correspondents: Christine Hinze (London), Christina
Lieberman (New York). Valuable assistance was also
provided by Liz Brown (New York).

Library of Congress Cataloging in Publication Data
Low maintenance gardening / by the editors of Time-Life Books.
 p. cm.—(The Time-Life complete gardener)
Includes bibliographical references (p.) and index.
ISBN 0-7835-4101-5   1. Landscape gardening. 2. Low maintenance
gardening. 3. Plants, ornamental. 4. Landscape gardening—United
States. 5. Low maintenance gardening—United States. 6. Plants, Or-
namental—United States. I. Time-Life Books. II. Series
SB473.L69 1995 635.9—dc20   94-40455   CIP
School and library distribution by Time-Life Education, P.O. Box
85026, Richmond, Virginia 23285-5026.

TIME-LIFE is a trademark of Time Warner Inc. U.S.A.

This volume is one of a series of comprehensive gardening books
that cover garden design, choosing plants for the garden, planting
and propagating, and planting diagrams.

Cover: Sun-warmed reed grass is a backdrop for such easy-care plants as purple coneflower, rudbeckia, and, in the foreground, a potted climbing shrub, allamanda. *End papers:* Miscanthus sinensis dominates a planting that includes nicotiana and Stewartia pseudocamellia, a small pest-resistant tree with year-round interest. *Title page:* Joe-Pye weed blooms at the center of this natural garden, surrounded by Miscanthus sinensis, yellow flowering cassia, Artemisia lactiflora, and the dried seed heads of Rudbeckia maxima.

CONTENTS

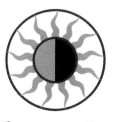

CHAPTER ONE

Designing for Low Maintenance

Few of us can dedicate endless time and energy to our gardens, however much we might like to. Fortunately, it's possible to have a garden that is beautiful and at the same time easy to care for. The secret of low-maintenance gardening is careful analysis and thoughtful design: You need to decide which areas of the garden and which functions are important to you and focus your attention on these.

Preparing your site to ensure good growing conditions and choosing plants that are in harmony with your environment will more than repay you in time saved over the years. Such initial investment has made the Atlanta garden shown here amazingly self-sufficient. Pests are rare, the grasses and perennials defy heat and drought, and there's little to do except a late-winter cleanup, when the grasses are cut to the ground.

Work is work. But with the techniques presented in this book, you'll be able to streamline routine chores. The burden they represent will seem lighter when the garden serves you well and gives you pleasure, season in and season out.

A. *Miscanthus sinensis 'Gracillimus' (3)*
B. *Pennisetum alopecuroides (1)*
C. *Rudbeckia fulgida sullivantii 'Goldsturm' (15)*
D. *Yucca sp. (2)*
E. *Verbena canadensis 'Rosea' (10)*

The key lists each plant type and the total quantity needed to replicate the garden shown. The diagram's letters and numbers refer to the type of plant and the number sited in an area.

Developing a Low Maintenance Approach

AN EASY, INFORMAL ENTRANCE
By opting to edge their front walk with informal, easy-care plants, including the summer-blooming tawny double kwanzo daylilies above, the owners of this Victorian home in Missouri avoid spending time staking, deadheading, and performing other labor-intensive chores that other, high-maintenance perennials would require.

Creating a garden that's easy to care for may mean retraining your eye and rethinking your concept of how a garden should look. Big lawns flanked by immaculate borders of perennials and annuals are a popular feature in the American landscape. The look can be lovely—but to keep it that way requires constant attention, especially during the growing season when the need to battle weeds, to water, to mow the grass, and to perform other tasks such as staking, deadheading, and cutting back flowering plants is at its peak.

The low-maintenance approach to such a garden would be to abandon the status quo. In conservative hands, some of the perennials and annuals would yield their places to shrubs and ground covers, plants that are handsome in their own right and require relatively little care. The work thus saved on weeding, dividing, and other tedious chores could make the upkeep of the lawn a manageable affair. In radical hands, the garden might undergo even more extensive changes, with mixed plantings of shrubs, small ornamental trees, ground covers, and perennials occupying widened borders and new island beds taking up much—even most—of the space originally given over to turf grass.

Also on the low-maintenance gardener's hit list would be such time-gobbling features as precision-trimmed edgings and foundation plantings and shrubs that have grown spindly and have stopped flowering in the increasing shade cast by once-small trees.

The Cost of Going Low Maintenance

Remaking a high-upkeep garden, whether in a total sweep or a bit at a time, is a demanding business, but if it's done right the payoff is a reduction in workload for years to come. Doing it right entails several critical processes—thoughtful design, intelligent plant selection *(pages 30-47)*, and good site preparation *(pages 66-73)*. All told, laying the foundation of a successful low-maintenance garden may require more time and labor than the initial

work for a conventional garden. Finally, a certain amount of courage is needed to tear out even part of an existing garden, unsatisfying though it may be.

Beginning the Design Process

The design process begins with an assessment of how your garden could serve you better and a realistic appraisal of how much time you'll have for tending it, especially during the growing season. Functional aspects to consider include how best to accommodate outdoor-living activities such as recreation

and entertaining. You'll also need to decide how much of the garden to leave in public view and how much to screen for privacy.

Other, more practical matters to take into account are traffic patterns linking house, garden, and street as well as convenient storage for garden equipment and furniture.

Keeping the list of such needs and desires in mind, the next step is to survey your garden's natural and constructed features (pages 14-17) to determine its assets and drawbacks. With this kind of preparation, you can tailor the garden to minimize the tasks you dislike and emphasize those you find satisfying. A garden should give pleasure, and low maintenance is one way to make that happen.

A TRIO OF RELIABLE PERFORMERS
An expanse of pachysandra encircling a Japanese maple reduces the area taken up by the lawn in this Richmond, Virginia, garden. The far side of the lawn is bordered with hosta, which, like the maple and the pachysandra, is a low-maintenance standby.

Keeping Your Garden's Water Needs in Bounds

NATIVE TEXANS
Undemanding native plants in this Austin xeriscape include yaupon hollies grouped around a Texas persimmon tree (below, right), blackfoot daisy, and yellow damianita. St. Augustine, a shade-tolerant non-native turf grass, needs less water if planted in dappled sunlight.

Watering is the most important gardening chore, and one that hardly any gardener can trust to nature alone. Erratic rainfall patterns or extended droughts during the growing season are the rule rather than the exception for most of the United States *(map, page 12)*.

When it comes to water, working with nature is far more rewarding and less complicated than trying to outwit it. And, if you design and plant your garden to make it not only beautiful but as self-sufficient as possible, you can count on reducing the time you spend on maintenance. This sensible, less adversarial approach to gardening is called xeriscaping.

The Xeriscape Approach

A new way of thinking about gardening, xeriscaping is a term that derives from *xeros*, the Greek word for dry and also the botanical term for drought, and from *landscape*. It

originated in the semiarid West in the early 1980s, but it is equally applicable to virtually every part of the United States.

There are seven basic guidelines to establishing a water-thrifty garden, all of which make good gardening sense:

- Plan and design comprehensively, taking your area's climatic conditions into account at every stage.
- Analyze your garden's soil and improve it to increase water retention.
- Create lawn areas of manageable sizes and shapes and plant them with grasses that are suited to the climate.
- Select plants that are well adapted to your area and group them according to their water needs.
- Irrigate efficiently by applying the right amount of water at the right time, using the right equipment.
- Use mulches extensively to keep the soil moist and cool and to reduce the growth of weeds.
- Adopt routine maintenance practices that conserve water. These include mowing turf grass high, weeding regularly so that ornamental plants don't compete with weeds for moisture, and fertilizing sparingly.

The Benefits of Xeriscaping

Avoiding unnecessary watering, in itself a timesaver, also has timesaving consequences. Because the excessive growth that often results from overwatering is curtailed, a plant's need for nutrients—and therefore the need for fertilizer—is reduced. Also curbed is the production of excessively soft, waterlogged tissue that is prone to attack by insects, so fewer applications of pesticides may be necessary. And since efficient irrigation practices concentrate water where ornamental plants need it most instead of applying it wastefully to the whole garden, another consequence is

COLOR FOR CALIFORNIA'S DRY COASTAL CLIMATE
The April display put on by a mixed planting of drought-tolerant perennials and shrubs includes, clockwise from lower right, pink-and-white-flowered Santa Barbara daisies; Jerusalem sage, with yellow flowers; the pink Mexican evening primrose; sweet pea shrub, with small pinkish purple blooms; yellow daylilies; and a pale-flowered, stiffly upright westringia.

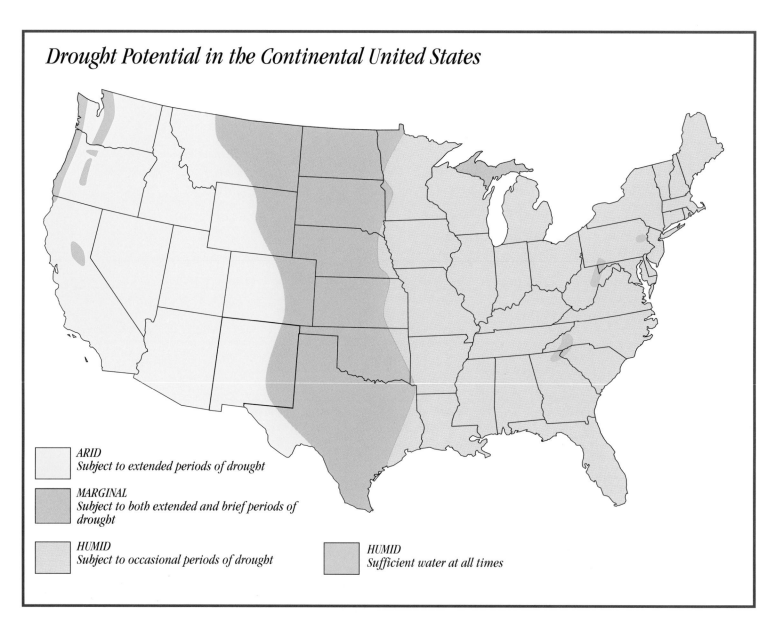

Drought Potential in the Continental United States

ARID
Subject to extended periods of drought

MARGINAL
Subject to both extended and brief periods of drought

HUMID
Subject to occasional periods of drought

HUMID
Sufficient water at all times

fewer weeds. Weed seeds that germinate readily in moist soil find the xeriscape garden's generally drier conditions inhospitable.

Besides the practical benefits of xeriscaping, there are aesthetic ones as well. When there's a good match between plants and their environment, there's a much better chance of strong, healthy growth and a fine display of flowers. In addition, a xeriscape remains in good condition even in the heat of summer, when more conventional landscapes all too often look parched and droopy.

Getting Started

Converting your garden to a xeriscape need not involve starting over. It may simply mean taking a close look at your garden's moisture supply and demand and replanting an area or two where those factors are out of balance. For instance, you may decide to plant daylilies or creeping mahonia on a steep, dry bank where keeping turf grass in decent condition has been a losing battle. Or you might remove the solitary but thirsty rosebush growing in the midst of trailing lantana, which blooms less profusely with frequent waterings.

Water-thrifty plants such as Russian sage, coreopsis, cotoneaster, catmint, and yucca are classic choices for a xeriscape. But there's no reason to restrict yourself solely to plants that tolerate drought. High-maintenance, water-demanding varieties can be part of a xeriscape without a burdensome amount of work as long as you plant them together instead of spotting them about here and there (*opposite*).

The Right Plants for the Right Place

Grouping plants with similar cultural and maintenance needs—a procedure known as zoning—is one of the surest ways offered by the xeriscape approach to cut work time in the garden. The major factor in dividing a garden into zones is water. You'll want to consider how convenient it is to irrigate different parts of your garden and whether you'll do it manually or with an automatic system *(pages 77-80)*. And, since the water-retentive capacity of soil varies greatly according to its structure and organic content, you'll need to familiarize yourself with your soil. Other factors to assess are soil pH and the distribution of light and shade.

Creating Zones

Unless a garden is unusually large, three zones—for high, moderate, and low water use—should suffice. The fewer zones you have, the easier watering will be. Too many zones also increase the chance of giving less thirsty plants too much water, which harms plants as much as not enough water. When you are blocking out your garden's zones and considering plant choices, keep these guidelines in mind:

- Limit the number of different kinds of plants.
- Keep lone-sited specimen plants to a minimum.
- Group plants in well-defined beds.
- Link zones by using transitional plants that tolerate different moisture levels.
- Use patios and other paved areas to separate water-use zones. Place drought-resistant plants next to pavement, which heats up in sunlight and causes the soil to dry out faster.

Sites for High Water Use

You may want to put your oasis, or zone of high water use, in an area close to the house, where plants will be both easier to water and harder to overlook. If your ground slopes,

you can take advantage of water's natural downward flow and place moisture-loving plants near the foot of the slope. Alternatively, site these plants in partial shade, which shields them from heat and direct sunlight and helps reduce water needs. But be flexible. If the best place for water- and sun-loving favorites such as roses lies at the periphery of your yard, and if you want them enough to be willing to spend the extra time and effort it will take to maintain them, then situate the oasis zone there.

Making the Most of Your Property's Unique Conditions

The more you know about the conditions prevailing in your garden, the more successful and satisfying your planting scheme will be. Some of the factors to be reckoned with operate on a very large scale—the temperature range in winter and in summer, the amount of rainfall and its distribution over the course of the year, and the intensity of sunlight.

At the opposite end of the spectrum is the highly localized environment, or microclimate, in which you live. Shaped by both climate and geography and the features of your property—the house and other structures, topography, existing vegetation, and the exposure to sunlight and wind—your microclimate may differ significantly from your next-door neighbor's.

In fact, you probably have not one but several microclimates to work with. The strip of shade beside a tall fence may be suitable for one group of plants, while another group will thrive in the brighter light of an open sunny area just a few feet away. These small-scale variations are not a curse but a blessing: They permit you to grow more kinds of plants than would be possible on a property with uniform conditions, and to grow them well.

Temperature in Your Garden

Nothing can kill a plant faster than temperature below the level it's adapted to, so be realistic when you're planning your garden. Keep the USDA hardiness zone in which you live firmly in mind *(zone map, page 108)* and choose from plants that have proved their ability to survive the winter in your region.

There are, of course, large variations within a zone, and you may enjoy a local climate that's milder than that of surrounding areas. Water acts as a buffer for temperature extremes—even a lake of modest size can moderate winter lows. And because cities are routinely warmer in summer and winter than their outlying suburbs, urban gardeners may be able to grow plants rated hardy only to the next zone south without any problem.

If you live near the limit of a plant's cold tolerance, search for a warm, sheltered pocket in which to grow it. South- or west-facing walls and fences absorb sunlight that is re-radiated as heat, thereby affording protection for cold-sensitive plants; heat transmitted from the house through a ground-level window can also create a hospitable spot. At the garden's edge, a tree canopy creates a sheltered environment, trapping the heat absorbed by soil during the day and making nights a little warmer than in an open area.

Just where warm and cool pockets are located isn't always obvious, however, so you may want to use a thermometer to check for variations. Leave it outside several nights in a row in different areas of your garden, recording the temperature early each morning. Close observation of your garden will also turn up clues. If, for instance, the seeds of the same annual germinate sooner in one part of your garden than in another, the difference may be due to temperature. In chilly weather, note where frost lingers in the morning.

Topography and Temperature

A garden's contours have a major impact on temperature, as well as on soil moisture. North-facing slopes, because they intercept less sunshine, are cooler year round than level ground and south-facing slopes. In winter, a north slope may be shaded virtually all day, and where winters are snowy, melting will be slower, allowing the ground more time to absorb the moisture. By contrast, a sunny, south-facing slope may get twice as much winter sun as a plot of level ground, or even more, depending on how steeply it rises. As a result, snow melts quickly, with more runoff and a greater chance of drought. The same holds true for rainfall.

Whatever the direction of a slope, its heights will be mild compared with the foot. Cold air, which is heavier than warm air, flows down and collects at the bottom of the incline. Rugged plants that withstand prolonged dormancy, such as rose of Sharon,

A Garden to Suit the Site

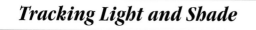

The landscaping on the north side of this house takes advantage of the summer shade. Erosion on the bank next to the terrace has been halted with a retaining wall on one side of the steps and a planting of daylilies on the other. Sited against the house's north wall, broadleaf evergreens are sheltered from winter sun and wind.

viburnums, lilacs, and inkberry, are good choices for these cold-air basins. If your garden lies at the bottom of a hill, Oregon grape holly may prove a more reliable broadleaf evergreen there than the winter daphne that will do nicely near the milder summit.

Tracking Light and Shade

A plant that lacks sufficient sunlight will never be a handsome specimen; its form will be distorted and its growth stunted. For a plant

Cold air flowing down a slope toward the south wall of this house passes over and around it (arrows). Part of the airflow is trapped between the slope and the house. The deciduous shrub planted there weathers the combination of low temperature and bright sun, which in winter might kill a broadleaf evergreen.

Planting a Windbreak

A wall of evergreens—eastern red cedars in this illustration—protects an area equal to at least double the height of the trees from damaging winds *(right)*. The long arrows trace the path of the wind that is deflected up and over the windbreak. Wind also blows through the trees, whose branches and foliage dissipate its force and slow it down, as indicated by the short arrows on either side of the trees. A solid wall of stone or brick makes a poor barrier against wind, producing strong eddies on the sheltered side that are harmful to plants. For an effective windbreak, plant two or three staggered rows of closely spaced trees *(inset);* the junipers shown here are set 5 to 6 feet apart.

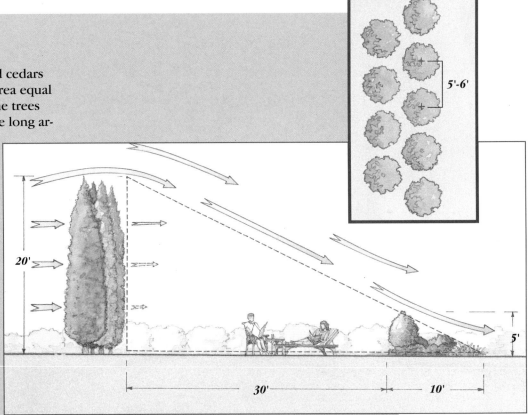

Clearing a Wind Channel

Removing the lower branches of large trees that impede air circulation—a process known as limbing up—allows a cooling breeze to flow into a garden. In the diagram at right, a pair of scarlet oaks has been limbed up to the level of the roof line. The dotted line indicates the extent of the growth that was pruned away. Good ventilation is particularly desirable in hot, humid climates, making the garden more livable and creating better growing conditions for plants.

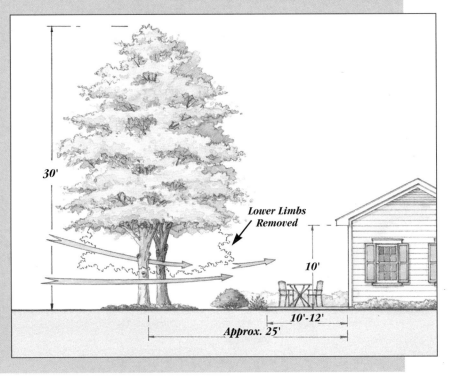

Evergreens for Windbreaks

Abies concolor (Colorado fir)	*Picea pungens* (Colorado spruce)
Cedrus atlantica 'Glauca' (blue Atlas cedar)	*Pinus strobus* (eastern white pine)
Juniperus scopulorum (western red cedar)	*Pinus sylvestris* (Scotch pine)
Juniperus virginiana (eastern red cedar)	*Pseudotsuga menziesii* (Douglas fir)
Picea abies (Norway spruce)	*Thuja occidentalis 'Nigra'* (American arborvitae)

Shade Trees to Limb Up

Acer rubrum (red maple)	*Quercus phellos* (willow oak)
Cladrastis kentukea (yellowwood)	*Quercus rubra* (red oak)
Nyssa sylvatica (black gum)	*Sophora japonica* (Japanese pagoda tree)
Quercus coccinea (scarlet oak)	*Tilia cordata* (littleleaf linden)

COMFORT ON WINDY DAYS
A slope rimmed with a windbreak of Pfitzer junipers and smothered by Algerian ivy protects this California terrace. Dwarf strawberry trees and pastel pansies ring the terrace.

needing full sun—some 6 hours of direct light daily—an unobstructed site facing south is, of course, ideal. However, a western exposure or an unobstructed eastern exposure usually provides enough light for sun-loving plants.

Bear in mind, though, that one important difference distinguishes east and west locations that receive equal amounts of light, and that is temperature: A site that receives afternoon sun will be hotter. In a garden that is near the southern limit of a plant's range, a bed with an eastern exposure is preferable to one with a western exposure that gets an equal amount of light during the day but may be too hot for the plant to perform well.

Heading Off Wind Damage

One factor that is easy to overlook when you're designing a planting is the impact of wind. Moving air can be highly beneficial to your plants, cooling them in hot weather and reducing the incidence of insects and diseases that sultry, stagnant air encourages. However, in a garden that is excessively windy, the cooling and drying effects may become so intensified that plants are harmed. Such damage is severest when wind is com-

bined with either freezing winter weather or summer drought.

Some broadleaf evergreens, including rhododendrons and camellias, are especially vulnerable to winter winds precisely because they retain their foliage year round. (Deciduous plants are nearly impervious to winter winds since they shed their leaves.) When sunshine warms a broadleaf evergreen, moisture is drawn out of its foliage. As long as the ground isn't frozen, the roots can replace the moisture lost. When the ground freezes, however, sun and wind together remove so much moisture that the plant suffers winterkill. The leaves turn brown and, if the desiccation is really severe, the plant dies.

A microclimate well suited to broadleaf evergreens is a bed against the north wall of a house or on the shady side of a tall hedge, either of which serve as shelter from the drying effect of the winter sun. You can create a microclimate in which a substantial portion of a garden will be shielded from the effect of cold winds by planting a windbreak. A windbreak is also in order if persistent winds in summer exacerbate drought. In either case, determine the prevailing direction of the wind and, as nearly as possible, plant the windbreak at a right angle to it *(opposite, top)*.

Taking the Work Out of a Lawn

A PLACE FOR PERENNIALS
Planting 'White Nancy' lamium, pink columbine, and other perennials between two grassy areas does away with the awkward job of mowing and trimming around the posts and along the base of the fence in this Richmond, Virginia, country garden.

Traditional turf-grass lawns remain the most popular garden treatment in the United States, and for good reason. Restful to the eye, cushiony underfoot, and remarkable in its ability to withstand wear and tear, an expanse of velvety lawn in the front yard serves as an inviting transition between the public reaches of a property and the security and privacy of the house.

As a design element, a lawn defines the open spaces of a yard. It provides a calm, green horizontal plane for the garden's verticals—trees and tall shrubs, house, fences, walls. Simple and monochromatic, a lawn helps unify the varied shapes, colors, and textures of other plantings into a pleasing, harmonious landscape.

Well-kept turf adds value to a property and often prompts appreciative comments from neighbors and passersby. Likewise, a badly maintained lawn may elicit reproach. A lawn beset with bare spots, overgrown with weeds, and riddled with anthills and vole runs can ruin a landscape.

The Environmental Impact of Lawns

Lawn grasses help purify the air, releasing oxygen and reducing pollutants such as sulfur dioxide and ground-level ozone. They also reduce glare, moderate temperatures, and control erosion. Like other kinds of dense, low-growing vegetation, turf grasses collect rain and irrigation water, and the underlying soil filters out impurities as the water percolates down. This filtering helps maintain the quality of underground aquifers. Of course, that quality will be compromised if the lawn has been treated with pesticides and fertilized excessively.

The Unpampered Lawn

The many benefits a lawn confers exact a price in terms of mowing, irrigating, edging, applying pesticides and herbicides, weeding,

Choosing a Turf Grass

The chart below describes 12 common lawn grasses—five cool-season grasses, which thrive in spring and fall; five warm-season grasses, which perform best in summer heat; and two native grasses noted for their adaptability. Grasses have two growth habits: Bunch grasses grow as single plants that clump together, and sod-forming grasses spread by runners. The growing zones recommended for each grass appear on the map at right. At zone borders, both cool- and warm-season grasses are grown.

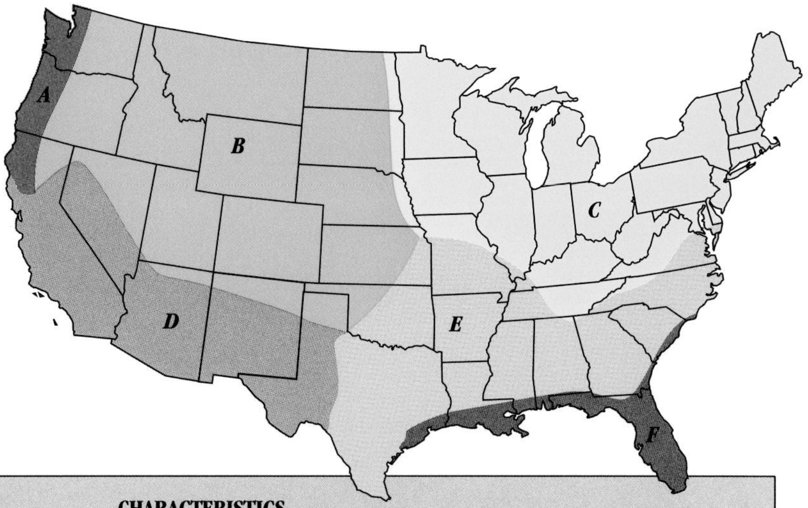

	GRASSES	CHARACTERISTICS								
		Texture & Appearance	*Drought Tolerance*	*Heat Tolerance*	*Cold Tolerance*	*Light Requirements*	*Disease Susceptibility*	*Fertilizer Needs*	*Wear Tolerance*	*Zones*
Cool Season	**Bent grass**	Very fine bladed; bright green; dense bunch or sod	Very low	Low	Very high; thrives in cool, humid climates	Full sun; tolerates very light shade	High	High; 4 to 6 lbs. per 1,000 sq. ft. per year	Moderate to low	A and northern parts of C
Cool Season	**Kentucky bluegrass**	Medium- to fine-bladed; medium green; dense sod	Moderate	Moderate	High	Full sun; tolerates very light shade	Moderate	Moderate to high; 3 to 5 lbs. per 1,000 sq. ft. per year	Moderate to high	A, B, C
Cool Season	**Fine fescue**	Very fine bladed; medium to deep green; bunch or sod	Moderate to high	Moderate	High	Full sun to part shade	Moderate to high	Low; up to 2 lbs. per 1,000 sq. ft. per year	Low	A, B, C
Cool Season	**Tall fescue**	Medium- to coarse-bladed; light to medium green; bunch	High	High	Moderate	Full sun to light shade	Moderate	Moderate; 2 to 4 lbs. per 1,000 sq. ft. per year	Moderate	A, B, C, western parts of D
Cool Season	**Perennial ryegrass**	Medium-bladed; shiny medium to dark green; bunch	Low	Moderate to low	Moderate	Full sun to light shade	High	High; 4 to 5 lbs. per 1,000 sq. ft. per year	High	Northern parts of D and E; southern parts of B and C
Warm Season	**Bahia grass**	Tough, coarse-bladed; light green; dense bunch	High	High	Low	Full sun to light shade; tolerates some part shade	Low	Moderate; 2 to 4 lbs. per 1,000 sq. ft. per year	Moderate	F, southern parts of E
Warm Season	**Bermuda grass**	Fine-bladed; medium to dark green; dense sod	High	High	Moderate to low	Full sun	Moderate	Moderate; 2 to 4 lbs. per 1,000 sq. ft. per year	High	D, E, F
Warm Season	**Centipede grass**	Medium-bladed; light green; sod	Moderate	High	Moderate to low	Full sun to light shade; tolerates some part shade	Low	Low; up to 2 lbs. per 1,000 sq. ft. per year	Moderate to low	F, southern parts of E
Warm Season	**St. Augustine grass**	Coarse-bladed; bluish green to medium green; sod	Moderate	High	Very low	Full sun to part shade	Moderate	Moderate to high; 3 to 5 lbs. per 1,000 sq. ft. per year	Moderate to low	D and F; southern parts of E
Warm Season	**Zoysia grass**	Medium-bladed; medium green; dense sod	Moderate to high	High	Moderate to high	Full sun to light shade; tolerates some part shade	Low	Low; up to 3 lbs. per 1,000 sq. ft. per year	Very high	D, E, F
American Native	**Blue grama grass**	Medium-bladed; grayish green; bunch or sod	Very high	Very high	High	Full sun	Low	Very low; less than 1 lb. per 1,000 sq. ft. per year	Moderate to low	B, D, western parts of C and E
American Native	**Buffalo grass**	Fine-bladed; light green to grayish green; sod	Very high	High	Moderate to high	Full sun; some new hybrids tolerate light shade	Moderate	Very low; less than 2 lbs. per 1,000 sq. ft. per year	Moderate to low	B, D

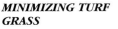

MINIMIZING TURF GRASS
In a reversal of conventional proportions, turf grass in the Lincoln City, Oregon, garden at right has been restricted to a narrow path between wide borders planted with a mixture of shrubs, perennials, and ground covers. The brilliant splash of red azalea and red and orange tulips is tempered by the cool blue spikes of ajuga in the foreground.

Rules for Designing Practical Turf Areas

- Reduce the size of the lawn. As a work saver, this step is second only to choosing the right grass type. It reduces the outlay for fertilizers, lime, and other lawn-care products and enhances the lawn's visual impact, making it an important feature rather than simply a background for plantings.
- Make the lawn compact, with a relatively small perimeter. Less water will be wasted in sprinkler overspray and in the faster evaporation that takes place at a lawn's edge. The most compact shape is a circle, followed by a shape with right angles.
- Make the lawn as level as possible to make mowing easier and to minimize water runoff.
- Don't plant grass along the base of a wall, a fence, or in any other hard-to-mow spots that will need hand trimming.
- Edge the lawn with masonry or rot-resistant wood set flush with the soil to eliminate the need for clipping and to prevent grass from encroaching upon neighboring plantings.

fertilizing, and reseeding. The price is high indeed for perfectionists who want a lawn that's as flawless as a putting green. For much less work, however, it's possible to have a perfectly satisfactory and healthy lawn. In fact, a less rigorous regimen can actually make turf grass more vigorous and self-sufficient, and it also results in reduced exposure to potentially toxic chemicals.

The practice of keeping grass mowed very short, for example, is abandoned in the low-maintenance garden. When grass is mowed high, it is softer and more luxurious. More important, the taller blades of grass cast shadows that cool the roots and retard the evaporation of soil moisture. The consequence is a lawn that is more resistant to heat and drought—and is less work, because it needs less watering and is better able to resist disease. Other maintenance practices, such as occasional dethatching and aerating *(page 83),* also help ensure the vigor and good looks of your lawn without resorting to chemical fertilizers, herbicides, pesticides, and disease controls that make turf increasingly reliant on human intervention.

Grasses for Your Climate

One of the best forms of insurance against unnecessary lawn tending is to plant a grass that's appropriate for your region. Grasses are divided into two types—cool-season and warm-season. Cool-season grasses perform best in northern climates, staying green in the winter and thriving in the spring and fall, but frequently turning brown during the hottest days of summer even when they're watered copiously. Warm-season grasses, on the other hand, are better in southern regions, where they grow vigorously during the heat of summer; in cool weather they turn tan and go dormant, and they are slow to green up in the spring.

In the hot, arid climates of the West or Southwest, attempting to grow a water-thirsty, cool-season turf grass such as Kentucky bluegrass is pointless. It would require intensive care and maintenance even to survive, let alone look good. A better choice would be buffalo grass or blue grama grass, both of which are natives that are adapted to

dry, alkaline soils. Buffalo grass formerly had to be sown from seed and tended to clump, but new cultivars of the grass such as 'Prairie' and '609' form a dense, springy sod that is extremely drought tolerant. Blue grama grass is equally tough. It can survive on as little as 5 inches of water a year, is hardy to -20 F, and tolerates light shade.

Selecting a Grass

The chart on page 19 describes the varieties of grass that are recommended for your climate. You can also use the chart to compare the demands that different types of grass will make on you. For instance, if you live in an area where both cool-season Kentucky bluegrass and warm-season zoysia can be grown, you may decide to forgo bluegrass despite its fine texture and the fact that it is green nearly year round. Zoysia, though tan in winter and somewhat coarser in texture, is easier to maintain because it needs less fertilizer, is less prone to disease, and is better able to tolerate drought.

A LAWN LOOK-ALIKE
Mowed just once a year before new growth appears in spring, the large planting of mondo grass in this Atlanta, Georgia, yard never needs fertilizing. A brick edging keeps the tough, drought-resistant ground cover from creeping into the adjoining bed filled with lavender hydrangeas and fronted with dwarf hollies. The edging doubles as a narrow footpath; unlike turf grasses, mondo grass doesn't stand up well to foot traffic. But if trampled, it will spring back in a few days.

The type of grass you choose will probably fit most conditions prevailing in your lawn area, but perhaps not all of them. For that reason, it's wise to buy a seed mixture containing several varieties of different grasses that may vary in their resistance or susceptibility to certain diseases and in their ability to accommodate different growing conditions and soil. Fortunately, improvements in vigor and in disease and drought resistance have been bred into many of the new strains now available.

Designs for Easier Care

The size and shape of a lawn, its contours, and its boundaries can be changed to lighten the maintenance burden it imposes on the gardener; the box on page 20 offers several design alternatives. Clearly, shrinking the lawn confers instant benefits. Island beds mixing shrubs, trees, perennials, and ground cover are handsome alternatives to turf, as are hard-surfaced areas such as patios, decks, or walkways *(pages 24-25)*.

You may want to go so far as to completely reverse the standard relationship between the lawn and other plantings. In such a design scenario, the turf area becomes no more than a wide pathway flanked by masses of perennials and shrubs. If you do convert part of the lawn to other uses, however, be careful not to create a patchwork of separate grassy areas lest you make watering and mowing more—rather than less—difficult.

Another design possibility retains the amount of space devoted to grass but uses it in two different ways. A lawn planted with a traditional turf grass, which requires relatively high maintenance, might go close to the house, where such a velvety carpet would be highly visible and accessible. A second area, sited at some distance from the house, would be planted with meadow grasses such as crested wheatgrass, smooth bromegrass, or little bluestem grass, depending upon the region in which you live. These grasses withstand temperature extremes, require little or no watering even during droughts, and have root systems dense enough to smother many weeds. The meadow grasses, which grow to a height of 1½ to 3 feet, should be mowed at least once a year to discourage woody invaders. A midsummer mowing is most effective, but if you don't want to sacrifice a display of summer wildflowers, wait until late fall, after a heavy frost.

A Place for Ground Covers

Whatever a gardener's appetite for work, there are places where lawns never belong, such as slopes that are too steep to mow safely, rocky, uneven ground, and excessively shaded areas. In such cases, the realistic gardener opts for a ground cover. There are many dozens to choose from, and they can be woody or herbaceous, evergreen or deciduous. The Plant Selection Guide on pages 102-107 and the Encyclopedia beginning on page 110 will help you make appropriate choices.

Given the large numbers of plants that can be pressed into service as ground covers, the look of them need never be dull. Some offer flowers, others handsomely tinted and textured foliage. You can have a flat carpet, low swells of arching branches, or a bed of spiky leaves. Growing low and wide, typically at a rapid rate, ground covers create a weed-free blanket of attractive vegetation. Under shrubs and trees, such plants act as a living mulch, preserving moisture in the soil and cooling the earth. Planted around the perimeter of a lawn, a strip of ground cover serves as a low-maintenance border. The edges of an area of vinca, for example, can be occasionally mowed along with the grass; the plants will soon put out new shoots.

Choosing the Right Plant

It is always important to restrict yourself to plants whose growing requirements are easily met. This is paramount with ground covers—having to fuss with them defeats their role as work savers in the landscape.

A new planting, of course, must have regular weeding and watering. Depending on how closely the plants are spaced and their growth rate, after as little as a year (more likely after two) a well-chosen ground cover will make few demands on your time.

COVERING A ROCKY SLOPE
A dense carpet of blue-gray woolly thyme (above),
purplish arcticus thyme, and white-flowering
'Snowdrift' thyme thrives in a Pacific Northwest garden on a dry, infertile bank. At the top of the bank
are clumps of pink and red clarkia, an annual
easily grown from scattered seed.

**A MOWABLE
PERIMETER**
The pachysandra grow-
ing alongside a lawn
of fine fescue and Ken-
tucky bluegrass puts out
new shoots to replace
the stems that are cut
off in the course of
mowing. In contrast
to most turf grasses,
pachysandra performs
well in part shade.

Durable Surfaces
for the Garden

Plants are the life of any garden, but there are many places where they should give way to something more durable and permanent. City dwellers, for instance, may confront so much shade and such poor soil that it makes sense to pave a large portion of the garden instead of undertaking a full-scale, backbreaking course of soil amendment. A suburbanite might find the bulldozer-compacted ground beside a house to be the perfect place for a brick terrace, and a soggy depression in the yard might be handily disguised by a low deck. And, beyond sheer practicalities, surfaces of brick, stone, concrete, wood, or gravel make the garden more livable and create visual links between your plantings and other areas of your property.

Easy-Care Surfaces

Although constructing a permanent, durable surface may mean a major initial expenditure of time, labor, and money, there are attractive trade-offs. Installing a walkway, terrace, or deck eliminates the effort involved, both short-term and long-term, in establishing and maintaining plants in the area. Paving, if properly installed, is virtually maintenance free. Sweeping off fallen leaves and occasional hosings are minor chores that can be accomplished quickly.

Gravel, crushed rock, and other loose surfacing materials have the advantage of being relatively inexpensive, but they usually require more upkeep. There are ways to minimize it, however. One is to lay the materials over landscape fabric. This will block weeds and make the stray weeds that do occasionally take root in the gravel or rock easier to rake or pick out. Don't, however, use loose surfacing materials where deciduous trees and shrubs will shed leaves on them; the leaves will be hard to rake.

For more on maintenance needs, characteristics, and tips on how to use the most popular surfacing materials, see the box on the opposite page.

Hardscaping Materials

GRANITE SETTS
These sturdy rectangular blocks, long used for paving streets, are available in the size of a brick or a half brick; the half-brick size works well in circular designs. Hand-hewn granite setts are more irregular in shape and more natural looking than the wire-cut variety.

BRICK
Easy to cut and lay in sand or in mortar, brick is the most popular kind of garden paver. Sand-finished, glazed-face brick has an especially smooth surface that is highly weather resistant and easier to keep clean than common brick, which is rougher textured and more porous.

COBBLES
Ranging from 2 to 12 inches in diameter and smoothed and rounded by water erosion, cobbles are generally gray or tan but sometimes have a pink, plum, or blue cast. They can be set in concrete or used loose in a dry watercourse, where they provide fast drainage.

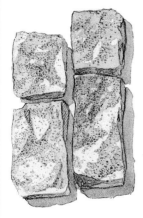

WOOD
The heartwoods of red cedar, bald cypress, and redwood are outstanding choices for decks and walkways because they resist rot and can be left to weather naturally. Woods that are more prone to decay must be sealed to repel water and reduce warping and cracking.

GRAVEL
These small, rounded, naturally occurring stones allow fast drainage but scatter easily. Paths or terraces of gravel need edgings to keep the stones in place. To control weeds, rake the gravel periodically.

CRUSHED ROCK
Rock crushed mechanically yields small, sharp-edged pieces. Available in a variety of distinctive colors and textures, crushed rock compacts well. It is used as a base for paths and terraces and as a surfacing material for high-traffic walkways, driveways, and parking areas.

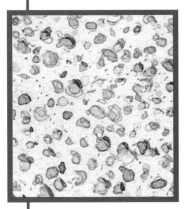

CONCRETE AGGREGATE
Economical for covering large areas, concrete aggregate is a mixture of sand, cement, and gravel. It is poured over an area and, when nearly dry, brushed to expose the gravel. The surface texture varies from fine to coarse, depending on the size of the gravel used and the depth of the brushing.

TILE
Terra-cotta, ceramic, and quarry tiles are suitable for use outdoors only in areas that are free of frost. Glazed tiles resist stains, but they are more slippery when wet than the unglazed kinds. Tile is a very expensive material, but it is highly prized for its decorative value.

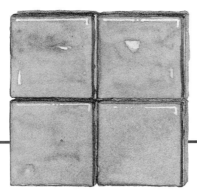

CONCRETE PAVERS
Concrete pavers come in many shapes, sizes, colors, and textures. Versatile, durable, and inexpensive, they can be laid in sand or mortar or, alternatively, placed atop level soil and interplanted with creeping herbs or ground cover.

STONE PAVERS
Ready-cut stone—usually granite, limestone, quartzite, sandstone, or slate—can be set in sand or mortar. It is available in geometric shapes suited to a repeat pattern or as irregularly shaped stones for free-form designs. Durability, slipperiness, and resistance to frost varies among stone types and should be considered when selecting stone pavers.

25

Forging a Partnership with Nature

A residential garden in which native plants are simply allowed to grow wild isn't much of a garden. By definition, gardening involves human intervention in nature. If, however, you draw inspiration from the terrain and climate that characterize your area, your garden will be an artful variation on the local theme. The look will be one of harmony rather than of competition.

TIPS FROM THE PROS

The Menace of Deer

White-tailed deer in the eastern United States and mule deer in the West can do enormous damage in your garden. Creatures of habit that feed from sunset to dawn, deer are especially likely to make regular feeding grounds of those places they pass on their way to water. Among their favorite foods are fleshy, moisture-laden leaves, buds and blossoms, and the bark of young stems. If a tree is girdled by a deer's gnawing—that is, a complete ring of bark is torn away—the plant may die.

To thwart these pests, gardeners have tried such deterrents as hanging nylon stockings containing scented soap or human hair in the garden. These may discourage deer if the animals can find ample food elsewhere, but not when food is in short supply. Commercial sprays applied to plants as soon as growth appears, after every rain, and at least once a week during the growing season are sometimes effective, but such frequent spraying is a lot of work. Chicken-wire cages can be placed around young plants,

and tree wrap will prevent bark stripping. A fence at least 7 feet high offers certain protection, but it's an expensive solution and may detract from the character of your garden.

Another tack is to choose at least some plants that deer find unappetizing. Few plants are totally safe from browsing, but there are a number that are unpalatable enough that they'll be eaten only if nothing else is available and the animal is very hungry. Deer sometimes leave favorite plants alone if they are planted with some of these more resistant types. Plants unattractive to deer include:
- Plants with tough, wiry mature growth (yucca, nandina)
- Strong-flavored herbs and perennials (rosemary, mint, santolina, artemisia, yarrow, salvia, lamb's ears)
- Spiny plants (holly, devil's-walking-stick). Unfortunately, deer feed on roses despite their thorns.
- Leathery-leaved trees and shrubs (mahonia, skimmia)
- Poisonous plants (oleander, mountain laurel)

Letting Nature Set the Tone

Perhaps the two best examples of this kind of collaboration with nature are a garden shaped by a woodland environment where rainfall is plentiful and a garden dictated by desert conditions. Beneath a canopy of trees, the air is more humid and its temperature is lower in summer and milder in winter than in open, unshaded spaces. The surface of the ground also remains cooler, and the litter of decaying vegetation makes the soil both high in organic content and acidic. A large variety of low-growing herbaceous plants, some valued for their flowers and others for their striking foliage, will thrive in the cool, moist conditions and filtered sunlight of the woodland floor. The shrubs and small trees, both deciduous and evergreen, that form the understory serve as windbreaks, privacy screens, and accent ornamentals. The overall

Building a Woodland Path

A path surfaced with woodchips or shredded bark and kept in place with a benderboard edging lends a casual, relaxed air to a garden. Once you've decided on an approximate route, use garden hoses as stand-ins for the edges of the path. Curve the path and vary its width to add interest; make it widest at areas where you want people to pause and look around. When you're satisfied with the layout, mark the path's edges with lime, remove the hoses, and clear all vegetation from the outlined path.

You'll need enough 1-by-4 rot-resistant benderboard to edge each side of the path. Along each edge dig a trench about 3½ inches deep. Remove roots and rocks from the trench.

A WOODLAND DESTINATION
An informal path surfaced with shredded bark leads to a hammock hanging between two massive Douglas firs in this Pacific Northwest shade garden. Softening the walkway's edges are irregularly spaced clumps of stinking hellebore, which spill their dark green fingerlike foliage onto the path. The shade-loving yellow corydalis in the foreground provides color for most of the summer.

1. Set a length of benderboard into one of the trenches, bending it to fit. *Drive stakes into the ground beside the board at intervals of no more than 4 feet; alternate placing the stakes on the inside and the outside of the board. Using a piece of 2-by-4 as a brace, nail each stake to the board (above). Saw off each stake top at a bevel, making the upper end of the bevel even with the benderboard's upper edge. Repeat for all of the benderboard, then fill the outside of the trench with soil.*

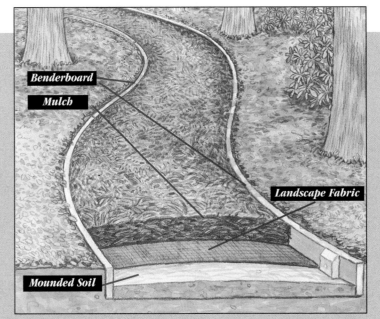

Benderboard

Mulch

Landscape Fabric

Mounded Soil

2. Excavate the area between the benderboards to a depth of 4 inches. *To ensure good drainage, mound some soil in the center and tamp it down so it is about 1 inch higher than the sides. Cover the soil with woven landscape fabric to discourage weeds, then add a mulch of bark or woodchips to within ¼ inch of the top of the benderboards. Let the material settle for a day or two, and fill in any depressions.*

effect of the garden is one of informality, serenity, and enclosure.

By contrast, in sunny, arid climates where erratic rainfall patterns, hot, drying winds, and alkaline soil prevail, spiny, sculptural cacti and succulents are at home. Their foliage is compact and has a waxy coating that reduces water loss. Following nature's example and allowing ample space between these sturdy specimens ensures they do not compete with each other for the little water and few nutrients available. This planting practice lends a spare, uncluttered look and an architectural character to the garden landscape.

Enhancing the Woodland Perimeter

An ideal site on which to establish a low-maintenance garden lies at the edge of a rural woodland or in a tree-shaded suburban setting. The garden forms a transition zone between two sheltered sites—the house and the woodland. Removing some trees or limbing them up to increase sunlight can enhance the natural environment by encouraging a greater diversity of plants. Native mountain laurels can then be partnered with shrubs that need slightly more light—azaleas, rhododendrons, and hydrangeas—and that offer a succession of bloom through spring and summer. Many viburnums also thrive in partial shade and provide red or orange fall foliage as well as berries for birds.

Constructing walls, terraces, and other architectural features from local materials underscores a woodland garden's relationship to the region. In the hill country of Texas, limestone would be a good choice for building a raised bed, whereas in the Northeast, schist and granite have been used for centuries to erect unmortared stone walls.

Paths of earth or shredded bark heighten the sense of the garden as a restful, private retreat. A wide range of plants can overflow the paths and provide year-round appeal. The early blooms of winter aconite and Siberian squill can be followed by daffodils. Dutchman's-breeches and ferns appear, to be followed in late spring and early summer by false Solomon's-seal. Still later come wild blue phlox and hardy amaryllis with blossoms that range in color from rose to lilac.

You may want to leave an area undisturbed to see whether native plants such as spotted

orange jewelweed or white wood aster appear. A brush pile, well screened from view, will provide shelter for birds and small mammals such as chipmunks; and a dead tree, if it poses no threat and is camouflaged with a vine, will draw woodpeckers. Some animals are less welcome—deer in particular, which are surprisingly common in well-populated suburbs and can devastate a garden. See the box on page 26 for tips on discouraging deer.

Gardening at the Desert's Edge

A garden at the edge of a woodland is an opening between two sheltered havens. A garden abutting the vast openness of a desert, however, acts as a gradual transition to the shelter of the house. Choosing well-adapted plants is especially critical in the unforgiving climate of a hot desert garden. Among the most valuable are the spiky evergreen yuccas, agaves, and aloes, whose stiff, fanlike shapes can be combined with fine-textured shrubs such as creosote bush and ephedra.

Adding organic matter to make the soil more water retentive is a priority, as is keeping plants mulched. Fertilizing should be done sparingly, however, since accelerating a plant's growth rate increases its need for water.

It's also important to create shade and shelter, for both plants and people. Planted in the open garden, deep-rooted trees such as carob, acacia, and olive can tap underground reserves of moisture and cast pools of shade that slow the evaporation of surface moisture and cool the soil a little. A high-walled courtyard shelters and shades less drought-tolerant species such as bearded iris, Texas bluebonnet, trumpet vine, and woodbine honeysuckle. These plants will give concentrated doses of color in a place where they're easy for the gardener to tend and enjoy.

A SIMPLE PLANTING FOR A HARSH HILLSIDE
Upright clumps of silvery green rubber rabbitbrush form a backdrop for purple-flowered spike gay-feather and a scattering of red and yellow gaillardia. Winter jasmine cascades down the wall beside the entrance to this Santa Fe home and into the courtyard.

Furnishing the Low Maintenance Garden

All gardeners by definition love plants. The gardener who aims to save time and work, however, tempers that passion. Instead of indulging in impulse buying or selecting plants on the basis of looks alone, he or she adopts a more methodical and ultimately more rewarding approach. Each shrub or tree, ground cover or perennial is evaluated in terms of its function in an overall plan, how well it is adapted to the conditions prevailing in the garden, and its resistance to pests and diseases.

In short, the gardener seeks out plants, both native and imported from other countries, that will largely take care of themselves. This in no way compromises the garden's beauty, as is demonstrated by the easy-care Charlotte, North Carolina, garden shown here. Pictured in springtime, the plantings remain a captivating composition of color, shape, and texture in every season.

A. *Hosta undulata (2)* **B.** *Aquilegia canadensis (3)* **C.** *Rhododendron hybrid (1)* **D.** *Lobelia cardinalis (4)* **E.** *Adiantum raddianum 'Grandiceps' (1)* **F.** *Pachysandra terminalis (3)* **G.** *Ajuga reptans 'Bronze Beauty' (7)* **H.** *Valeriana officinalis (1)* **I.** *Nandina domestica 'Harbour Dwarf' (1)* **J.** *Iris sibirica 'Alba' (1)* **K.** *Magnolia virginiana (1)* **L.** *Acer palmatum 'Dissectum Atropurpureum' (1)* **M.** *Rhododendron hybrid (1)* **N.** *Prunus laurocerasus 'Schipkaensis' (1)*

Easy Care Plants for Your Low Maintenance Garden

Any plant you consider for your low-maintenance garden should meet a fairly stringent set of requirements. It has to look good through a long season without a lot of up-keep; it must be reasonably tolerant of less-than-perfect soil and climate conditions; and it should be resistant to common pests and diseases. Of course, no garden will thrive in the absence of any care whatsoever. But you can minimize the maintenance chores by starting with the right plants.

Good Looks with Little Fuss

The foundation of a low-maintenance garden usually includes nicely behaved trees, as well as shrubs and ground covers. Once established, woody plants need only modest attention, and ground covers help reduce routine tasks like weeding. While many hardy perennials, including daylilies and peonies, add color with little fuss, you can also enjoy flowers blooming on your ground covers, shrubs, and trees. In addition, berries on pyracanthas, hollies, and viburnums add bright summer or fall accents that may last into winter. Other low-maintenance plants—Japanese maple and the purple-leaved smokebush, for example—display beautiful foliage during spring, summer, or fall.

Some longtime favorites won't meet the conditions for low-maintenance gardening, however. Varieties of roses that host a number of pests, for instance, and succumb to intractable ills like black spot are out. Choose instead from the few hardy rose varieties that do make excellent easy-care plants *(page 155)*. Similarly, common lilac *(Syringa vulgaris)* fails the low-maintenance test. It is susceptible to disfiguring mildew and deadly borer and scale, and it tends to produce an abundance of suckers from its roots, which require pruning to keep the shrub in its place. Other plants you'll want to avoid are the messy ones, like the female ginkgo tree, which drops particularly foul-smelling fruit. The well-mannered male, however, makes an excellent shade tree.

Soil, Climate, and Site

Even the easiest-care plants perform better when their soil requirements are considered. Mountain laurel does best in acid soil similar to that of its woodland habitat, and drought-tolerant plants such as lamb's ears grow well in dry places but tend to rot in wet ones. You should also take into account your climate. A winter daphne might thrive in a warm garden microclimate, but the plant will die in severe cold. The sturdier fragrant viburnum, on the other hand, will reawake from those same conditions to produce its deliciously scented white flowers.

Your choice of plants will also depend on the job you want them to do. Most forsythias are fast-growing, large shrubs that need plenty of room; as a result they aren't suitable as foundation plants, where they would need to be tamed by barbering. A 'Heritage' river birch makes a fine tree for a garden because its light shade won't impede plant growth, but if you want to protect your house from the hot sun you will want the denser shade of an oak or a maple.

Knowing the Right Name

Although learning the Latin, or botanical, names of plants may seem like a lot of trouble, the knowledge will serve you well when you shop. Many plants have several common names, so you may not get what you want unless you know the botanical term. In addition, you'll need to know the names of cultivars. Variations in hardiness, size, and performance can be broad within a species. The crape myrtle cultivar 'Tuskegee', for instance, resists the mildew that often besets the species, *Lagerstroemia indica*. A final point to keep in mind as you wander the aisles at the garden center or thumb the pages of a catalog is that as a low-maintenance gardener, you won't be shopping for bargains. The most expensive plant in the garden is the bargain that died and had to be replaced.

Ornamental Grasses

Ranging in size from the 1-foot-tall *Imperata cylindrica* (Japanese blood grass) to the 12-foot *Erianthus ravennae* (plume grass), grasses make outstanding all-season easy-care plants. In fact, they practically thrive on neglect. Grasses are virtually disease and pest free and, once established, most of them are drought tolerant. As a rule they are also sunloving, but a few species do well in part shade *(Plant Selection Guide, pages 102-107)*.

While some grasses form slow-growing clumps, vigorous varieties like *Miscanthus sacchariflorus* (eulalia, or Amur silver grass) need space to expand and show off their bold plumes. These plants seed prolifically and should be used in an area bordered by a hard surface where they cannot get out of hand.

Grasses take two seasons to fill out but probably won't need to be divided for 5 to 10 years. The principal maintenance chore is cutting back the larger varieties to 6 inches above the ground in early spring before new growth starts.

A SUBTLE BEAUTY
Ornamental grasses display their fall color in this handsome Baltimore garden. Pale, low-growing fountain grass and Miscanthus sinensis 'Gracillimus', with its reddish flowers, nod in the breeze in the foreground; behind them a clump of bronze reed grass stands tall.

The Well-Adapted Plant

A native plant is, by definition, one that was growing and reproducing in an area before humankind put down its own roots there. Often attractive, tolerant of neglect, and flexible about soil and climate, native plants are a natural choice for the low-maintenance garden. And as a bonus to the gardener, native species often attract birds and butterflies.

A Plant for Every Place

The United States has many different habitats, with varying soil types and qualities, temperature ranges, amounts of rainfall, and available sunlight. These habitats include forests, swamps, grasslands, seacoasts, and mountain meadows—and native plants have adapted to grow in all of them. However, not all natives make good garden plants. Some are lusty weeds that will take over the garden; and others, though pleasing to the eye, are too specialized to live in a garden. The lady's-slipper orchid *Cypripedium acaule,* for example, grows in woodlands from Canada to Alabama, but to survive the plant requires the aid of a fungus found only in those woodlands.

The best native plants for a home garden are those that are broadly tolerant, such as *Potentilla fruticosa* (bush cinquefoil), which is native to cooler areas over much of the northern hemisphere. A twiggy shrub with small yellow, pink, or cream flowers that appear from early summer to fall, it serves well as a

low hedge or in borders, growing in a variety of soil conditions from wet to dry. Other high-performance native plants for low-maintenance gardens are listed below, right.

Purchasing Native Plants

It is best to buy your native plants locally whenever possible because you will get the plants that are the most highly adapted to your region. *Cercis canadensis* (redbud), one of the prettiest small native trees, has a wide-ranging habitat, but a seed taken from a redbud growing in northern Florida will not produce a seedling hardy enough for the tree's northern range. Nurseries will offer a selection of plants appropriate for your climate and may also stock natives that have been improved over the wild stock; that is, plants that have been bred selectively for better garden characteristics. For example, two cultivars of *Hydrangea quercifolia* (oakleaf hydrangea), 'Snow Queen' and 'Snowflake', bloom more handsomely and more profusely than the species while retaining the native's brilliant fall color and low-maintenance characteristics.

Adaptable as most natives are, some have preferences based on their natural habitats. For instance, buttonbush *(Cephalanthus occidentalis),* a shrub with pretty, glossy foliage and 1-inch globe-shaped clusters of creamy little flowers, needs moist soil or, even better, a wet spot. Check with your nursery about any special considerations a plant may have before you buy.

Naturalized Plants

Naturalized plants are natives of other locales that have adapted to similar environments in this country. Olive and almond trees, laurestinus viburnum, and lavender, all of which originated around the Mediterranean, are equally at home in southern California. Many of the most popular ornamentals grown in American gardens are Asian imports, such as certain species of cherry, dogwood, and crabapple. Unfortunately, there are cases where the visitors have gone native all too enthusiastically and threaten to swamp the local flora. China's rampant kudzu is enshrouding much of the southern woodlands, and Japanese honeysuckle, though wonderfully fragrant, is now a pernicious weed in many areas of the country.

High-Performance Native Plants

Amelanchier arborea
(shadblow)
Amsonia tabernaemontana
(bluestar)
Aquilegia canadensis
(wild columbine)
Arctostaphylos uva-ursi
(common bearberry)
Aronia arbutifolia 'Brilliantissima'
(red chokeberry)
Asclepias tuberosa
(butterfly weed)
Calycanthus floridus
(sweet shrub)
Ceanothus 'Dark Star', 'Ray Hartman'
(wild lilac)
Cercis canadensis
(redbud)
Chrysogonum virginianum

(goldenstar)
Crataegus viridis 'Winter King'
(green hawthorn)
Echinacea purpurea
(purple coneflower)
Fothergilla spp.
(fothergilla)
Heuchera micrantha 'Palace Purple'
(alumroot)
Hibiscus moscheutos
(swamp mallow)
Ilex opaca
(American holly)
Ilex verticillata
(winterberry)
Kalmia latifolia
(mountain laurel)
Leucothoe fontanesiana
(drooping leucothoe)
Liatris spicata

(spike gay-feather)
Lonicera sempervirens
(trumpet honeysuckle)
Magnolia virginiana
(sweet bay magnolia)
Oxydendrum arboreum
(sourwood)
Rhododendron catawbiense
(Catawba rhododendron)
Rudbeckia fulgida var. *sullivantii 'Goldsturm'*
(orange coneflower)

Note: The abbreviation "spp." stands for the plural of "species"; where used in lists it means that many, but not all, of the species in a genus meet the criterion of the list.

Lonicera sempervirens (trumpet honeysuckle)

Temperature in the Garden

All plants prefer certain temperature ranges. For some species, the range in which they flourish is broad: For instance, inkberry *(Ilex glabra)* grows from Nova Scotia to upper Florida. For others, the range is very narrow: Pittosporum is a tender evergreen shrub that thrives only in the milder parts of the southern states and on the West Coast.

Because you cannot choose the temperatures in your garden, you must choose plants that are adapted to the temperatures you have. One widely used aid for this purpose is the USDA Plant Hardiness Zone Map *(box, opposite),* which divides the United States into 11 climatic zones based on average minimum temperatures. The plants sold by reputable nurseries are labeled to indicate the northernmost zone to which they are adapted.

There is more to consider than cold hardiness alone, however. Heat tolerance complicates the picture, and so does humidity. Some plants, such as the olive trees that grow in California gardens, tolerate high daytime temperatures but need cool nights and low humidity. In the warm, muggy nights of the Southeast, such plants suffer heat stress, declining over time.

Plant Dormancy

Cold-climate plants have a survival mechanism not shared by warm-climate species. Called dormancy, it is a state roughly analogous to human sleep. First the plant stores nutrients to see it through the winter and to fuel spring growth. Then it gradually slows its physical activity in a process called hardening off, which is triggered by the waning daylight of late summer and fall. To help cold-hardy plants prepare for winter, avoid pruning or fertilizing late in the growing season, since these practices stimulate growth. A plant using its stores of energy to put forth a burst of new shoots when it should be going dormant will be less able to survive the winter.

Protecting Your Plants

When unusually cold winter weather descends on mild zones, gardeners can be hard-pressed to protect their plantings. Such freezes, although mercifully infrequent, can destroy established plantings that have

Winter Protection for a Young Shrub

To erect an effective barrier against winter wind, *you'll need a length of tough, loosely woven material such as burlap; two or more wood stakes 8 to 10 inches taller than the evergreen; and a heavy-duty stapler. Drive the stakes firmly into the ground on the windward side of the shrub, as shown; the stakes should project slightly above the shrub. Fix the material to each stake with staples spaced about 4 inches apart. One large screen can protect several evergreens planted in a row.*

USDA Plant Hardiness Zone Map

Zone 1: Below -50°F
Zone 2: -50° to -40°
Zone 3: -40° to -30°
Zone 4: -30° to -20°
Zone 5: -20° to -10°
Zone 6: -10° to 0°
Zone 7: 0° to 10°
Zone 8: 10° to 20°
Zone 9: 20° to 30°
Zone 10: 30° to 40°
Zone 11: Above 40°

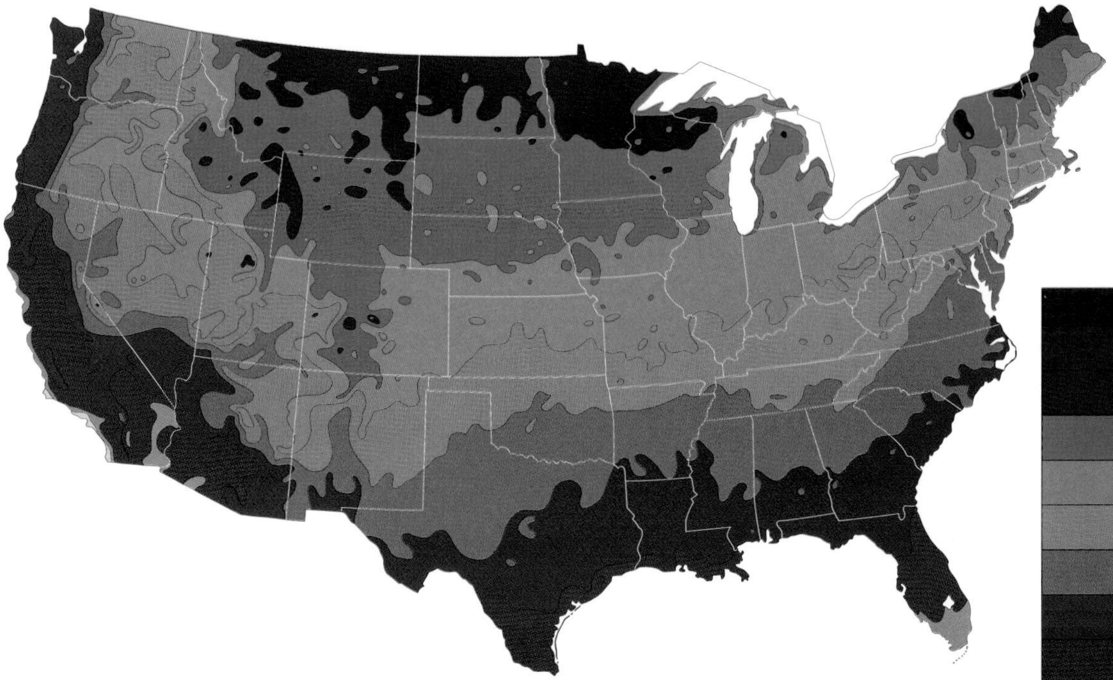

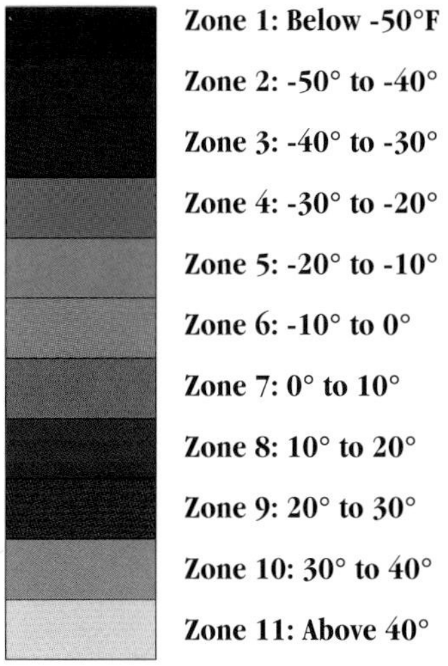

The USDA Plant Hardiness Zone Map divides the North American continent into 11 zones on the basis of average annual minimum temperatures. In Zone 1, the coldest, the temperature routinely falls below -50°F, while in Zone 11, the warmest, low temperatures average above 40°F—a difference of almost 100°F. Most of the continental United States lies within Zones 3 through 10.

The zone map is an invaluable aid to the gardener, but it simply isn't detailed enough to tell the whole temperature story. For instance, only the largest of the heat islands generated by metropolitan areas can be shown. Nor does the map include countless significant local increases in altitude, which can push average minimums down roughly 1°F per 300 feet—the equivalent of moving 300 miles north along the Atlantic seaboard. The warming effect of water is indicated only along coastlines and very large lakes.

Moreover, sheer depth of cold is not always the most important determinant of plant survival. In the Rocky Mountain region, for example, extreme temperature swings in spring and fall kill more plants than do stretches of unrelievedly frigid weather in winter.

thrived for many years. Watering the garden thoroughly before a cold front arrives offers some protection; a moisture-laden plant is better equipped to withstand cold. An additional measure is a loose covering of burlap or old sheets draped over stakes or a cylinder of chicken wire. Make sure the covering doesn't touch the plant, and remove it as soon as the weather has warmed to a safe level.

If a plant sustains a moderate amount of damage, with some branch or twig dieback, prune back to healthy-looking wood in early spring. If the damage is severe, however, don't be hasty about pruning or discarding the plant; branches that fail to leaf out in

spring may revive, even as late as midsummer.

In northern zones, cold-hardy deciduous trees and shrubs can look after themselves during a normal winter. However, shallow-rooted broadleaf evergreens such as rhododendron, azalea, and mountain laurel that are in exposed, windy sites benefit from protection in the first year or two after planting. Water these plants regularly as the date for the first hard frost approaches, and apply a thick layer of mulch to retain moisture and to prevent alternate freezing and thawing from breaking their roots. For added protection, an antidesiccant, renewed halfway through the season in Zones 3 and 4, where winters are especially severe, is helpful.

Sun and Shade in the Garden

If plants are to do their best in your garden, you must carefully consider their light requirements and find places where those needs will be met. Experienced gardeners know that the light in even a small garden may vary much more than might be imagined from a casual glance, and in ways that significantly affect the health of the plants. Take the time to observe the changing distribution of light and shade in different parts of your garden over the course of the day and in different seasons. Note the reach of a shadow cast by a house or fence, and pay attention to the quality of the light beneath a tree canopy; the open, dappled shade of a ginkgo will call for one plant community, while the denser shade of a row of white pines will dictate another. It's helpful to keep a record of your observations as a guide for future planting.

Defining Light Gradations

There are many kinds and degrees of light and shade. Seasonal changes and the unique features of a particular garden come into play, as does latitude. The southern part of the United States enjoys more intense sunshine year round than do the northern states, and plants that thrive in full sun in the cool North may need a more shaded—and therefore cooler—site in the South. Another influential factor is humidity: Sunlight in a clear, dry climate will be more intense than in a cloudy, humid one at the same latitude because water vapor in the air blocks some of the sun's rays.

Although light intensities can't be exactly defined, the term *full sun* is generally taken to mean a total of 6 hours or more of direct, unobstructed sunlight between 9:00 a.m. and 4:00 p.m. Sunlight is strongest during this period and peaks at noon, when the sun is at its highest point. In early morning and late afternoon, the sun's rays are relatively weak: Because their angle is low, they traverse a greater thickness of atmosphere, which absorbs or scatters some of the rays.

Most perennials and deciduous shrubs need full sun, especially to flower well. Forsythia, for instance, is a dull disappointment in partial shade. Light level can also make a difference in leaf color. 'Crimson Pygmy' barberry and 'Royal Purple' smokebush, for instance, need full sun to develop and maintain their richest color; both are greenish in lower light. Similarly, the pink and rose tints that make 'Burgundy Glow' ajuga a standout are muted in shade.

Since sunny gardens have a tendency toward dryness, it makes sense to give first consideration to plants noted for their drought tolerance. Some good choces are *Lagerstroemia indica* cvs. (crape myrtle), *Cornus alba* 'Sibirica' (Tartarian dogwood), *Myrica* spp. (bayberry), and *Taxus* spp. (yew).

Plants for Dry Shade

Acanthopanax sieboldianus
(five-leaf aralia)
Aquilegia canadensis
(wild columbine)
Brunnera macrophylla
(brunnera)
Epimedium spp.
(barrenwort)
Geranium macrorrhizum
(bigroot geranium)
Hedera helix
(English ivy)
Ilex cornuta 'Burfordii'
(Burford holly)
Liriope spp.
(lilyturf)

Mahonia aquifolium
(Oregon grape)
Nandina domestica
(nandina)
Ophiopogon japonicus
(dwarf mondo grass)
Pittosporum tobira
(Japanese pittosporum)
Vinca minor
(periwinkle)

Note: The abbreviation "spp." stands for the plural of "species"; where used in lists it means that many, but not all, of the species in a genus meet the criterion of the list.

Brunnera macrophylla (brunnera)

Establishing a Bed of Moss

1. Choose a shady site with moist, acid soil, and clear it of all vegetation and roots. Dig in a 2-inch layer of peat moss and soak the soil until it is muddy.

2. Dig up clumps of moss several inches across; for a mosaic effect, gather a number of varieties. Keep the moss wrapped in moist cheesecloth until you are ready to plant it. Working with one clump at a time, gently rinse the soil from the underside to expose the tiny, hairlike roots. Press the clump firmly onto the prepared soil to remove any air pockets. Seal the edges with mud. Repeat with the other clumps, laying them in a loose patchwork. Water the finished bed well. If only a little moss is available, use this method: Put a handful of moss into a blender with a cup of buttermilk or beer; if you're using beer, add ½ teaspoon of sugar. Blend the ingredients thoroughly and spread the mixture ¼ inch deep on the prepared soil.

3. Check the bed frequently to make sure it remains constantly moist while the moss is becoming established. Remove any weed seedlings promptly.

Tough Plants for Low Light

At the other end of the light spectrum is full shade. This describes an area that gets fewer than 4 hours of direct sun a day; in the dimmest places—under a low, dense tree canopy or at the foot of a high north wall of a building, for example there may be indirect light only. Some attractive low-maintenance plants perform well under such daunting conditions, among them English ivy, pachysandra, epimedium, yew, and some ferns and hostas. Don't value shade-loving hostas only for their delicate blooms; instead, exploit them for the color, shape, and texture of their leaves. Another good choice for cool, moist, full shade is a carpet of moss, which you can establish using the method described in the box above.

Of all garden situations, none is more difficult than dry shade. A list of shrubs, ground covers, and perennials to grow in such an area appears opposite.

The Possibilities of Partial Shade

For areas in partial shade, where direct sun amounts to somewhere between 4 and 6 hours each day, the plant palette expands enormously. Oakleaf hydrangea, climbing hydrangea, rhododendrons and azaleas, camellias, mountain laurel, redbud, shadblow, witch hazel, and fothergilla thrive in partial shade and flower beautifully. This is also the best situation for 'Bloodgood' Japanese maple, a cultivar prized for its reddish purple leaves. (Don't be tempted to try it in full shade, however; there the foliage will be greenish.)

Plants That Adapt to a Range of Light

High on any low-maintenance gardener's list are those plants that perform creditably in a range of light levels. Oakleaf hydrangea, for instance, is suited to full sun as well as partial shade, and both environments have something special to recommend them to the gardener: In partial shade, the shrub's flowers last longer, while in sun the fall foliage color is richer. Other similarly accommodating shrubs and trees are Virginia sweetspire; American summer-sweet and its exotic cousin, Japanese clethra; 'Otto Luykens' cherry laurel; and five-leaf aralia. Among ground covers, English ivy, Algerian ivy, ajuga, liriope, periwinkle, and goldenstar are all remarkably adaptable.

Low-Growing Plants for the Garden Floor

In the easy-care garden, ground covers have two roles to fulfill: They must hold their own aesthetically, and they must be hardworking. Ground covers offer an enormous range of attractive features to choose among: Some are prostrate creepers, others mounded, knee-high shrubs; some flaunt beautiful flowers, while others are prized for their handsomely colored or richly textured foliage, which may be evergreen or deciduous. As a utilitarian garden element, a ground cover, whatever its appearance, grows into a dense, weed-suppressing carpet of foliage that shades the soil and helps to conserve moisture. When planted on a slope, it prevents erosion.

Don't limit yourself to old reliables when choosing ground covers. Ajuga, English ivy, periwinkle, and Japanese pachysandra have their merits, but there are dozens of other low-growing shrubs, vines, and herbaceous perennials that will carpet the ground in a timely way—but not so fast that they become problems rather than solutions.

Shrubby Ground Covers

If shrubs are planted where you can take full advantage of their ground-covering potential, they will demand little upkeep once established. Creeping junipers, for example, need plenty of space between them since they may eventually reach 10 feet in width.

Other shrubs to consider as ground covers are the mound-shaped dwarf Gumpo azaleas, which do well in shade; 'Crimson Pygmy' bar-

Determining How Many Ground-Cover Plants to Buy

To avoid overbuying or underbuying when you are adding a ground cover to your garden, it's important to calculate in advance the planting area and the number of plants needed for proper coverage. In the chart at right, distances to allow for between plants, measuring from center to center, are recommended for each of 12 popular ground covers (list, bottom right). Spaced as suggested, the ground covers should give complete coverage in 2 years.

The chart also shows how many plants to buy on the basis of the area to be covered and the recommended spacing.

NUMBER OF PLANTS NEEDED BASED ON AREA AND SPACING

SPACING \ AREA IN SQ. FT.	9	18	27	36	45	54	63	72	81	90
8"	20	41	61	81	101	122	142	162	182	203
12"	9	18	27	36	45	54	63	72	81	90
18"	4	8	12	16	20	24	28	32	36	40
24"	2	5	7	9	11	14	16	18	20	23

Ajuga reptans
(bugleweed)
Ceratostigma plumbaginoides
(leadwort)
Echeveria agavoides
(hens and chicks)
Epimedium x *rubrum*
(barrenwort)
Geranium macrorrhizum
(bigroot geranium)
Hedera canariensis
(Algerian ivy)

Iberis sempervirens
(candytuft)
Lamium maculatum
(dead nettle)
Liriope muscari
(big blue lilyturf)
Liriope spicata
(creeping lilyturf)
Phlox stolonifera
(creeping phlox)
Stachys byzantina
(lamb's ears)

berry for sun or part shade; prostrate abelia, which has glossy semi-evergreen to evergreen foliage and blooms from midsummer until frost; and lace shrub.

Perennial Ground Covers

Of the perennials that make good ground covers, the most sedate form mound-shaped foliage clumps that gradually increase in diameter. Hostas, bergenias, 'Palace Purple' heuchera, and big blue lilyturf *(Liriope muscari)* are clump formers.

If you want a plant that will colonize an area faster and continue to expand outward until checked, choose one that grows by throwing out either surface runners or underground shoots. The surface runners are comparatively easy to control, since the runners are in plain sight and can be easily pulled. Ajuga, sea thrift, bigroot geranium, lamb's ears, and the native foamflower are all surface runners.

Some plants that increase by underground shoots proceed at a modest pace—epimediums, for instance, and the wild gingers. However, others of this type often become a maintenance headache. One example is variegated goutweed. In addition to its rampant shoots, it seeds prolifically if not deadheaded.

A word of caution about English ivy: Although it is valued for its ability to take hold quickly under adverse conditions, from Zone 6 south it is all too likely to become a weed. Luckily, there are many easy-to-grow cultivars of English ivy that lack their parent's invasive vigor. Two such are 'Aureo-variegata' and the silvery-edged 'Glacier'. It's best to plant variegated ivies like these in the shade, since they can be damaged by winter sun and wind.

Buying and Planting Ground Covers

How quickly a new bed of ground cover will fill out depends on its growth rate and how closely you space the plants. The box at left suggests planting distances for 12 popular ground covers. Prepare the bed in advance so you can install the plants promptly after buying them. When firming soil around each plant, create a slight depression around the stem that will catch water. Once planting is complete, water the bed thoroughly and add a layer of mulch.

A MOSAIC OF GROUND COVERS
The distinctive textures, shapes, and colors of five ground covers create a rich composition. Moving clockwise from lower right, the planting includes lamb's ears, variegated lilyturf, 'Crimson Pygmy' barberry, blue lyme grass, and a hardy geranium.

The Garden's Midstory

Growing to a mature height of only 20 feet or so, shrubs and small trees are the midstory of the garden, spreading their branches between the carpet of lawn and ground cover and the canopy of tall trees. These two groups of woody plants are the backbone of the low-maintenance garden, the permanent structure into which herbaceous plantings—turf grasses, perennials, bulbs, and annuals—are integrated. Shrubs and small trees can be used to divide your garden into distinct areas and to give you privacy from your neighbors and from passersby. They also link the vertical lines of your house to the ground, and contribute form, line, and color in winter when perennials have disappeared from view and the lawn's summer green has been subdued.

Essential as basic building blocks, shrubs and small trees can serve as a low-mainte-

nance garden's principal ornaments. With a knowing choice, it's possible to have bloom from late winter until frost, beginning with the spidery yellow, orange, or red flowers of witch hazel and ending with the fragrant little trumpets of abelia.

These plants shouldn't be looked to just for their flowers, however; perennials, bulbs, and annuals throw more of their energy into flowering and generally produce more vivid displays. Choose woody plants for the color, texture, and shape of their leaves; for beautiful bark and fruit; for sculptural lines of trunk and branch; for narrow forms that are bold punctuation marks set against dense, round masses of comforting solidity. Guidelines for composing a border that capitalizes on such characteristics appear at right; a selection of shrubs and small trees that are outstanding

COLOR FROM FLOWER AND FOLIAGE
In a Pacific Northwest shrub border, Point Reyes ceanothus spreads a carpet of blue at the feet of yellow 'Moonlight' Scotch broom. A solid-looking dark green mugo pine anchors the border's center, and the new growth of Japanese photinia adds a coppery red accent at upper left.

ornamentals in three seasons can be found in the list below, right.

Plants for the garden's framework are relatively expensive and, unless you buy very large specimens, it will take several years of growth for them to come into their own. If you've planned well, the result is worth the wait. But if a plant turns out to be inferior or unsuited to your garden, you'll have to decide whether to get rid of your mistake and start over or whether to live with it if it's grown too large to transplant.

Choosing Wisely

When you're planting for the long term, limit yourself to species and varieties that are sturdy, neat, and long-lived. First, though, you must satisfy yourself that a plant will thrive in your garden's climate, soil, and light conditions. In cities and heavily trafficked suburbs, air pollution and compacted or poor-

Plants for Three Seasons of Beauty

Acer griseum	(oakleaf hydrangea)
(paperbark maple)	*Ilex vomitoria*
Acer palmatum	(yaupon)
(Japanese maple)	*Mahonia aquifolium*
Amelanchier arborea	(Oregon grape)
(shadblow)	*Malus 'Donald Wyman'*
Arbutus unedo	(crabapple)
'Compacta'	*Nandina domestica*
(dwarf strawberry tree)	(nandina)
Aronia arbutifolia	*Oxydendrum arboreum*
'Brilliantissima'	(sourwood)
(red chokeberry)	*Prunus sargentii*
Berberis julianae	(Sargent cherry)
(wintergreen	*Pyracantha coccinea*
barberry)	*cultivars*
Cornus kousa	(scarlet firethorn)
(Japanese dogwood)	*Viburnum dilatatum*
Crataegus viridis	(linden viburnum)
'Winter King'	*Viburnum plicatum*
(green hawthorn)	var. *tomentosum*
Hydrangea quercifolia	(double file viburnum)

Mahonia aquifolium (Oregon grape)

ly drained soils make it hard or impossible for certain plants to succeed. The pollution-tolerant plants listed opposite are good choices for urban gardens.

Beyond ensuring appropriate growing conditions, the single most important work saver may be barring from your garden any shrubs and small trees that are subject to serious insect problems or diseases. You must be discriminating even among plants that are very closely related. For instance, the beautiful flowering dogwood *(Cornus florida)*, native from eastern Oklahoma to the Atlantic coast, is under serious attack by anthracnose, a disease that can kill an infected tree in just 2 years. However, the kousa dogwood and the new hybrids between the kousa and flowering dogwoods are apparently immune.

The viburnums, a large family of shrubs with showy spring flowers and, in many cases, colorful fruit and fall foliage, are generally trouble free. However, the European cranberry bush—so called because of its bright red fruit that lasts into winter—is prey to infestations of aphids and borers. Likewise, planting euonymus species is an invitation to devastation by scale insects. The only exception is the winged euonymus *(E. alata)*, a massive shrub with spectacular rose red fall foliage.

Crabapples and flowering cherries are similarly mixed lots. Beautiful as they are in spring flower, because of serious pest and disease problems only a few—including the 20-foot 'Donald Wyman' crabapple, with white blossoms and red fruit, and the dainty little 'Hally Jolivette' cherry tree—are worthwhile subjects for the low-maintenance garden.

Even a tree with good resistance becomes vulnerable to diseases, pests, and environmental stress when its bark is injured. The lawn mower is a common source of such injuries, so instead of trying to grow grass up to the trunk of a tree, surround it with a ground cover or with mulch.

Judging Plants for Neatness

Fruit that collects beneath a shrub isn't likely to make work, but under a small tree set in a lawn, it can create an unsightly mess. Crabapples with large fruit are major offenders. Both flowers and fruit dropped on paved walks and patios can make them dangerously slippery. Prolific seed producers also make work for you. One such nuisance is the old-fashioned rose of Sharon *(Hibiscus syriacus)*, a tough, adaptable large shrub or small tree that produces sizable white, red, or purple flowers in midsummer—and countless weedy seedlings. However, hybrids of the species such as 'Diana' and 'Helen' have all of their parent's virtues but set few if any seeds and thus qualify as truly low-maintenance plants.

The Importance of Place

Whether or not a characteristic is a problem often depends on where a plant is sited. A case in point is suckering shrubs, which produce widening clumps of stems that spring from their roots. In the close quarters of a bed or border, they have to be pruned frequently, but they are good choices for naturalistic plantings. A valuable suckering shrub is Japanese sweetspire *(Itea)*, which spreads quickly and has fragrant white flowers in spring and rich green foliage that turns purple in fall. Three excellent colonizers are the glossy-leaved 'Gro-lo' fragrant sumac *(Rhus*

Siting Shrubs beside a House

Plant a shrub with its center far enough from the house that the branches won't touch the wall when the plant is mature. Make sure the center of the shrub is beyond the edge of the eave, as indicated by the dotted line, so that most of the roots will be exposed to rain, reducing the need for watering.

Choosing a High-Quality Shrub

Use the following guidelines when you shop for shrubs:

- Branches should be arranged symmetrically around the plant's center. Avoid plants that have been pruned, which may indicate that unhealthy growth has been cut off.
- Evaluate the proportion of roots to top growth. For balled-and-burlapped plants, the root-ball should be about two-thirds the width of the top growth. A too-small root system won't supply enough water and nutrients for vigorous growth.
- Except for new leaves, foliage should be uniform in color and evenly distributed. Pass by plants with shriveled, wilted, or dead foliage, buds, or stems.
- Bark should be unblemished, with no abnormal fissures that could harbor insects or disease.
- On a dormant plant, gently scrape away a tiny bit of bark to make sure that the stem tissue beneath is a healthy green.
- Avoid a container-grown shrub that has numerous roots protruding above the soil's surface *(right)*. The plant has been growing in the pot so long that its roots are tangled and would have to be cut before planting.
- If you are allowed to, lift a container plant out of its pot and look for evenly distributed roots with a healthy white or tan color; black or dark brown roots are probably diseased.
- The soil ball of a balled-and-burlapped shrub should feel tight and firm; if the soil is loose, the roots may have dried out or been injured.

aromatica), which is adapted to both sun and shade, and the chokeberries *(Aronia)*. The fast-growing black chokeberry makes thickets in soils that range from boggy to dry; because it is slower to increase, red chokeberry can be used in a shrub border.

Taking Size into Account

When you're setting out small, young shrubs and trees it takes discipline to allow sufficient room for each one to grow since the planting is bound to look a little bare. During the 4 or 5 years in which shrubs and trees are getting established and filling out, perennials or annuals can be used to give the spaces around them a more finished look. As a rule, you can expect a width of about 10 feet for plants with a mature height of 10 feet; in the 5- to 10-foot range, allow for a width three-quarters the height; for heights of 2 to 5 feet, allow for a width of 3 feet. Keep in mind that closely related plants can have radically different sizes. For instance, Japanese holly *(Ilex crenata)* matures at about 10 feet tall and wide, but its 60 or so cultivars vary widely.

Pollution-Tolerant Shrubs

Acanthopanax sieboldianus
(five-leaf aralia)
Berberis thunbergii
(Japanese barberry)
Cotinus coggygria
(smoke tree)
Forsythia spp.
(forsythia)
Hibiscus syriacus cultivars
(rose of Sharon)
Hydrangea arborescens 'Grandiflora'

(hills-of-snow hydrangea)
Hydrangea paniculata
(panicle hydrangea)
Ilex crenata
(Japanese holly)
Ilex glabra
(inkberry)
Magnolia stellata
(star magnolia)
Myrica pensylvanica
(bayberry)
Nerium oleander
(common oleander)
Pieris japonica

(Japanese andromeda)
Potentilla fruticosa
(shrubby cinquefoil)
Taxus spp.
(yew)
Viburnum carlcephalum
(fragrant snowball)

Note: The abbreviation "spp." stands for the plural of "species"; where used in lists it means that many, but not all, of the species in a genus meet the criterion of the list.

Hydrangea arborescens 'Grandiflora'
(hills-of-snow hydrangea)

Shade Trees for the Lawn and Garden

Think of a shade tree as a long-term investment: Although a good sapling is likely to be one of the most expensive plants you'll ever buy, it will reward you—and generations to come—by being among the longest-lived and most maintenance-free plants in your landscape. Moreover, trees planted to shield your home from the summer sun not only offer cooling comfort but also help pay for themselves over time by reducing your energy bills.

Selecting the Right Shade Tree

Before choosing a tree, take some time to observe those already growing in your community, and, if possible, visit an arboretum or park where trees are labeled to get acquainted with the various species. After you've noted which ones appeal to you and seem appropriate for your site, start paring down the prospects by eliminating any that are not compatible with your soil and light conditions, and are not naturally pest and disease resistant. Likewise, rule out trees with shallow roots, such as silver maples, because they compete with other plants for moisture and nutrients, make mowing difficult, and can buckle pavement. Finally, choose strong-wooded trees over weak-limbed varieties such as Siberian elm or the Bradford pear, and exclude trees that litter, such as the sycamore, which drops debris all summer.

Experts consider the 12 shade trees shown below to be excellent easy-care candidates that are hardy over most of the United States. The birch, ash, and tupelo will tolerate wet conditions, while the ginkgo, zelkova, and Japanese pagoda tree can adapt to dry areas. The ash, ginkgo, red oak, and pagoda trees can also endure the salt that is used on icy roads in wintertime.

Size, Shape, and Shade

One of your major considerations in selecting a tree should be its ultimate size. Knowing the growth habits of different trees will help you avoid choosing one that will eventually outgrow its space or cast shadows on your sun-loving plants. The trees illustrated below are shown at the height and width they typically achieve after about 20 years if grown from seed. Nursery saplings could reach these sizes

The 12 Best Shade Trees

The illustrations below show the height and shape after 20 years of 12 top-performing shade trees grown from seed.

Acer rubrum 'October Glory' (red maple): *Medium to fast growth rate; prefers moist, slightly acid soil but tolerates others; full sun or part shade. Mature size: 40-60 feet tall by 35-50 feet wide. Zones 3-9.*

Betula nigra 'Heritage' (Heritage river birch): *Medium to fast growth rate; prefers moist, acid soil and full sun. Mature size: 40-70 feet tall by 40-60 feet wide. Zones 4-9.*

Carpinus caroliniana (American hornbeam): *Slow growth rate; prefers moist, slightly acid soil and full sun to shade. Mature size: 25-30 feet tall by 25-30 feet wide. Zones 2-9.*

Cladrastis kentukea or C. lutea (American yellowwood): *Medium growth rate; soil tolerant; prefers well-drained site, full sun. Mature size: 30-50 feet tall by 40-55 feet wide. Zones 3-8.*

Fraxinus pennsylvanica 'Marshall's Seedless' (green ash): *Fast growth rate; soil tolerant; requires full sun. Mature size: 50 feet tall by 40 feet wide. Zones 3-9.*

Ginkgo biloba (ginkgo, maidenhair tree): *Slow to medium growth rate; soil tolerant; prefers moist site, full sun. Mature size: 50-80 feet tall by 30-40 feet wide. Zones 3-8.*

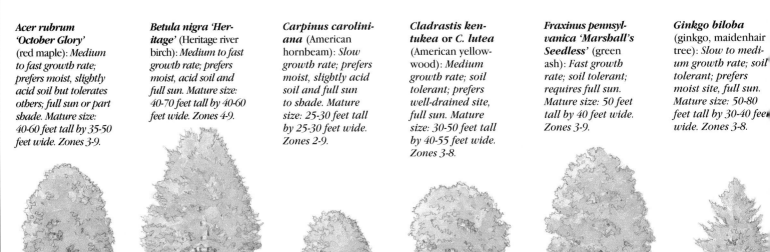

in 10 years or less, depending on their size at planting, the quality of the soil, and the care they are given. The red and willow oaks are especially fast growers—making them a good choice for gardeners who want to shade a house as quickly as possible.

The tree's overall shape is another aspect to consider. As a focal point of your garden or as a feature that will accent—or conceal—the architecture of your home, the most aesthetically pleasing tree may be either vase-shaped, like the zelkova, or round and broad, like the red maple, whose wide-reaching branches will also provide many hours of shade.

The shade cast by the different trees varies according to the density and size of the leaves as well as the tree's shape. The large, overlapping foliage of the maple, for example, creates a solid shadow, while the finer, more widely spaced leaves of the ginkgo and the river birch provide dappled shade.

You should also take into account the other ways in which trees might enhance your garden. Both the American yellowwood and the pagoda tree produce beautiful blossoms; the tupelo and the red maple display vibrant fall color; and the interesting bark of the river birch and the American hornbeam ornament the winter landscape. Factoring in these variables will help ensure that the tree you finally decide on brings you many years of pleasure.

Siting and Planting a Tree

If your aim is to block summer sun from a house or patio, site your tree to the south and west. A basic rule of thumb when planting is to situate the tree at a distance of one-third to one-half its ultimate height from the house or other structure. In other words, a tree that matures at 30 feet should be planted 10 to 15 feet away from the building. If the tree's shape is narrower and more upright, you may be able to plant it closer, but bear in mind that branches overhanging a house will drop leaves into gutters, adding to the upkeep of the house, and could even be dangerous: Heavy branches can do damage during a storm. Also be sure not to plant a shade tree where its branches will someday interfere with utility lines.

The same guidelines for identifying a healthy, high-quality shrub *(page 45)* also apply to shade trees. Instead of planting a new tree yourself, you may want to pay the nursery to install it: The rootball of an 8- to 10-foot sapling can weigh as much as 150 pounds.

A CHOICE NATIVE
The American yellowwood—so named for the color of its heartwood—produces fragrant white blooms among bright green leaves in spring. Its medium size, hardiness, and resistance to diseases and pests make it an excellent choice for home landscapes.

Nyssa sylvatica
(black tupelo, also called black gum, sour gum): *Slow to medium growth rate; prefers moist, well-drained, acid soil and full sun to semishade. Mature size: 30-50 feet tall by 20-30 feet wide. Zones 3-9.*

Quercus phellos
(willow oak): *Medium to fast growth rate; soil tolerant but prefers a moist, well-drained site; full sun. Mature size: 40-60 feet tall by 30-40 feet wide. Zones 5-9.*

Quercus rubra
(red oak): *Fast growth rate; prefers sandy, well-drained, acid soil and full sun. Mature size: 60-75 feet tall by 60-75 feet wide. Zones 4-8.*

Sophora japonica
(Japanese pagoda tree): *Medium to fast growth rate; prefers loamy, well-drained soil and full sun. Mature size: 50-75 feet tall by 50-75 feet wide. Zones 4-8.*

Tilia cordata
(littleleaf linden): *Medium growth rate; soil tolerant but prefers moist, well-drained soil; full sun. Mature size: 60-70 feet tall by 30-40 feet wide. Zones 3-7.*

Zelkova serrata
(Japanese zelkova): *Medium growth rate; soil tolerant; prefers moist, deep site and full sun. Mature size: 50-80 feet tall by 50-80 feet wide. Zones 5-8.*

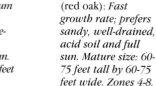
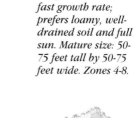

Easy Care Gardens

Of primary importance to successful low-maintenance gardening is finding plants that suit your environment, be it the desert Southwest, a rainy northern coast, or the midwestern prairie. If the plants are a good fit, they can thrive with minimal care. Even some varieties of roses, which are often associated with many hours of toil, can prosper under these conditions.

Most reliable are plants that are native to your area or are imported from a similar climate. The gardens pictured here not only match the plants to their environment but also were designed with the growth habits and grooming needs of the plants in mind. As a result, maintenance is largely a matter of occasional watering, tidying up, and trimming back—leaving plenty of time for the gardener's pure enjoyment.

STAR OF A RAIN-SOAKED GARDEN
In Portland, Oregon, this 'Old Dawson' climber rose blooms from late June to late July. The plant is disease resistant and needs only occasional pruning.

A DESERT OASIS

A surprising variety of textures, shapes, and colors abound in this sun-scorched Arizona garden, where a scant 7 inches of rain fall in a year. The coarse granite mulch that covers the bed lasts indefinitely and helps keep the soil moist and the roots cool; a drip-irrigation system takes care of the twice-weekly watering. Many of the plants are imports that are well adapted to the American desert: The Cape marigold with its white daisylike flowers and the bright yellow bulbine (foreground) are from South Africa, and the medicinal aloe, bearing tall stalks topped by bright orange blossoms, is native to North Africa. American desert natives include ocotillo, a shrub with tall, unbranched stems (upper left); rounded bunny-ears cactus; and pinkish purple desert penstemon and moss verbena. Along the fence at the rear of the garden is a mass of tall, yellow-blooming brittlebush.

RESPITE FROM THE CITY

Overlooking Long Island Sound and Manhattan, the large New York coastal garden at left blends evergreens, grasses, and perennials for a rich show that changes throughout the growing season. A wide stand of rudbeckia just beginning to show its golden flowers is the backdrop for a low juniper spilling gracefully over a boulder; at the boulder's base, several clumps of annual 'Daybreak Mix' gazania have burst into bloom. Farther back, tall, arching maiden grass mixes with pastel clumps of 'Blue Lacecap' hydrangea and 'Betty Prior' shrub roses, here in their July splendor. Successful in part because they tolerate wind and salt spray, the plants receive further protection from a thick layer of cedarbark mulch that is refreshed every 18 to 24 months. The plot is watered by an automatic irrigation system, so the gardener's most demanding chore is deadheading.

BEAUTY AT WATER'S EDGE

Proclaiming the start of the summer season, a red Oriental poppy adds drama to this lush Bridgehampton, New York, garden located on a pond near the Atlantic shore. Deep pink and bright white salt-tolerant rugosa roses are just beginning to produce blossoms that will continue through late summer, when the clumps of daylilies flanking the poppy will commence their own spectacular show of color. The thin, willowy stems of phragmites at the rear of the 4-foot-wide border will last into winter. Although the garden is a full 80 feet long, it requires only an hour a week of care— namely, weed pulling. Once a year, in spring, the garden is top-dressed with rotted manure. Should the need arise, an underground watering system augments the local rainfall, which usually measures a generous 45 inches a year.

COLORFUL AND CAREFREE
*Nestled amid broad, crinkled leaves
of borage in this southern California garden, patches of purple
cranesbill and red valerian form
vibrant splashes of color. Frost-free
winters and pleasantly warm summers are perfectly hospitable to
the exotic plants the gardener has
chosen, such as the silvery green
licorice plant to the left of the bench,
the large rosemary at right, and the
lavender sprinkled throughout. The
clay soil is regularly enriched with
compost made from kitchen scraps
and garden waste, and an automatic watering system helps keep
the ground moist in a region that
receives just 12 inches of rainfall a
year. The garden can thus be left
unattended for 3 weeks at a time
with no threat to its survival.*

A NATURAL LANDSCAPE
In midsummer, 6 years after it was planted, this prairie garden composed exclusively of Wisconsin natives boasts large drifts of spiky white Culver's root, pink bergamot, and black-eyed Susan. Over the years, next to nothing has been done to the 90-by-20-foot hillside plot, which is in bloom from early spring through October. The only routine maintenance is carried out in March, when everything is cut to the ground to make way for new growth. Since the annual rainfall averages 30 inches and winter snows amount to between 40 and 50 inches, watering is almost never necessary.

SHADES OF GREEN

Shrubs ranging in hue from the blue-green of the blue spruce at the center of the border to the deep green of the San Jose holly at the back give a cool feel to this informal Maryland garden. The plants were chosen to withstand the mid-Atlantic region's steamy summer temperatures, erratic periods of drought, and winter lows that regularly approach zero. The garden requires just 2 hours of maintenance a week.

A RAINBOW OF COLOR

'Pink Gumpo' azaleas, reddish orange gaillardias, and feathery rose pink astilbes blooming among hostas and other foliage plants light up this small Richmond, Virginia, garden with bright springtime color. Later, annuals and daylilies, chosen to stand up to the area's high heat and humidity, will keep the garden in bloom through October. After spring planting, only an hour's worth of cleanup is required each week to maintain the quiet elegance.

A Guide to the Gardens

STAR OF A RAIN-SOAKED GARDEN
pages 48-49

A. *Rosa 'Old Dawson'* (2)
B. *Euonymus japonica* (1)
C. *Saxifraga fortunei 'Wada'* (2)
D. *Iris sp.* (1)
E. *Rhododendron hybrid* (1)

F. *Iris douglasiana hybrid* (3)
G. *Primula x Juliana* (12)
H. *Magnolia x loebneri 'Merrill'* (1)
I. *Digitalis purpurea* (2)

J. *Rhododendron schlippenbachii* (1)
K. *Molinia caerulea 'Variegata'* (5)
L. *Geranium nodosum* (9)

A DESERT OASIS
pages 50-51

A. *Bulbine caulescens* (2)
B. *Cereus hildmannianus* (1)
C. *Simmondsia chinensis* (2)
D. *Fouquieria splendens* (1)
E. *Encelia farinosa* (3)

F. *Opuntia microdasys* (2)
G. *Penstemon parryi* (1)
H. *Aloe barbadensis* (1)
I. *Verbena tenuisecta* (12)
J. *Dimorphotheca sinuata* (5)

NOTE: The key lists each plant type and the total quantity needed to replicate the garden shown. The diagram's letters and numbers refer to the type of plant and the number sited in an area.

**RESPITE FROM
THE CITY**
pages 52-53

A. *Gazania 'Daybreak Mix'* (3)
B. *Juniperus chinensis 'Nana'* (5)
C. *Pinus mugo* (1)
D. *Rudbeckia fulgida
   'Goldsturm'* (8)

E. *Ilex glabra 'Compacta'* (2)
F. *Hibiscus 'Lord Baltimore'* (1)
G. *Miscanthus sinensis
   'Gracillimus'* (3)

H. *Amelanchier x 'Cumulus'* (1)
I. *Hydrangea 'Blue Lacecap'* (3)
J. *Rosa 'Betty Prior'* (4)
K. *Alyssum 'Carpet of Snow'* (7)

**BEAUTY AT WATER'S
EDGE**
page 53

A. *Rosa rugosa* (2)
B. *Papaver orientale* (1)
C. *Hemerocallis fulva
   'Europa'* (7)

D. *Hibiscus moscheutos* (1)
E. *Phragmites communis* (6)

COLORFUL
AND CAREFREE
pages 54-55

A. *Rosmarinus officinalis* (5)
B. *Chamaemelum nobile* (1)
C. *Borago officinalis* (3)
D. *Geranium sp.* (1)
E. *Centranthus ruber* (1)

F. *Selago thunbergii* (1)
G. *Iris sibirica* (1)
H. *Lantana montevidensis* (2)
I. *Helichrysum petiolatum* (1)
J. *Chamelaucium uncinatum* (1)

A NATURAL
LANDSCAPE
pages 56-57

A. *Solidago rigida* (10)
B. *Rudbeckia hirta* (30)
C. *Silphium laciniatum* (1)
D. *Asclepias tuberosa* (3)

E. *Heliopsis helianthoides* (3)
F. *Echinacea purpurea* (8)
G. *Veronicastrum
virginicum* (6)

H. *Ratibida pinnata* (12)
I. *Parthenium integrifolium* (5)
J. *Echinacea pallida* (12)
K. *Monarda fistulosa* (10)

SHADES OF GREEN
pages 58-59

A. *Liriope 'Silver Dragon'* (36)
B. *Picea pungens 'Hoopsii'* (1)
C. *Rhododendron 'Koromu Shikibu'* (5)

D. *Ilex x attenuata 'Foster #2'* (2)
E. *Ilex 'San Jose'* (1)
F. *Zelkova serrata* (1)

G. *Ligularia dentata* (3)
H. *Impatiens wallerana* (6)
I. *Hosta undulata 'Albo-marginata'* (6)

A RAINBOW OF COLOR
page 59

A. *Cornus florida* (1)
B. *Astilbe simplicifolia 'Bronze Elegans'* (3)
C. *Buxus sempervirens* (1)
D. *Paeonia lactiflora 'Sarah Bernhardt'* (3)
E. *Coreopsis verticillata 'Moonbeam'* (1)
F. *Salvia farinacea 'Victoria'* (7)
G. *Rhododendron 'Pink Gumpo'* (3)
H. *Rosa 'Blaze'* (1)
I. *Hibiscus syriacus* (1)
J. *Hemerocallis 'Hyperion'* (3)
K. *Tagetes erecta 'Primrose Lady'* (5)
L. *Lilium regale* (7)
M. *Rhododendron 'Spring Dawn'* (2)
N. *Impatiens 'New Guinea hybrid'* (3)
O. *Gaillardia sp.* (1)

CHAPTER THREE

Maintaining Your Garden

The reward of developing an easy-care garden is a long-term reduction in routine maintenance chores. The brainwork of planning your garden (pages 6-29) and informing yourself about plants (pages 30-47) does away with much of the backbreaking work. But one task that cannot be omitted is that of properly preparing your soil. The better it is, the healthier your plants will be and the better they'll perform for you. This chapter takes you through the basics of soil preparation and offers options such as building raised beds (pages 66-69) if you have problem soil, or terracing a slope (pages 70-73) if you have problem terrain.

There are plantings that come close to self-sufficiency, such as the mature, evergreen-filled Baltimore garden shown here, but watering, occasional pruning, and the like are inevitable. There are various ways of doing them, however, and in this chapter you'll discover tricks used by master gardeners that will make life easier for you. Something as simple as the height at which you mow your grass, or finding the right pruning tool or a mulch that's appropriate for your climate, will make caring for your garden a quicker and more satisfying process.

A. *Lonicera pileata (1)* **B.** *Muscari sp. (12)* **C.** *Hedera helix (5)* **D.** *Lysimachia punctata (3)* **E.** *Ilex opaca (1)* **F.** *Fargesia nitida (1)* **G.** *Ilex pedunculosa (1)* **H.** *Taxus cuspidata (2)* **I.** *Fargesia nitida (2)* **J.** *Tulipa (15)* **K.** *Epimedium versicolor 'Sulphureum' (1)* **L.** *Liriope sp. (8)* **M.** *Ilex x attenuata 'Fosteri' (3)* **N.** *Lonicera pileata (2)*

Choosing and Caring for Tools

"Buy the right tools of good quality and then take care of them properly," advises John Stevens, estate manager and longtime gardener from Alexandria, Virginia. And good advice it is, since even experienced gardeners can fall prey to purchasing the wrong equipment. It's easy to understand how this can happen when you confront store shelves filled with an eye-catching array of spades, shovels, rakes, and the latest multipurpose gadgets that promise to do all your work for you.

In truth, the basic tools for preparing your garden have changed little over the past century: a medium-point, general-purpose shovel; a square-tined spading fork; a sharp, square-bladed spade; a mattock; an onion hoe; and a steel flat-headed rake will easily take you through most of your cultivation work.

Keeping your tools in top condition ensures that they will always be ready to use and also extends their life span. Clean off any encrusted debris and dirt after use and apply a thin coat of light oil to the blades to keep them from rusting. Store

your tools out of the elements, in a shed, garage, or basement.

Hoes, spades, and mattocks also require occasional sharpening. This chore is easily accomplished with a sharpening file, which, when pushed over the edge of the tool blade, sharpens by removing metal *(right)*. Files come in a range of coarseness levels; for hoes, spades, and mattocks, use what is called a bastard mill file.

Finally, to avoid hurting yourself while digging with shovels and spades, let your body weight and gravity drive the tool into the ground as you press your foot onto the back blade edge. Lift your loaded shovel or spade with bent knees and straight back to keep from straining muscles. Use a mattock to break up soil that is too compacted or rocky for spades and shovels. Hold the mattock with both hands *(overleaf)* and raise the tool over your head, then in one fluid motion let the weight of the mattock fall toward the ground in front of you. Reverse hand positions on the mattock every three or four swings to reduce fatigue.

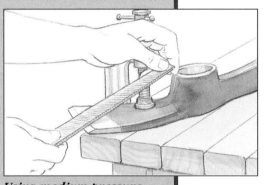

To sharpen a mattock, *remove the head from the handle and secure it to a flat surface with a C-clamp or vise. Grasp each end of the file and place it at a 30° to 35° angle against the edge of the mattock blade (inset).*

Using medium pressure, *stroke the file over the blade's edge. Repeat until the blade attains the angle of its original bevel and has a good but not too sharp edge.*

once you've decided on raised beds, you can give your imagination free rein to create the sort of garden you really want because you will be able to create the soil conditions for plants and flowers that suit your personal style; you won't be limited to just those that would grow in your soil's normal conditions. In the Southwest, for example, you might tailor a bed for camellias or azaleas—plants you could never cultivate naturally in the native alkaline soil—by filling it with acid soil.

Unless your raised bed is a very large square, you should be able to maintain it without stepping inside its boundaries, thus avoiding compacting the soil. In this way your

soil will always remain porous and loose, making it easy for water, fertilizer, and air to penetrate. Because raised beds can be built high enough to be accessible from a sitting position, they are also the perfect alternative for gardeners in wheelchairs.

Finally, raised beds allow you versatility when planning a garden. By building beds at various heights, flowers and plants are better positioned to delight the eye. The neat lines of the beds add a sense of order to your garden, and since soil in a raised bed tends to warm up sooner than ground soil, your beds become the perfect place for a vibrant display of early spring color.

A RAISED BED FOR FAST-SPREADING PERENNIALS
A bed built of narrow landscape timbers and filled with drought-tolerant oxeye daisies (Chrysanthemum leucanthemum) lends an informal, rustic charm to this Texas garden. The white-bloomed perennials spread by creeping rhizomes and reseed prolifically, so they need be planted only once.

How to Build a Raised Bed

A raised bed can easily be constructed from landscaping timbers, which come in varying dimensions and are available at most large garden centers or lumberyards. To ensure longevity, use only pressure-treated wood. For the bottom tier, select timbers labeled "ground-contact"; these have been treated to make them more resilient. For the upper tiers, regular pressure-treated wood is fine. Buy enough timbers to build a bed about 2 feet high.

1. Prepare your site by first measuring and marking off the perimeter of the bed with stakes and string. *Cut the timbers to size. Then, beginning at one end of the bed and working your way to the other, remove the existing turf, making sure no plant roots remain in the soil. Next, use a mattock (above) to break up the soil to increase drainage and encourage root growth below the level of your raised bed. Finally, along the inside perimeter of your staked area, dig a framing trench 1½ to 2 inches deep and 2 to 3 inches wider than your landscape timbers.*

2. Check the border trench with a carpenter's level to make sure the ground is even (inset). *If it is not, fill in with soil and tamp down, then check again. Lay out the base tier of timbers in the border trench, alternately butting the end of one timber against the side of another to create a squared-end rectangle as shown above. Use the level to double-check that each piece of timber is evenly laid. If you are building your bed with timbers smaller than 6 inches in diameter, you may wish to support the base level with wooden stakes; place them outside the frame, 6 to 12 inches from the end of each timber.*

Designing the Bed

A raised bed will become a permanent part of your garden design, so you should give careful thought to where you place it and to such aesthetics as style and shape. If your bed will have border trim, there are a variety of materials from which you can create a simple edging or a more formal construction. Stone, bricks, wood, or landscape timbers are all good choices. Railway ties may also be used, but, if you decide on them, be sure they have not been treated with creosote, which is harmful to plants.

When planning a bed's size and shape, keep in mind a few basic guidelines. If the bed will be accessible from two sides, make it no wider than 6 feet; if accessible from only one side, make the bed no wider than 3 to 4 feet. Widths any greater than these would require you to step on the beds in the course of tending them. The depth of a raised bed is determined by the types of plants you wish to grow. For shrubs and perennials, beds should be 18 to 24 inches deep; for vegetables plan on 12 inches; and for annuals, 8 to 10 inches will do fine. In deciding the length of your bed, keep in mind the scale and balance of your house. With a little planning and attention to such details, you can create raised gardens that will provide you with a long-lasting, easy-to-maintain, and beautiful addition to your landscape.

3. Nail abutting timbers horizontally with 8- or 10-inch galvanized spikes (A, above). Use a heavy-duty hammer to make this job easier. Begin laying your second tier, making sure the joints between timbers are offset from those of the base tier. As you lay each timber, use 6- or 8-inch galvanized nails to toenail the upper piece of timber to the lower piece (B, above). Once the second tier is in place, nail abutting timbers horizontally as you did with the base level. Repeat the process until all tiers are in place.

4. To determine the amount of soil needed to fill the bed, multiply length times width times depth, in feet. Then divide your answer by 27 to calculate cubic yards, which is how large quantities of soil are usually sold. Fill the bed and dig in organic amendments, such as peat moss and compost. Adding these amendments will raise the total volume in the bed. Try not to mound it higher than 25 percent above the top tier; over time, the soil will settle.

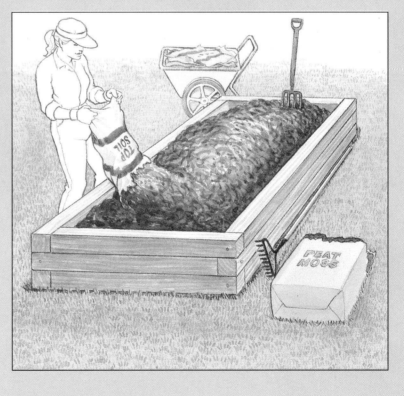

Easy Terracing for Hard-to-Work Slopes

A TERRACED HILLSIDE WALKWAY
Bluestone granite rocks support terraces bisected by a brick walkway. The tiered slope displays begonias, catharanthus, and red geraniums amid a background of hostas, ferns, and other perennial foliage.

Working a garden situated on a hill may seem to be a discouraging prospect. However, by building a few steps, or terraces, that cut across the slope, a resourceful gardener can transform a troublesome landscape into a multilevel spectacle of imagination and beauty. Terraces are essentially miniature retaining walls, and installing them on a slope will not only enhance your property's appearance but will also solve any problems with erosion and water runoff caused by the natural terrain. And it helps that the job is not a difficult one to undertake.

When to Terrace

Deciding whether to terrace a hillside depends on several factors. First, how steep is your incline? You don't need to take formal

measurements; just consider how difficult it is to perform your existing gardening chores. Does standing on the hill require some extra effort? If the slope is grass covered, is mowing it unduly tiring? Does the mower slip out of your control? If you cannot work easily on the hill, then terracing may be the perfect solution for you.

If your slope is excessively steep, you may want to consult a professional landscape architect, who can quickly determine whether terracing is advisable. Your property may require sturdy retaining walls or banks instead, especially if you live in an area that experiences severe rains and mud slides. Other options for steep inclines include holding the slope back with ground covers *(box, overleaf)*, and planting shrubs and trees into the side of your slope *(box, page 73)*.

Making a Terracing Plan

Terraces can be built of stone, railroad ties, landscaping timbers, or bricks. Choose a buttressing material that suits your garden design; for instance, you might select bricks for a formal air, or railroad ties if you want a more rustic look.

Figuring out the number of terrace steps you should install will depend on the slope's length, or run. The dimensions of your terraces—how high they will stand and how deep you make them—will vary with the run and the height, or rise, of the slope. How wide you make the terraces depends on the site and the amount of planting you'd like to do. In any case, all the terraces should be uniform in size. As a rule, terraces should be at least 1 foot deep, that is, 1 foot from the terrace's front edge to the rise where the next terrace begins. For visual definition and stability, each terrace should be at least 5 inches but no more than 12 inches high. Because they drain so well, terraces may dry out too fast if they are higher than 12 inches. Also, you don't want to be climbing and working on steps more than a foot tall. Terraces with 8-inch rises and 2-foot depths work well on most slopes. To calculate the rise and run, see the box at right.

As you develop your terracing plan, take into account any features such as trees and shrubs that presently exist on the slope. Can they be included in the terrace structure, or do they need to be removed? Large trees and

How to Size Your Terraces

Calculating the number of terraces your slope can accommodate and their dimensions is a matter of simple arithmetic. First you need to measure the rise (height) and the run (horizontal length) of your slope. For the rise, have a helper hold a 2-by-4 board horizontally, with one end resting on the top of the slope, as shown below. Check to see if the board is level. Then measure the vertical distance from the ground at the foot of the slope to the board. Measuring from one end of the board, mark off that distance. To calculate the run, reverse the position of the board so that it stands upright at the foot of the slope, and measure the horizontal distance from the top of the slope straight across to the point on the board that corresponds to the slope's rise. For a slope with a more gradual rise, measure the slope in increments and add the resulting figures together.

Next, divide the rise measurement by the height you want each terrace to be. For example, if the rise is 32 inches and you want terraces 8 inches high, divide 32 by 8, for a result of 4 steps. To find the depth of each terrace, divide the run measurement by the number of steps you want to build. If the run is 96 inches, divide 96 by 4; your terraces will be 24 inches, or 2 feet, deep. The numbers rarely work out this neatly, but you can adjust the measurements an inch or two this way or that to come up with some usable dimensions.

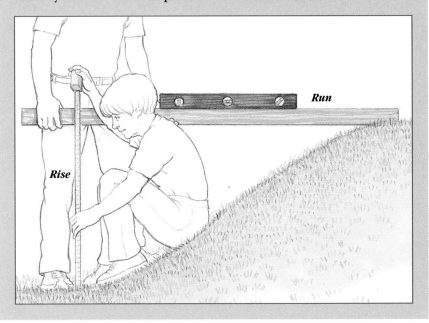

shrubs are best left in place since removing them could exacerbate erosion or runoff problems. Also, if the incline descends toward your house, plan on leaving a flat area at the bottom. This will keep water that is running off the terraced hill away from your foundation. An added benefit of this open space is that it may allow more daylight to enter your home. Planting ground cover or shrubs along the outer embankments of your terraces will also slow runoff and erosion.

Building a Stone Terrace

One of the easiest ways to build terraces is to construct the tiers with large stones. They are available at local quarries and are relatively inexpensive. Select stones with at least one flat side; you'll place this side up so that the top edges of all the terraces look uniform.

Before starting your first tier, clear the slope of its existing plants, including all sod. Terraces will have to be built around permanent features such as trees. Taprooted trees pose less of a problem than shallow-rooted ones, whose roots extend out just below ground surface and interfere with construction. If you have shallow-rooted trees, you may want to consider alternatives, such as building raised beds around the trunks or planting some kind of ground cover.

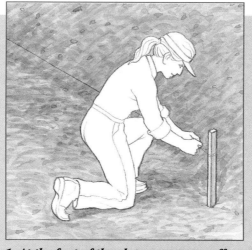

1. At the foot of the slope, measure off the width of the first terrace and drive a stake into the ground at either end. *Mark the height level of the terrace on each stake. Stretch a string between the two stakes at the marked points. Use a line level or lay a carpenter's level lightly across the string to make sure that the guideline is exactly horizontal.*

2. Start laying the stones for the first terrace. *If necessary, scoop out some soil with a trowel to fit large or irregularly shaped stones neatly and solidly into the earth. Build up the rows of stones until the terrace wall lines up with the string. To ensure drainage, pour coarse gravel behind the stones until it reaches about three-quarters of the height of the terrace.*

Planting Ground Cover

Planting an erosion-controlling ground cover on a slope is sometimes the only option, especially on a short, steep drop. If you choose creeping juniper or another low-lying woody shrub whose branches grow horizontally, consider laying down landscape fabric to control weeds *(right)*. Avoid the fabric, however, with a ground cover such as vinca or ivy that roots as it grows.

Clear the slope of existing vegetation, and if grass abuts the edges, install mowing strips. Then lay panels of landscape fabric across the slope; overlap the lengths by 4 to 6 inches. To hold the fabric in place, stake it with bent wire. Then measure and mark the correct spacing for your plants and cut Xs into the fabric at the marks. Dig holes large enough to accommodate the rootballs, then plant. Do not cover the fabric with chunky mulch; heavy rains may cause it to slide down the incline.

3. Fill in the first terrace by scraping soil from farther up the slope *and shoveling it behind the stones until the entire terrace is at the right height and even. Make sure the terrace is flat by laying a carpenter's level across it, as shown above. Use a measuring tape to check that the terrace is as deep as you planned.*

4. Move the stakes and string up and back to mark the position and height of the next terrace. *Lay stones as described in Step 2, then pour in gravel and level off the terrace with shovelfuls of earth. Repeat the process until you have terraced the entire slope. Amend the soil and let it settle for a few days before planting.*

Preparations for Planting

When selecting plants for the terraces, you'll generally want to keep to low growing types that creep or form mounds. Plants that cascade create a lovely display and also help unite the levels of the terraced area. Good choices are creeping phlox *(Phlox stolonifera)* or moss phlox *(P. subulata),* creeping juniper, sedums with trailing stems, small-leaved ivies, and herbs such as thyme. Mounded plants such as winter jasmine, prostrate abelia, and dwarf cutleaf stephanandra (lace shrub) help soften the edges of the terraces without obscuring them.

As is true for any new garden bed, you will need to work the soil in each of your terraces before planting. Amend it as necessary, keeping the soil level 1 to 2 inches below the top edge of the border. This prevents soil from being washed over the front of the terrace during heavy rains.

Planting Trees

A slope offers you the chance to nurture a lovely tree or shrub in a spot you may not otherwise be inclined to plant. Too often trees and shrubs list aimlessly off the sides of hilly slopes, but you can avoid this problem with proper planting. First, dig a hole deep enough so that the top of the rootball is flush with the uphill side of the slope. Fill in the hole and mound soil on the downhill side of the rootball until the entire rootball is well covered. Make a water basin for the trunk by building up a rim of earth around the top of the mound. Then cover the area with mulch and water slowly but thoroughly. If you plant a tree on a very steep incline, you may want to stake it from the uphill side.

Mulching and Weeding

The work required to keep a garden well mulched pays off handsomely. Besides contributing to optimum growing conditions, a mulch minimizes watering and weeding and gives beds and borders a finished look.

Organic Mulches versus Stone

Mulches best suited to the ornamental garden include numerous organic materials—shredded bark, cocoa shells, woodchips, and leaves, among others—and one inorganic material—stone. Stone mulch is available in different forms, most commonly gravel, crushed rock, or stone chips. Another inorganic mulch, the long-lasting, porous synthetic material called landscape fabric, blocks weeds but, because it is unattractive, should be covered with a decorative mulch *(opposite)*, except on a steep slope, where the mulch would likely be washed downhill by rain.

Both organic and stone mulches slow the evaporation of soil moisture and moderate soil temperature. Organic mulches are especially effective shields against heat—on a 100°F day, the soil beneath a 3-inch layer may be as much as 30°F cooler than the air above. Organic mulches also improve the soil, decaying into humus. Because they decompose, however, they have to be replenished.

AN EYE-CATCHING ORGANIC MULCH
Unfit for brewing because they were roasted too long, coffee beans find an alternative use as an unusual mulch in a Seattle garden.

HEADING OFF DISEASE WITH THE RIGHT MULCH
An expanse of fine stone chips provides a hospitable setting for sand phlox, a spring-blooming native perennial that thrives in fast-draining sandy or rocky soil. The heat and light a stone mulch reflects help keep foliage dry, reducing the likelihood of crown rot in susceptible plants.

Stone mulches have the virtue of permanence. And only 1 inch of rock or gravel may be enough for good coverage. But there are drawbacks. When used under a deciduous tree, the mulch makes fallen leaves difficult to rake up. It can also become hot enough in bright sun to raise the ambient air temperature by 10°F or more, and the stones themselves can burn any plant stems they touch. In addition, sunlight hitting pale-colored stones can produce an unpleasant glare. And lastly, the very permanence of stone means that it doesn't improve soil structure.

Choosing and Applying a Mulch

Looks, longevity, site, and price are all factors to consider when selecting and using organic mulch. Combining materials is also an option: A serviceable but unsightly layer of newspapers, ground corncobs, or ground sugarcane stalks can be concealed beneath chunks of bark or pine needles. Avoid using peat moss as a mulch, however. Although it's a good soil amendment, when placed on top of the soil it blows around, is hard to rewet when it dries out, is a fire hazard, and is expensive to boot.

There are no across-the-board rules governing how deeply to mulch. Soil type must be taken into account; a loose, sandy soil, for instance, dries out more quickly than clay soil and consequently needs a thicker layer of mulch. The density of the mulch itself is important—the coarser and airier it is, the deeper you can apply it. Be careful, however, not to use a mulch so dense that little air and water can pass through it into the soil.

Whatever material you pick, lay it thickest between plants, tapering it down to soil level within an inch or two of the base of the plants. Avoid piling mulch against trunks or stems lest it encourage pests and diseases. As a rule of thumb, use a 1- to 2-inch layer for a mulch with particles measuring ½ inch in diameter. Particles ranging from ½ inch to an inch or so should be spread at least 2 to 3 inches deep, and dry leaves, pine needles, and woodchips deeper still. If the woodchips are fresh, mix each cubic yard with 3 pounds of controlled-release nitrogen fertilizer before putting the mulch in place. Otherwise, microorganisms proliferating in the woodchips will draw nitrogen from the soil.

If weeds continue to appear, you've proba-

Laying Landscape Fabric in an Existing Bed

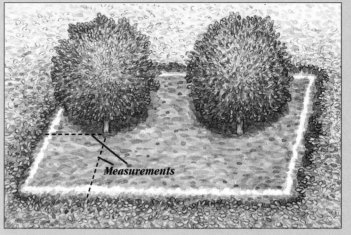

Measurements

1. Use lime to outline the area that is to be mulched, then remove any weeds and debris from around the plants. Measure the bed's length and width to determine how many lengths of fabric to cut, allowing for a 4- to 6-inch overlap between adjoining sections. Correctly position the fabric in an area adjacent to the bed. Next, measure the distance from a plant's center to the two closest edges of the bed that form a right angle. Transfer this measurement to the fabric and mark the point where the two lines intersect.

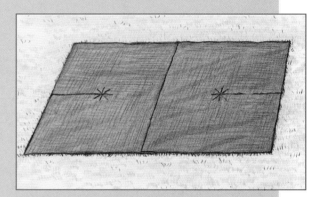

2. Cut from one edge of the fabric to the point where the two lines intersect, then make a series of radiating cuts around it (above). The cuts should equal the radius of the plant's trunk or stem cluster, plus about 3 inches.

3. Slip the fabric around each plant, then fold the pie-shaped wedges under to make a neat circle. When all of the sections of fabric are in place, cover them with a decorative mulch.

Using an Onion Hoe

A lightweight onion hoe that is well sharpened and properly wielded requires little effort to use. To sever a weed just below ground level, position the blade a few inches above the soil *(inset)* and pull it toward you in a shallow arc. In tight spots, turn the hoe sideways and use one of its narrow edges to slice off a weed. A blade used in rocky soil will need more frequent sharpening than one used in sandy soil.

Using a Dandelion Digger

Working when the soil is moist, thrust a long-handled dandelion digger into the ground deep enough to reach the tip of a weed's root (inset). Then push down on the tool's handle to pry the weed out. Examine the root; if it isn't intact, dig out the portions that broke off to prevent regrowth.

bly skimped on mulch and should add more. However, if slugs and snails are a problem, additional mulch may draw still more of them. In such cases, it's better to use a combination of landscape fabric hidden by a thin covering of mulch. Plan on renewing bark and leaf mulches annually. Woodchips can last 2 years and pine needles up to 3 years.

When Weeds Appear

Although keeping soil mulched is an excellent preventive, no garden is ever completely free of weeds. Perennial weeds are a worse problem than annual ones. Their more extensive root systems are harder to dig out, and any fragments left behind may produce new growth. Use a digging fork with ground ivy, Bermuda grass, and other perennial weeds that have wide-spreading runners; a narrow-bladed dandelion digger *(left)* is the best choice for weeds with deep roots such as Canada thistle and dandelion. An onion hoe works well for cutting larger shallow-rooted annual weeds such as chickweed *(above, left)*. For weeds in spots that are hard to get at with a digging tool, try pouring boiling water on them. Several applications may be needed.

Herbicides should only be used as a last resort against persistent weeds, and then only to spot-treat. Glyphosate is one of the less toxic and most useful herbicides, but if carelessly applied will attack ornamentals.

Techniques of Efficient Watering

Water is critical to plant life, and keeping soil moisture at a healthy level is one task that can't be postponed without risking injury to the garden. If you know your soil, however, and pay attention to equipment and techniques, you'll get the job done much more efficiently and in a timely way.

Deep Watering for Drought Resistance

Plants are most demanding while they're becoming established—a year or so for perennials, twice as long for shrubs and trees. Give new plantings relatively light, frequent waterings and monitor for signs of stress, such as drooping or dull-looking leaves. The soil should dry out slightly between waterings so that oxygen can reach plant roots.

As plants mature, progressively deeper and less frequent watering is called for. This encourages the roots to penetrate far into the soil, where they can tap into moisture reserves and come through dry spells in good condition. Established plantings of drought-tolerant trees, shrubs, and perennials may need only minimal watering during such periods—or even none at all, depending on the soil's structure. A good rule of thumb, though, is to moisten soil to a depth of 12 inches two to three times a month for woody plants, and every 7 to 10 days for perennials. Unless an extended drought occurs, the soil below that point usually has enough moisture to supply deep-growing roots.

Shallow watering can actually be worse for a plant than no watering at all because roots will tend to remain concentrated near the surface. As a consequence, the plant is more vulnerable to damage during spells of heat and drought.

The Best Watering Methods

Watering large areas with a hand-held, high-pressure hose is a waste of time because so much of the water runs off instead of sinking

77

into the soil. Similarly, moving hoses and sprinklers from place to place is tedious work. For the best results with the least effort, consider a system of low-flow, low-pressure hoses and delivery devices that's tailored to your site. These systems can be installed above ground or buried, and not all of them require installation by a professional. Some can be easily devised by the homeowner from materials available in a local garden center *(opposite)*.

There are two basic ways to apply water to your garden: by sprinkling or by soaking. Sprinkling is by far the better method to use with a lawn, and it also works well with perennials and ground covers, especially those that thrive in a humid environment. The overhead action helps wash dust and pollutants from foliage, and it also discourages undesirable insects such as spider mites.

A major disadvantage of sprinklers is that they waste water if the pressure isn't appropriate to the soil. For clay, where runoff is a problem, pick a sprinkler that has a low delivery rate. A sprinkler with a higher delivery

Testing Soil Moisture

To determine how well a watering regimen delivers moisture to the root zone of your plants, use a soil auger *(below)* to collect a sample of earth. The auger, basically a hollow cylinder with a handle and a window cut in one side, is pushed into the ground vertically, twisted to free a core of soil, then pulled out at an angle, window side up. Feel the soil; if only the top few inches are moist, adjust your watering regimen to get deeper penetration.

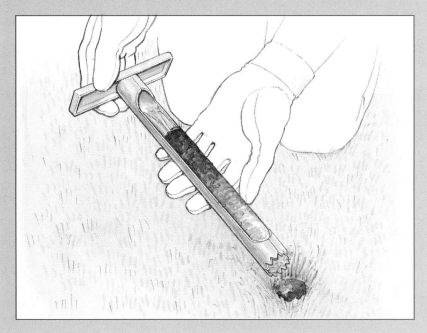

An Off-the-Shelf Irrigation System

At a very reasonable cost, you can put together an irrigation system using garden hoses, soaker hoses, sprinklers, timers, and other accessories widely available at garden centers and hardware stores. The property illustrated at right has a series of setups that are configured to suit the plantings in different parts of the garden. Except for two garden hoses that need to be moved into position when it's time to water, the system can be left in place year round.

The system uses two different kinds of soaker hose. One has metal fittings at each end that are identical to those of a conventional garden hose. The other kind allows the gardener maximum flexibility in customizing an irrigation system because it is cut to the lengths appropriate for particular areas.

The various pieces of the system are joined with specially designed tubular fittings. Virtually any layout can be assembled. In the example shown here, a timer—either electronic or mechanical—is attached to each of the three outdoor faucets supplying water to the garden.

The system supplies different areas as follows:

1. The backyard lawn and most of the surrounding perennial border are irrigated simultaneously by a single impulse sprinkler, which is stored beside the house between waterings, along with the garden hose *(brown)* that supplies it. A soaker hose with brass fittings on its ends *(green)* is operated off the same faucet via a Y-connector and waters the back of the border, to the left of the lawn.

2. Custom-cut lengths of soaker hose are placed in a ring around each of the trees planted behind the garage *(red)*, and are joined by tubular connectors to nonporous supply pipes *(blue)*.

3. The garden hose *(brown)* running from the faucet beside the driveway does double duty, supplying the backyard trees and the hedge flanking the driveway. Two-part metal couplings at either end of the hose make the hose easy to connect and disconnect.

4. A Y-connector attached to the faucet on the front of the house allows the sunny street-side perennial bed and the shrubs in the partly shaded side yard to be watered independently with soaker hoses *(green)*.

ELECTRONIC TIMER
This device switches water on and off automatically. Because it can be programmed to water at any time, it is particularly useful during vacations.

IMPULSE SPRINKLER
This sprinkler's spring-loaded arm disperses water evenly over an area ranging from a small wedge to a full circle.

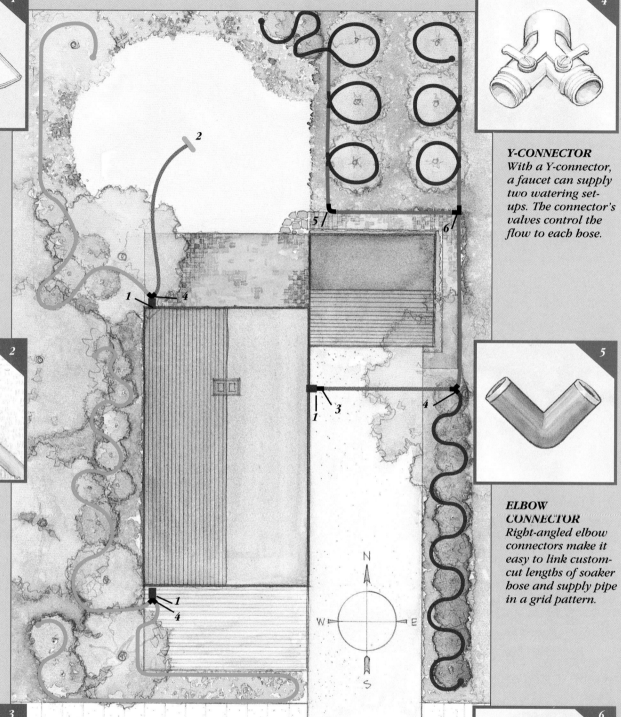

TWO-PART SNAP COUPLING
This coupling eliminates the need to screw threaded devices together, making connecting and disconnecting a hose easy.

T-CONNECTOR
A T-connector can link three hoses, either custom-cut or with brass fittings, which attach to its threaded ends.

Y-CONNECTOR
With a Y-connector, a faucet can supply two watering set-ups. The connector's valves control the flow to each hose.

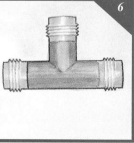

ELBOW CONNECTOR
Right-angled elbow connectors make it easy to link custom-cut lengths of soaker hose and supply pipe in a grid pattern.

rate suits a sandy soil, providing a fast soaking that minimizes evaporation.

Whatever the soil type, a sprinkler head should produce droplets rather than a readily evaporated fog or mist. (The easiest time to check a sprinkler's output is when it is illuminated by the low, slanting rays of an early-morning or late-afternoon sun.) In addition, the droplets should be emitted at a low angle; sprayed high into the air, water is more likely to drift out of the target area or evaporate. All told, as much as 50 percent of the output of an ill-chosen and ill-used sprinkler can go to waste.

A Soaking for Trees and Shrubs

The most water-efficient method to use with trees and shrubs is a slow soaking. One way to accomplish this is by installing a drip-irrigation system operated manually or, more conveniently, by an electronic timer. Flowing slowly through plastic supply tubing underground or beneath a layer of mulch, water oozes out by way of emitters placed near individual plants. How much water a plant receives is determined by the type and number of emitters supplying it; thus more water can be supplied in a hot, sunny spot, less in a moist, cool corner of the garden. As a plant grows, you can change the emitters to suit the plant's changing requirements. A bonus of such a system is less weeding, since areas beyond the reach of emitters remain dry and don't foster lush weed growth.

Another watering option for trees, shrubs, and borders is the soaker hose. Made of recycled tires, soaker hoses ooze water along the entire length of their porous walls. How far apart to space them depends on your soil: 1 to 1½ feet in sandy soil, 1½ to 2 feet in loam, and 2 to 3 feet in clay soil, where water spreads farther in a lateral direction.

A drawback to both drip-irrigation systems and soaker hoses is the potential for clogging by debris, insects, or mineral salts in the water supply; locating a blockage can be time-consuming. And with either system, keep the water pressure low; high pressure can weaken parts or cause a blowout.

Watering a Slope

The chart at right shows how a garden's contours and its soil type—sandy, loamy, or clay—affect the rate of water absorption. A sandy, level area, for instance, can absorb up to 1.7 inches of water per hour. But on a sandy 10 percent slope—one whose elevation rises 1 foot for every 10 feet of run—only 1.02 inches are absorbed; the remainder runs off before it can soak into the ground. When the slope increases to 20 percent, the maximum amount of water absorbed in an hour falls still further, to 0.68 inch.

To give a slope a proper soaking without excessive runoff, apply water more slowly than on level ground. In addition, water the top of the slope more heavily than the bottom, since as much as half of that water may move downhill, either on the surface or underground. If you're using soaker hoses, minimize runoff by laying them across the slope.

SOIL TYPE	INCHES OF WATER ABSORBED PER HOUR ON THREE GRADES		
	LEVEL	10% SLOPE	20% SLOPE
SANDY	.5"-1.7"	.3"-1.02"	.2"-.68"
LOAMY	.25"-1.0"	.15"-.6"	.1"-.4"
CLAY	.1"-.2"	.06"-.12"	.04"-.08"

Maintaining Your Lawn

A lawn typically requires more time to maintain than any other part of the garden of equal size. However, if you have limited the lawn area, prepared the soil with plenty of organic matter, and planted a variety of grass that's appropriate for your climate, lawn chores will be much less demanding.

When and How Much to Water

The precise amount of water a lawn needs varies with the climate, season, and type of grass *(page 19)*. A typical demand is for 1 to 2 inches of water weekly in summer and about half that in spring and fall, including any rainfall. As in other parts of the garden, aim for thorough watering. The soil should be moistened to a depth of at least 6 to 8 inches; 12 inches is better, however, and will stimulate robust, deep-rooted, drought-resistant turf.

According to many experts, it's preferable to let a lawn go dormant during a dry spell if the alternative is scanty watering that allows weeds to flourish but isn't sufficient to keep the grass growing well.

Several visual cues indicate when a lawn is suffering from lack of moisture. The blades turn bluish or metallic-looking, lose their sheen, and may roll into cylinders. And, instead of springing back when it is walked on, the turf retains footprints.

The Right Way to Mow

Paying attention to mowing height and frequency helps keep the lawn in good health and actually makes maintenance easier in the long run. How tall to let the grass grow varies by type and also by season, as shown in the

PROTECTING THE LAWN AGAINST WEAR
Steppingstones laid in a frequently trod garden corridor eliminate the chore of restoring turf damaged by foot traffic. The upper surfaces of the stones have been placed slightly below the level of the soil so they don't interfere with the lawn mower.

chart below. If allowed to grow taller in hot, dry weather, the blades of grass shade the soil and slow the evaporation of soil moisture.

Yellow or brownish areas that appear after a mowing in summer suggest that the grass has been cut too short. For mowers on which heights are indicated, set the machine's levers to the correct positions. If settings aren't marked on your mower, check the adjustment by mowing a test patch of grass; then measure the distance from the soil level to the tip of the blade. If the grass is too short or too long, place the mower on a smooth paved surface such as cement and adjust the blades to a higher or lower setting. Measure the distance between the paving and the bottom edge of the lowest blade to check whether it's the same as the height you want to cut the grass.

To avoid stressing the roots, mow your lawn often enough that no more than a quarter to a third of each blade is removed at one time. If your lawn has grown too tall, get it back in line with several mowings separated by a day or two of recovery time.

With frequent mowings, it isn't necessary to bag or rake grass clippings. You can simply leave them in place to form a fine mulch that adds organic matter and nutrients to the soil and cuts down on the amount of fertilizer you have to apply.

Maintaining Your Lawn Mower

Power lawn mowers come in two basic types, reel and rotary. Reel mowers can be adjusted to cut much closer, but they're harder to take care of than the more commonly used rotary mower. An alternative for small lawns is the nonpowered reel mower. Silent and nonpolluting, it does a good job on fine-textured, cool-climate lawn grasses but not the tougher, more wiry warm-climate grasses, which need a rotary mower. A special type of rotary mower called a mulching mower eliminates the need to rake altogether. It has extra blades that cut grass clippings into very small bits that sift down to soil level and decay quickly.

Whatever type of lawn mower you use, it's important to keep the blades sharp. A dull

	GRASSES	MOWING HEIGHTS OF TURF GRASSES	
		COOL WEATHER	HOT WEATHER
COOL SEASON	BENT GRASS	½"	1"
	KENTUCKY BLUEGRASS	1½"	3"
	FINE FESCUE	1½"	2"- 2½"
	TALL FESCUE	2½"	2½"- 4"
	PERENNIAL RYEGRASS	1½"	2"- 2½"
WARM SEASON	BAHIA GRASS	2"	3"
	BERMUDA GRASS	½"	2½"- 3"
	CENTIPEDE GRASS	1"	2"
	ST. AUGUSTINE GRASS	2"	3"
	ZOYSIA	½"	1"
NATIVE	BUFFALO GRASS	3½"- 5"	3½"- 5"
	BLUE GRAMA	4"	4"

A Pattern for Efficient Mowing

Mowing in a spiral pattern eliminates the tiring, time-consuming backtracking demanded by parallel swaths. Work from the outside inward, as shown below, saving any areas outside the spiral course for the end. Reverse directions from one mowing to the next to minimize soil compaction.You can adjust the pattern to fit the lawn's shape—an elliptical course, for instance, works better for a long, narrow area. The height at which you cut the grass will depend on the type of grass you have *(right)*.

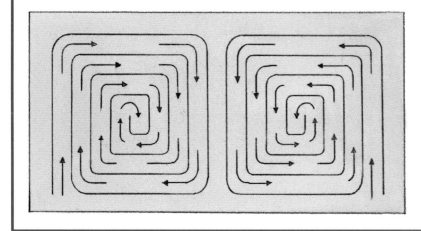

blade tears the tips of the grass, making them slow to heal and the grass more vulnerable to disease than cleanly cut turf. In addition, the ragged tips give the lawn an unattractive brownish cast.

Steps to Improve Compacted Soil

Because a lawn invites foot traffic, over time the soil may become too compacted to supply the roots with adequate air, water, and nutrients. Thinning grass, numerous weeds, and a thick mat of undecayed clippings, stems, and runners known as thatch *(below)* are all symptoms that the soil needs to be aerated.

Carry out this treatment while the grass is actively growing. If the ground is dry, water it the night before to soften it. The fastest and most efficient way to aerate your lawn is to use a powered aerating machine, which can be rented from a garden-equipment center. As it is run back and forth across the lawn, the aerator pulls up small plugs of sod and soil and throws them aside. When you've gone over the lawn, rake up the plugs and crumble them to separate the soil from the bits of sod. Mix the soil with coarse sand and peat moss or sieved compost. Scatter a half-inch-deep layer of this mixture, called a top dressing, over the lawn. With the back of a garden rake, spread the top dressing evenly and push it down into the aeration holes. Then water the lawn to a depth of at least 6 inches.

Raking the Easy Way

The best tool for clearing a lawn of fallen leaves is a bamboo rake. Use the rake as you would a broom, sweeping it across your body instead of pulling it toward you. To keep the rake flexible, soak it in water overnight every 2 or 3 months.

Checking for Thatch

Dig up a small plug of turf and inspect it for dead stems and runners matted between the grass blades and the soil. More than a ½ inch of thatch forms a barrier to water, air, and fertilizer. Use a dethatching machine or a rake to remove excess thatch.

Pruning Shrubs and Trees

In a well-planned low-maintenance garden, pruning isn't a burdensome task. Shrubs and trees are chosen with an eye to their shape, growth rate, and mature size, and they are planted in accommodating spots where they won't loom out of scale, cast too large a pool of shade, or crowd their neighbors. But the surest way to shrink the pruning workload is to adopt a naturalistic style. This means simply allowing a shrub or tree to achieve its natural shape and size, with only an occasional pruning to encourage new growth or eliminate a wayward branch or stem. By contrast, when hedges and specimen shrubs are sheared into formal, geometric shapes, they require tending throughout the growing season; it takes only a scattering of new shoots to make them look messy.

Pruning for Health and Vigor

Even when the need for routine pruning is kept in check, the gardener should watch out for and promptly remove abnormal or undesirable stems or branches that threaten a plant's health. Examples include:

- Insect-infested or diseased growth. Cut back to healthy tissue.

Cutting Back

When a branch is cut back, or shortened, the plant puts out new growth, usually from the vegetative bud located just below the point where the branch was pruned. You can steer the new growth in a desired direction by choosing where to cut. The risk of disease or injury to the plant is minimal when a cut is made properly.

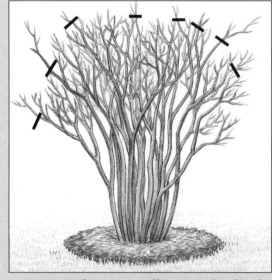

1. Examine the winter silhouette of a deciduous shrub for any overlong, rangy branches in need of cutting back. *In the example shown above, cuts made at the points indicated by the colored bars will neaten the shrub while preserving a natural look.*

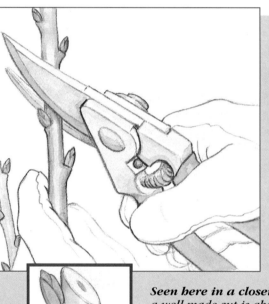

2. Inspect the branch to be cut and find a bud pointing in the direction in which you want a new shoot to grow. Using clean, sharp pruning shears, align the blades parallel to the direction in which the bud points and cut through the branch with one smooth stroke; twisting can tear the wood and bend the blades.

Seen here in a closeup view, a well-made cut is about ¼ inch above the bud and slopes down and away from it at a 45° angle. Water flowing over the cut surface drains away from the bud, reducing the likelihood of rot.

BAD CUTS. The sharply slanting cut at far left exposes an excessive amount of heartwood to infection and drying. The cut at center is too far from the bud, leaving a long stub that won't heal well. The third cut is so close to the bud that damage is likely.

Choosing the Right Time to Prune

These plants should be pruned in winter or early spring:

Abelia x grandiflora
(flowering abelia)
Hibiscus syriacus
(rose of Sharon)
Hydrangea spp.
(hydrangea)
Itea spp.
(sweetspire)
Lagerstroemia indica
(crape myrtle)
Nerium oleander
(oleander)
Oxydendrum arboreum
(sourwood)
Potentilla fruticosa
(shrubby cinquefoil)

These plants should be pruned immediately after flowering:

Chaenomeles speciosa
(flowering quince)
Cornus spp.
(dogwood)
Deutzia gracilis
(slender deutzia)
Forsythia spp.
(forsythia)
Fothergilla spp.
(fothergilla)
Hamamelis x intermedia
(witch hazel)
Kalmia latifolia
(mountain laurel)
Kerria japonica
(Japanese kerria)

Pieris spp.
(andromeda)
Prunus 'Hally Jolivette'
(Hally Jolivette cherry)
Rhododendron spp.
(azaleas, rhododendrons)
Spiraea spp.
(spirea)
Syringa spp.
(lilac)
Viburnum spp.
(viburnum)

Note: The abbreviation "spp." stands for the plural of "species"; where used in lists it means that many, but not all, of the species in a genus meet the criterion of the list.

Rhododendron sp. (azalea)

- Dead, broken, damaged, or winter-killed stems or branches. Cut back to healthy tissue.
- Basal shoots, or suckers, that emerge from roots near the base of a plant. These grow faster than the rest of the plant and divert water and nutrients. Cut off at the ground.
- Water sprouts, a type of sucker that grows straight up from a branch or trunk. Water sprouts seldom produce flowers or fruit, and their soft tissue provides an entry point for pests. Cut off at the sprout's base.

Enhancing a Plant's Looks

At times you'll need to prune to correct flaws in shape or structure—for instance, awkwardly angled branches, two upright stems competing to be a tree's leader, or stems that are crowded on one side of a shrub and sparse on another. This pruning is best done when the shoots and branches are still young, slender, and pliable. Cutting immature growth takes less effort, and it's also better for the plant. Because the wounds left by the pruning shears are small and the tissue is growing rapidly, healing takes place quickly. Consequently, the opportunity for infection or insect invasion is less than it would be in larger, woodier growth. In addition, scarring is minimal or nonexistent, a boon for the long-term appearance of the plant.

Thinning

Eliminating a branch or a stem improves a plant's form, opens its center to more light, and reduces the risk of disease by improving air circulation. Cut off at its base as shown below, the shoot doesn't grow back because no dormant buds remain below the cut. When heavily thinned, a plant sends up more vigorous growth from its roots.

1. Branches growing at an awkward angle or in an undesirable direction, shown here in dark brown, are slated for removal from the shrub at left; the colored bars indicate where to make the pruning cuts. In cases where an entire stem is to be removed, the pruning cut is made as close to the ground as possible.

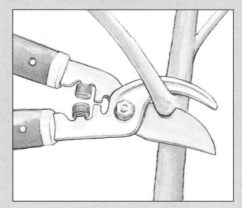

2. To avoid leaving a stub that could sprout or invite rot, place the blades of the loppers around the branch with the large cutting blade against the parent stem. It's best to cut from the bottom, as shown here; otherwise the blade may get wedged in a narrow crotch and make a ragged cut.

Pruning a Young Tree

The payoff for correcting a tree's structural flaws early is sounder health and better looks in maturity. Prompt attention to common defects such as those illustrated here will save you trouble and money in the long run, preventing small problems from burgeoning into large, expensive ones requiring a professional.

1. Remove any branch in competition with the tree's central stem. Multiple leaders make the tree prone to breaking.

2. Cut back disproportionately long branches.

3. Prevent bark injury by cutting off any branch that crosses and rubs the tree trunk or another branch.

4. Remove one of a pair of closely spaced parallel branches to prevent crowding later on.

5. Cut off any vertical unbranched shoots, or water sprouts.

6. Remove low branches for more headroom or better light for underplantings.

How to Prune

There are two basic pruning techniques— cutting back and thinning. When you cut back, only part of a branch or stem is removed, with the cut made just above a bud *(page 84)*. The procedure stimulates the buds remaining along the stem to develop and thicken the plant with new foliage.

The more radical of the two techniques is thinning, which opens up the center of a plant to more light and better air circulation by reducing the total number of branches or stems. When you thin, you remove a stem or branch completely by cutting it off at ground level or at the point where it springs from a trunk or parent branch *(page 85)*; ideally, this removal is permanent. You can safely thin up to a third of a plant's wood in a year. Such a thoroughgoing pruning will rejuvenate an aging, overgrown plant and restore its flowering potential.

The Right Tool for the Job

For any pruning job you undertake, do the work with hand tools such as hedge shears or, preferably, pruning shears *(opposite)*. Although electric hedge shears save time, it's easy to prune unevenly or more heavily than you meant to simply because the shears cut so fast. They also pose the danger of electric shock, and should never be used during or shortly after a rain or when standing on wet

Removing a Tree Limb

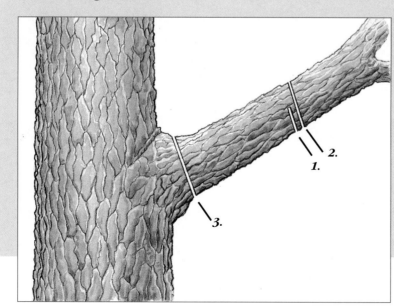

1. To prevent the tree's bark from tearing when the limb is removed, first saw halfway through the underside of the limb about 10 inches from the trunk.

2. Just beyond the first cut, start sawing from the top of the limb and saw completely through it, leaving a stub.

3. Remove the stub by sawing downward just beyond the collarlike bulge around the base of the limb; cutting into the branch collar, as it is called, would disrupt healing. Unlike an intact branch, the stub isn't heavy enough to strip bark from the trunk as it begins to fall.

soil. (As a matter of practice, avoid pruning right after a heavy rain, since walking around a plant at that time compacts the soil).

The Right Time to Prune

The best time to prune depends on the plant *(list, page 85)*. If a deciduous or broadleaf evergreen tree or shrub needs a thorough pruning of mature wood—wood that is a year or more old—the least risky time to do it is from midwinter to very early spring, while the plant is still dormant. Some spring bloomers, such as lilacs, are exceptions to this rule, however. Since early pruning would sacrifice buds for the current year's display, wait to cut back or thin until immediately after flowering. Prune summer-flowering plants, whose buds form on the current year's growth, early in the season; needled evergreens, just as new growth begins in spring. Use a very light hand with conifers, since if you cut back into mature wood new growth will rarely develop.

The Essential Pruning Tools

Three hand tools will see you through most pruning jobs—pruning shears for small branches, a pair of long-handled loppers for medium-size ones, and a pruning saw for bigger jobs. Of the three, pruning saws come in a greater variety of designs and sizes *(below)*; you may want to have more than one so that you can pick the tool best suited to the task at hand. Unlike carpenters' handsaws, pruning saws have wide triangular teeth that keep them from binding when cutting through sappy green wood.

Buy the highest-quality tool you can afford. Forged steel blades cut better, are much more durable, and keep their edge better than inexpensive tools made of cast or stamped metal.

LONG-HANDLED LOPPERS
Branches as large as 1½ inches in diameter are pruned with loppers. Handles range from 1 to 2 feet or more in length. Although heavier, the longer-handled models provide more leverage and greater reach. Bypass loppers (near right) generally make a closer, cleaner cut, but anvil loppers (far right) require less strength to operate.

PRUNING SHEARS
Both bypass pruning shears (below) and anvil pruning shears (below, right) can handle branches up to ¾ inch or so in diameter, depending on whether the wood is green or dead—deadwood is harder to cut. Because of the anvil pruner's chopping action, the blade needs more frequent sharpening than that of the scissor-action bypass pruner.

A VARIETY OF PRUNING SAWS
Because it has a thin blade of hardened steel that creates little friction, a bow saw (top) cuts large branches with relatively little effort. The curved blade of the saw at center can fit into tight spaces, and it has a comfortable pistol-grip handle. A latch on the folding saw at bottom keeps the blade securely fixed in the open position.

Answers to Common Questions

CHOOSING LOW MAINTENANCE PLANTS

Is it true that native plants are better bets for low-maintenance gardening than exotic plants from other parts of the world?

Not necessarily. Many exotics actually outperform natives when brought into cultivation in American gardens. The forsythia, for example, is an Asian plant that generally thrives, with very little attention. Provided your garden supplies a plant's basic cultural needs, you should choose on the basis of such qualities as growth form, flower color and size, season of bloom, hardiness, and disease resistance rather than country of origin.

When selecting plants for my garden, how do I know which ones will grow best in my area?

One of the best ways to learn which plants grow well in your area—exotics as well as natives—is to visit as many local gardens as you can. Garden clubs often give garden tours, especially in the spring, and your local community college may offer horticulture courses that include visits to area gardens. Also, visit an arboretum or a botanical garden if there is one close by.

Are fast-growing plants the best for low-maintenance situations since they cover the ground quickly?

Yes for the short term, but sometimes no for long-term low maintenance. Fast-spreading plants tend to fill in quickly but then need more fertilizing than other plants as well as pruning to keep them from taking over. The same is true of many species of shade trees that grow fast, such as willows and Norway and silver maples. The roots of these trees are so shallow and invasive that growing plants beneath the trees becomes a real challenge.

I am confused about which lawn-grass mixture I should buy for easy care. How can I decide among "playground mix," "park mix," or "estate mix" when those terms do not apply to my little yard?

The complex process of selecting the proper grass mix is not helped by the sales jargon you mention. There is no one lawn grass that can be planted throughout the United States. Like other perennials, grass species have unique requirements for moisture, light, temperature, and so on. The fine-bladed grasses that give the thick, luxurious lawns that most people prefer are bluegrass, Chewings and red fescues, and some of the new perennial ryegrasses. Use the chart on page 19 to determine what will grow in your area, and choose a grass mixture that includes those types. A combination of grasses in a mixture is best because some varieties will survive even if others have difficulty taking hold.

I have a large silver maple and am always picking up branches that have fallen to the ground. Should I cut it down, and if so, what should I plant in its place?

The silver maple presents many cultural problems because of its invasive surface roots. Only a few ground covers will grow, reluctantly, in its shade. The tree also is brittle and subject to storm damage. To top it off, it has no great landscape attributes such as brilliant fall color. Many other superior species could take its place *(pages 46-47)*. Choose a tree that is resistant to pests and disease and has supple branches. And when selecting a site for any new tree, consider its spread at maturity so you can avoid placing it too close to power lines and gutters.

Are there certain garden designs that are more maintenance free than others?

Garden styles definitely affect maintenance requirements. In general, the more formal your design, the more upkeep the garden will need, because formality requires balance, symmetry, and exactness—and that means more pruning and trimming of shrubs and trees. Informal designs, on the other hand, allow plants the freedom to follow their natural growth patterns.

What designs would you advise for someone who has a limited budget as well as a limited amount of time?

After you decide which low-maintenance trees, shrubs, and evergreens you like, repeat them throughout your garden. The same holds true for herbaceous perennials: Limit the types of plants you choose and plant more of them. However, you'll want to have a certain amount of plant diversity so that if disease strikes, you won't lose everything. Select and site your plants carefully to ensure against cultural, disease, or insect problems.

My home is located in a wooded glen. How can I create a more interesting shady landscape without increasing upkeep?

Use evergreen ground covers such as vinca and pachysandra intermixed with clumps of large-leaved hosta or ligularia. In addition, you might try the lily-of-the-valley cultivar 'Fortune's Giant', which produces beautiful, fragrant flowers on long stems.

What's the easiest way to tackle the job of planting a steep bank?

Soil preparation is a must since most banks have inadequate soil. For each plant, dig a deep hole and add amendments to the soil; stagger the placement of the holes to achieve a less linear effect. To control the growth of weeds on a slope, lay down landscape fabric and put the plants into the ground through slits cut in the fabric *(page 72)*. Spread pine needles or shredded bark on top of the fabric. These materials tend to stay in place, whereas a chunky mulch like pine bark nuggets will slide off a steep slope. Terracing with landscape timbers or stone *(pages 70-73)* reduces potential erosion and increases moisture retention but requires a bigger investment of both labor and money.

Plant choices aside, are there certain garden designs that are more maintenance free than others?

Styles definitely affect maintenance. In general, the more formal your design, the more maintenance the garden will need, because formality requires balance, symmetry, and exactness, which means more pruning and trimming of shrubs and trees. Informal designs allow plants more freedom to follow natural growth patterns.

How can I prevent winter damage on my broadleaf evergreens—rhododendrons, azaleas, and hollies—and also on evergreen perennials such as bergenia and Christmas and Lenten roses?

Sun and wind are usually the culprits in winter injury to evergreen plants. Leaves are most susceptible to damage when the plant becomes dehydrated, and drought conditions often can exist in the winter garden. Even though your neighbors may think you're crazy, water your evergreen plants in winter to help prevent injury to leaves and tender twigs. If you know that a plant is susceptible to winter damage, select a sheltered site that will provide some protection from wind and afternoon sun, such as against the north wall of the house or on the shady side of a tall hedge.

The perennial loosestrife and false dragonhead I planted in my garden have spread everywhere. Is there any way to control their growth?

The two loosestrife species (*Lysimachia clethroides* and *L. punctata*) and false dragonhead (*Physostegia virginiana*) cultivars are extremely invasive. One way of controlling them is to place them in containers, which can then be buried in the soil. However, there are times when invasive plants can work to your advantage in difficult spots. For instance, plant them on a slope that is bordered by a lawn at the top and a sidewalk at the bottom to control the plants' growth, and you will have a low-maintenance ground cover that requires very little weeding.

My huge clump of pampas grass has developed a big hole in the center. How can I rejuvenate it without digging it up?

Cut the top of the clump off close to the ground. Dig out the soil in the center and replace it with new, amended soil. Fertilize the grass with a cup of blended organic fertilizer, and water it well. In a short time grass around the periphery will fill in the center, and your plant will look normal again.

I am putting in an underground sprinkling system to save time. How long and how frequently should I water?

Water deeply and gently at the rate of 1 inch over 6 hours, slowly enough that all the water enters the soil with little runoff. You do not need to water again for another 7 to 10 days to 2 weeks—even longer if you have had rain. Deep watering produces deep roots that protect plants during drought conditions. Also, deep-rooted perennials are less likely to heave out of the ground when the soil freezes and thaws during snowless winters.

What is the least time-consuming way to fertilize a garden?

Blended organic fertilizers are the backbone of any fertilizing program for low maintenance. They contain a great variety of mineral nutrients and organic molecules that are released slowly into the soil. Gardeners can also turn to timed-release fertilizer pellets; when applied in late winter, the pellets deliver nitrogen, phosphorus, and potassium evenly over an entire growing season.

Are there any shrubs that don't have to be pruned?

Unfortunately, no. You can start by buying shrub cultivars that have been selected specifically for their compact growth form and neat branching habits. But in any event the conscientious gardener should follow the three Ds of pruning: Remove dead, diseased, and deformed branches at any time in a plant's life. To reduce the amount of pruning that you have to do, plant shrubs in a space large enough to allow them to achieve their adult dimensions without becoming obstacles. Also, try to remove no more than a third of the top growth at any time—this will limit the amount of suckering that occurs—and let shrubs assume their natural shape rather than pruning them into geometric globes and boxes.

Is there an alternative to staking my herbaceous perennials?

Improper culture often leads to plants that need to be staked. To minimize staking, give sun-loving plants the right amount of light; keep plant feedings, especially with high-nitrogen fertilizers, to a minimum; space your plants widely for good light and air circulation; and water deeply, thoroughly, and not too often. By following these guidelines you should grow plants that are as compact as their genes allow them to be.

I have tried to garden organically, and I compost all my plant debris—trimmings, old foliage, and weeds that I hoe from the garden—but it seems I have more weeds, disease, and insects every year. I thought organic gardening was going to be beneficial; what's wrong?

You are probably composting weeds that have seeds, giving them a fertile place to germinate before returning them to the garden to grow strong. Instead, put weeds that have gone to seed into the trash. Also, take care not to compost any diseased plant foliage. Many disease-causing organisms have resistant spores or go through resting stages that can survive the rigors of the composting process, particularly if your pile doesn't heat up sufficiently. Lacing your compost with 5-10-5 fertilizer or a compost activator, and turning it so that the outer, cooler portions are moved inward will help generate the heat necessary to kill insect larvae and disease organisms that may find their way into your compost pile.

MULCHING AND WEEDING

I am continually mulching my garden to keep down weeds and conserve moisture. It not only costs a lot of money but is also time-consuming. Do I have any alternatives?

One alternative is to switch from an organic mulch, which needs to be replenished periodically, to a stone mulch. Although stone doesn't have the soil-enhancing properties of an organic mulch, it is fairly permanent: One to 2 inches of uniform-size stones in earth colors provides a good-looking mulch that will last for decades. The best fertilizer to use for stone-mulched beds is one of the blended organics.

I would like to mulch all of my plants—trees, shrubs, and flower beds. When is the best time to do this?

Mulching after a recent rainfall would be ideal, and the best months are those during which the garden is dormant. Mulching later may bury and damage young bulb and perennial foliage. If you wait until the garden is actively growing to mulch, you'll spend a lot of extra time and effort working around your growing foliage so that you can apply the mulch evenly. The ground should be weed free and clean before mulch is applied.

It seems I am always pulling weeds. Can I use the weed-killer glyphosate to control weeds in my perennial garden without hurting the plants?

Yes, you can use glyphosate in your perennial beds, but first place paper bags or plastic pots lined with plastic bags over all of your plants, then spray between them. Microorganisms break glyphosate down into carbon dioxide, nitrogen, phosphate, and water, which are environmentally safe end products. This weed-killer will not leach through the soil into the ground water.

How can I control weeds that keep coming up among the wildflowers and on the bark paths of my woodland garden?

One of the best weed barriers is woven landscape fabric; place it on the pathways before spreading bark *(page 27)*. To block weeds under shrubs such as azaleas and rhododendrons, underplant them with a solid carpet of ground covers such as hosta, ajuga, epimedium, and chrysogonum.

I'm a person who hates to weed. What can I do to keep weeding to a minimum?

It is much easier to remove a tiny weed seedling than a full-grown weed that has had time to develop long, tough roots. By weeding when the plants are young, you also remove them before they have a chance to go to seed, a situation that makes your weeding problems even worse.

I love my lawn, but weed control is driving me crazy. What can I do to make things easier?

In temperate climates, cut your grass high. This promotes much deeper roots and a greener lawn, and the taller grass shades out many weeds such as crab grass. Also, keep the soil pH level between 6 and 6.8 to encourage grass growth and discourage weeds, and apply the appropriate amounts of fertilizer for your grass type. Leave lawn clippings in place to recycle into the ground.

SOIL AND DRAINAGE

One spot in my lawn stays wet, and I am always getting my riding lawn mower stuck in it. Is there anything I can do short of putting in a tile drain?

There are many trees that thrive in wet areas, where they take up and transpire lots of water, thus drying the area. Some members of the willow family—pussy willow *(Salix discolor)*, weeping willow *(S. babylonica)*, and the corkscrew willow *(S. matsudana* 'Tortuosa')—are good choices. Be sure, though, that there are no walkways, terraces, or drainfields close by because willow roots are extremely invasive and can damage them.

I have a very dry area in my yard. What plants can I use in this situation so that I don't have to water extensively with a hose or install a sprinkler system?

Some of the best herbaceous perennials for you would be Spanish sword, sedum, butterfly weed, prickly pear cactus, and blanket-flower. If you want woody plants, all of the *Juniperus horizontalis* cultivars, Scotch broom, bayberry, rosemary, *Rosa rugosa* cultivars, and lavender are good choices. Time your planting project after a rainfall so that digging will be easier.

How can I prepare a soil that will suit a wide number of plant varieties?

Every species of plant has its own range of tolerance for environmental factors such as pH, moisture, and nutrients, and it is impossible in a mixed planting to provide the ideal conditions for each one. Instead, try to achieve a happy medium by creating conditions that most plants can put up with. A pH of 5.8 to 6.5 will benefit the widest number of garden plants, and good drainage usually benefits all of them. Prepare a soil that is loose and crumbly and rich in nutrients; add organic matter in the form of compost and blended organic fertilizers.

PESTS AND DISEASES

My neighbor lost an entire planting of shrubs, perennials, and annuals after mulching with shredded bark. What happened?

The garden was a victim of "sour mulch syndrome." Mulches that become wet and are improperly stored foster the growth of anaerobic bacteria (those that grow without oxygen); the bacteria produce such gases as methane and ammonia, which are very toxic to plants. Death is swift and little can be done after the damage occurs. When storing a mulch, turn it periodically to replenish oxygen and dry it out. Good mulch smells fresh and woody, not sour.

What can I do to get rid of mildew on my garden phlox, monarda, and lilacs?

The low-maintenance way is to plant only disease-resistant varieties. Many new cultivars of garden phlox *(Phlox paniculata),* such as 'David', 'Katherine', and 'Prime Minister', have shown superior mildew resistance in field tests. Place plants in sunny areas with good air circulation, and avoid overcrowding. If you still have a problem, try spraying plants with an antitranspirant or with a mixture of 1 tablespoon each of baking soda and horticultural oil per gallon of water, which recent research has shown will effectively control not only mildew but other fungal diseases as well.

How can "spreader/stickers" save me time?

These liquids, technically known as surfactants, are useful when applying pesticides and fertilizers. When added to a solution, they cause the intended product to spread over the plant's surface and stick to it, increasing the product's effectiveness and reducing the need for frequent spraying. Besides saving you time and money, using surfactants is helpful to the environment.

My flowering dogwoods are dying throughout my property. I have been doing a lot of feeding and pruning, but it's not helping. I have heard the disease is terminal. Any solutions?

You are more than likely wasting your time, but it's too early to predict the final outcome of the anthracnose epidemic that is causing dieback in our native *Cornus florida.* Some resistant individuals may survive to provide new stock. In the meantime, the gardener looking for replacement trees can turn to the Korean dogwood (*Cornus kousa*) and its cultivars, which are more resistant. Some anthracnose-resistant hybrids of *C. kousa* and *C. florida* have also been developed.

Troubleshooting Guide

Even the best-tended gardens can fall prey to pests and diseases. To keep them in check, regularly inspect your plants for warning signs, remembering that lack of nutrients, improper pH levels, and other environmental conditions can cause symptoms like those typical of some diseases. If wilting or yellowing appears on neighboring plants, the source is probably environmental, whereas damage from pests and diseases is usually more random.

This guide is intended to help you identify and solve most of your pest and disease problems. In general, good drainage and air circulation will help prevent infection, and the many beneficial insects, such as ladybugs and lacewings, that prey on unwelcome pests should be encouraged. Natural solutions to garden problems are preferred, but if you must use chemicals, treat only the affected plant. Try to use horticultural oils, insecticidal soaps, and the botanical insecticide *neem;* these products are the least disruptive to beneficial insects and will not destroy the soil balance that is at the foundation of a healthy garden.

P E S T S

PROBLEM: Leaves curl, are distorted in shape, and may be sticky and have a black, sooty appearance. A clear, shiny, sticky substance often appears on stems and leaves. Buds and flowers are deformed, new growth is stunted, and leaves and flowers may drop.

CAUSE: Aphids are pear-shaped, semitransparent, wingless sucking insects, about ⅛ inch long and ranging in color from green to red, pink, black, or gray. Aphids suck plant sap, and through feeding may spread viral disease. Infestations are severest in spring and early summer, when the pests cluster on tender new shoots, undersides of leaves, and around flower buds. Winged forms appear when colonies become overcrowded. Aphids secrete honeydew, a sticky substance that fosters the growth of a black fungus called sooty mold.

SOLUTION: Spray plants frequently with a steady stream of water from a garden hose to knock aphids off plants and discourage them from returning. Ladybugs or lacewings, which eat aphids, may be introduced into the garden. In severe cases, prune off infested areas, and use a diluted insecticidal soap solution or a recommended insecticide. *SUSCEPTIBLE PLANTS: MANY PERENNIALS, ESPECIALLY ASTER, CHRYSANTHEMUM, COLUMBINE, DELPHINIUM, IRIS, AND POPPY; ROSES; SHRUBS, SUCH AS COMMON GARDENIA, FLOWERING QUINCE, AND VIBURNUM; AND MANY TREES, INCLUDING ALDER, DOGWOOD, MAGNOLIA, MOUNTAIN ASH, SILK TREE, TULIP POPLAR, AND WILLOW.*

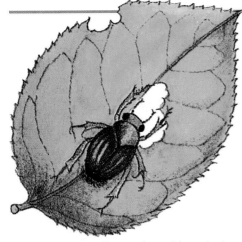

PROBLEM: Small round or oblong holes are eaten into leaves, leaf edges, and flowers. Leaves may be reduced to skeletons with only veins remaining.

CAUSE: Japanese beetles, iridescent blue-green with bronze wing covers, are the most destructive of a large family of hard-shelled chewing insects ranging in size from ¼ to ¾ inch long. Other genera include Asiatic garden beetles (brown), northern masked chafers (brown with dark band on head), and Fuller rose beetles (gray), as well as blister beetles (metallic black, blue, purple, or brown) and flea beetles (shiny dark blue, brown, black, or bronze), which are noted for their jumping ability. Japanese and other adult beetles are voracious in the summer. Larvae, the white grubs, feed on roots of plants and are present from midsummer through the following spring, when they emerge as adults.

SOLUTION: Handpick small colonies *(Caution: Use gloves when picking blister beetles),* placing them in a can filled with soapy water. Japanese beetles can be caught in baited traps. Place traps in an area away from susceptible plants so as not to attract more beetles into the garden. The larval stage can be controlled with milky spore disease, which can be applied to the whole garden. For heavy infestations, contact your local Cooperative Extension Service for information on registered pesticides and the best times to apply them in your region. *SUSCEPTIBLE PLANTS: ALL TURF GRASSES; MANY PERENNIALS; ROSES, ESPECIALLY THOSE WITH LIGHT-COLORED BLOSSOMS; SHRUBS; CRAPE MYRTLE, ELM, JAPANESE MAPLE, AND SYCAMORE TREES.*

CAUSE: Caterpillars, the wormlike larvae of moths, butterflies, and sawflies, come in a variety of shapes and colors and can be smooth, hairy, or spiny. These voracious pests are found in gardens during the spring.

SOLUTION: Handpick to control small populations. *Bacillus thuringiensis* (Bt) kills many types of caterpillars without harming plants. Identify the caterpillar species to determine the control options and timing of spray applications. Several species are susceptible to sprays of insecticidal soap, which must directly hit the caterpillar. Keep garden clean and cultivate frequently. Destroy all visible cocoons and nests.
SUSCEPTIBLE PLANTS: MANY PERENNIALS; ALL ROSES AND SHRUBS; MANY TREES.

PROBLEM: Holes appear in leaves, buds, and flowers; stems may be eaten as well.

PROBLEM: Small patches of the lawn turn brown and die. In affected areas, grass blades have jagged holes along the edges, and some may be severed at the soil surface. In the garden, stems of tender, emerging plants are cut off near the ground, and seedlings may be completely eaten. Leaves of older plants show ragged edges and chewed holes.

CAUSE: Cutworms, the larvae of various moths, are fat, hairless, and gray or dull brown in color. These 1- to 2-inch-long night feeders do the most damage in the spring. In the daytime, they curl up into a C-shape and are found under debris or below the soil surface next to the plant stem.

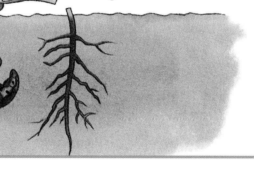

SOLUTION: Place barriers called cutworm collars around the base of plants. Force cutworms to the surface of the soil by flooding the area, and then handpick them. To reduce hiding places, keep the area weeded and clear of debris. Spade the soil in late summer and fall to expose and destroy cutworms. Apply *Bacillus thuringiensis* (Bt) in the evening, when the worms and moths are active.
SUSCEPTIBLE PLANTS: ALL TURF GRASSES AND PERENNIALS, ESPECIALLY ANEMONE, CHRYSANTHEMUM, DELPHINIUM, AND DIANTHUS; ALL YOUNG SEEDLINGS AND TRANSPLANTS.

PROBLEM: Leaves become stippled with white dots, then turn yellowish brown or have a burned look around the edges. Leaves and stems curl upward; young leaves become distorted. Plant growth may be stunted.

CAUSE: Leafhoppers are small (¼ inch long), yellow-green, cricketlike, wedge-shaped sucking insects that jump quickly into flight when disturbed. Most active in spring and summer, they feed on the undersides of leaves and, like aphids, secrete a sticky honeydew that fosters sooty mold. The aster leafhopper spreads the disease *aster yellows.*

SOLUTION: Spray with water to knock exposed leafhoppers off plants. Remove and destroy damaged foliage. In the fall, rake up leaves and remove weeds that can harbor leafhopper eggs through the winter. Direct spraying with insecticidal soap will give short-term control, but leafhoppers migrate freely, so repeated applications may be necessary. A labeled systemic insecticide will provide the longest control.
SUSCEPTIBLE PLANTS: MANY PERENNIALS, INCLUDING BABY'S-BREATH, CATMINT, CHRYSANTHEMUM, COREOPSIS, AND GERANIUM; ALL ROSES; SHRUBS; ELM, LOCUST, NORWAY MAPLE, POPLAR, AND WILLOW TREES.

PROBLEM: White or light green tunnels are bored through leaves; older tunnels turn black. Leaves may lose color, dry up, and die. Seedlings may be stunted or die.

CAUSE: Leaf miners—minute (⅟₁₆ to ⅛ inch long) translucent, pale green larvae of certain flies, moths, or beetles—are hatched from eggs laid on the leaves of plants. During spring and summer, the larvae eat the tender interior below the surface of the leaf, leaving behind serpentine trails of blistered tissue known as mines.

SOLUTION: Damage may be unsightly but is usually not lethal. Pick off and destroy infested leaves as they appear. In the fall, cut the plant to the ground and discard stalks. Remove and destroy leaves with egg clusters. Keep the garden well weeded. Use a systemic insecticide before leaf mining becomes extensive. Spray conifers in early summer, boxwoods in late spring, and hollies in midspring when new leaves develop. *SUSCEPTIBLE PLANTS: MANY PERENNIALS; MANY SHRUBS, INCLUDING AMERICAN HOLLY AND BOXWOOD; CONIFERS, ESPECIALLY ARBORVITAE, CYPRESS, AND JUNIPER; MANY TREES.*

PROBLEM: Leaves become stippled or flecked, then discolor, turning yellow or nearly white with brown edges; the leaves of some shrubs become speckled with gray. Entire leaves may turn yellow or bronze and curl. Flowers and buds discolor or dry up. Webbing may be seen on undersides of leaves and on the branches of shrubs. Growth is stunted; leaves may drop.

CAUSE: Mites are pinhead-size, spiderlike sucking pests that can be reddish, pale green, or yellow. These insects can become a major problem in hot, dry weather when several generations of mites may occur in a single season. Adults of some species hibernate over the winter in sod, in bark, and on weeds and plants that retain their foliage.

SOLUTION: Damage is worst to plants in full sunlight and hot areas. Keep plants watered and mulched. Regularly spray the undersides of leaves, where mites feed and lay eggs, using water or a diluted soap solution. Horticultural oils can also be applied to undersides. Insecticidal soaps control nymphs and adults but not eggs. Introduce natural predators such as green lacewing larvae. *SUSCEPTIBLE PLANTS: MANY PERENNIALS; ROSES; SHRUBS SUCH AS ANDROMEDA, AZALEA, BOXWOOD, AND JUNIPER; ELM, HOLLY, FIR, AND PINE TREES.*

PROBLEM: Plants turn yellow, drop leaves, and eventually die if infestation is severe. Shrubs cease to grow, and the tips of branches may die. Foliage wilts and loses its color. Branches, twigs, or leaves are covered with small rounded or oval masses.

CAUSE: Scale insects have hard or soft shells, ranging in size from ⅟₁₀ to ⅜ inch long, that may be white, yellow, green, red, brown, or black. Adult females appear on stems or leaves as bumps, always without appendages; some are so small they look like gray ash. Males are minute flying insects with yellow wings. The insects suck plant juices.

SOLUTION: Prune out severely infested branches. Scrub off the shells with a plastic scouring pad. Spray shrubs with horticultural oil in early spring to smother the eggs. If insects appear in summer, spray with an insecticide. *SUSCEPTIBLE PLANTS: PERENNIALS, ESPECIALLY GERANIUM AND PEONY; ROSES, ESPECIALLY CLIMBERS THAT ARE NOT PRUNED ANNUALLY; SHRUBS, PARTICULARLY EVERGREENS AND EUONYMUS; MANY TREES, INCLUDING ALDER, BAUHINIA, CHERRY, CRABAPPLE, DOGWOOD, MAGNOLIA, MOUNTAIN ASH, PLUM, POPLAR, SILK TREE, AND WILLOW.*

PROBLEM: Ragged holes are eaten in leaves, especially those near the ground. Telltale silver streaks appear on leaves and garden paths. Small plants may be entirely consumed.

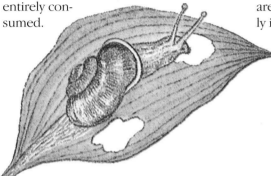

CAUSE: Slugs or snails hide during the day and feed on low-hanging leaves at night or on overcast or rainy days. They prefer damp soil in a shady location and are most damaging in summer, especially in wet regions or during rainy years.

SOLUTION: Keep garden clean to minimize hiding places. Handpick, or trap them by placing saucers of beer near plants. Slugs will also collect under grapefruit halves or melon rinds. Salt kills slugs and snails but may damage plants. Because slugs and snails find it hard to crawl over rough surfaces, barrier strips of coarse sand or cinders placed around beds will deter them. Spading in spring destroys dormant slugs and eggs. *SUSCEPTIBLE PLANTS: VIRTUALLY ANY PLANT, ESPECIALLY THOSE WITH YOUNG OR TENDER FOLIAGE.*

PROBLEM: Buds do not open, or flowers are tattered or deformed. Petals may be darkened or have brownish yellow or white streaks and small dark spots or bumps. Leaves and stems may be twisted, and plants may be stunted. Leaves of broadleaf evergreens have a dull, silvery appearance.

CAUSE: Thrips are quick-moving sucking insects that are barely visible to the naked eye; they look like tiny slivers of yellow, black, or brown wood. Emerging in early spring, thrips are especially active in hot, dry weather. The larvae are wingless and feed on stems, leaves, and flower buds. Adults are weak fliers but are easily dispersed by wind and can therefore travel great distances.

SOLUTION: Control of thrips is difficult, especially during a migratory period in early summer. Lacewings, minute pirate bugs, and several predaceous mites feed on them; late in the growing season such predators often check thrips populations. Remove and destroy damaged buds and foliage. In severe cases, spray plants with an insecticidal soap or systemic insecticide. *SUSCEPTIBLE PLANTS: MANY PERENNIALS; ROSES, ESPECIALLY WITH WHITE OR PINK BLOSSOMS; LILAC AND PRIVET SHRUBS; TREES, ESPECIALLY BEECH, BIRCH, AND MAPLE.*

PROBLEM: Small patches of dead brown grass appear throughout the lawn in spring and enlarge to several feet across by summer. Grass blades may be cut off at the soil surface. Small whitish tunnels appear at the soil surface. At night, moths fly over the lawn in a zigzag pattern. On trees and shrubs, a light webbing appears around leaves, which may be eaten with holes.

CAUSE: Webworms, the larvae of moths, usually feed at night. Sod webworms chew off grass blades and pull them into tunnels of soil and webbing; adult moths do not damage the lawn but drop their eggs onto the grass. On trees and shrubs, other forms of webworm larvae chew leaves, feeding on the undersides and eating out holes, and spin webs around leaves and over ends of branches.

SOLUTION: Proper maintenance, including watering, aeration, and dethatching, will reduce lawn infestation; damaged grass may recover if the webworms are controlled as soon as symptoms appear. Remove webs from trees and destroy them by burning or immersing them in soapy water. Apply an insecticide in the evening and repeat applications if necessary. *SUSCEPTIBLE PLANTS: TURF GRASSES, ESPECIALLY BENT GRASS, BLUEGRASS, HYBRID BERMUDA GRASS, AND ANY NEW LAWN PLANTING; EVERGREEN SHRUBS; TREES, ESPECIALLY AMERICAN ELM, ASH, CHERRY, MAPLE, MIMOSA, SYCAMORE, AND WILLOW.*

PROBLEM: Leaves turn yellow and plants are stunted. When plants are shaken, a white cloud appears. Parts of shrubs may be covered with a clear, sticky substance.

CAUSE: Whiteflies, sucking insects ¹⁄₁₆ inch long that look like tiny white moths, generally collect on the undersides of young leaves. Found year round in warmer climates but only in summer in colder climates, they like warm, still air. Both adults and nymphs suck sap from stems and leaves, causing an infested plant to wilt. Whiteflies are often brought home with greenhouse plants and can carry virus and secrete honeydew, which promotes sooty mold.

SOLUTION: Keep the garden weeded. Spray affected plants with a diluted soap solution or, in extreme cases, an insecticide. Whiteflies are attracted to the color yellow, so flypaper can be hung in the garden to help control the population. *SUSCEPTIBLE PLANTS: PERENNIALS, INCLUDING CHRYSANTHEMUM, COLUMBINE, HIBISCUS, LUPINE, PRIMROSE, AND MALLOW; ROSES; SHRUBS, ESPECIALLY AZALEA, CAMELLIA, AND RHODODENDRON.*

PROBLEM: Foliage develops irregular, yellow to purplish brown spots that darken with age. These spots may also expand and join to cover the leaves. Leaves turn brown and drop. Purplish lesions form along stems, and plant growth is often stunted.

CAUSE: Anthracnose is a fungus disease that is particularly severe in wet weather.

SOLUTION: Grow resistant varieties. Thin stems and tops to improve air circulation, and water plants from below to keep the disease from spreading. Remove and destroy infected plants. For trees, prune out deadwood and water sprouts. Water them during dry spells and keep the root zone mulched to prevent drought stress. To keep a severe infection from spreading, spray plants with a fungicide according to directions while new leaves are growing in spring. *SUSCEPTIBLE PLANTS: PEONY; ROSES; SHRUBS; MANY TREES, INCLUDING ASH, BOX ELDER, DOGWOOD, ELM, MAPLE, AND OAK.*

PROBLEM: Circular black spots that are ¼ inch in diameter and surrounded by a yellow halo appear on upper leaf surfaces of rose plants. The spots enlarge and coalesce until the entire leaf is yellow and falls from the plant.

CAUSE: Black spot, a fungus disease, is most often found under humid and rainy conditions because fungus spores germinate in water. Once rose plants are infected, the fungus will remain on the canes through the winter and reappear on the next season's growth.

SOLUTION: Choose roses that are less susceptible, and plant them in a sunny location. Water early in the day. Avoid splashing leaves. Clean up all refuse after pruning. Prune canes of infected plants farther back than normal to eliminate fungus that survives over the winter, and apply a lime-sulfur spray before leaves open. If symptoms appear, remove and destroy all infected leaves, including those on the ground. Spray a fungicide to keep fungus from spreading. *SUSCEPTIBLE PLANTS: ROSES, ESPECIALLY HYBRID PERPETUAL, HYBRID TEA, POLYANTHA, AND TEA ROSE.*

PROBLEM: A brownish gray, moldy growth appears on flowers and foliage. Stalks are weak and flowers droop. Buds may not open. Discolored blotches appear on leaves, stems, and flowers. Stem bases blacken and rot. Affected plant parts eventually turn brown and dry.

CAUSE: Botrytis blight, also known as gray mold, is a fungus disease that thrives in moist air and cool temperatures. The blight survives the winter as hard, black lumps in the soil or on dead plant parts.

SOLUTION: Water early in the day. Place plants in well-drained soil. Thin out plants so they get more light and air circulation, or transplant them to a dry, sunny location. Cut off and destroy all infected plant parts. To keep the disease from spreading, spray with a fungicide in spring when growth starts.
SUSCEPTIBLE PLANTS: MANY PERENNIALS, SUCH AS LILIES AND PEONIES; ROSES, ESPECIALLY THEIR YOUNG CANES; SHRUBS, ESPECIALLY PYRACANTHA; TREES, INCLUDING HAWTHORN, JAPANESE CEDAR, AND JUNIPER.

PROBLEM: Red or brown sunken spots with dark margins develop on rose canes or on the stems, branches, and trunks of shrubs and trees. Leaves and stems above the damaged area turn yellow, wilt, and die.

CAUSE: Canker, a fungal or bacterial disease, spreads in water and enters plants through cuts or wounds in stems. The common bacterial canker diseases strike in early to middle spring when plants come out of dormancy, whereas fungal cankers typically form during plant dormancy.

SOLUTION: Prune out infected parts, disinfecting tools with alcohol after each cut. For roses, prune canes to the node below the canker. Removing infected branches promptly will help to prevent the spread of the disease. There are no chemical preventives or cures.
SUSCEPTIBLE PLANTS: ROSES, ESPECIALLY HYBRID TEA, HYBRID PERPETUAL, AND TEA ROSE; MOST EVERGREEN SHRUBS; ASH, BIRCH, DOGWOOD, ELM, MAPLE, MOUNTAIN ASH, OAK, PLUM, POPLAR, AND WILLOW TREES.

PROBLEM: Corky galls about 2 inches in diameter appear at the base of the plant and on stems and roots. Growths are light green when young and turn brown and woody as they age.

CAUSE: Crown gall is a disease caused by bacteria that live in the soil and enter a plant through wounds at the root area. The bacteria cause abnormal cell growth, which produces the galls, thus stunting the plant's normal growth.

SOLUTION: Prune and destroy galled stems; sterilize shears with alcohol after each cut. Destroy severely infected plants. Bacteria will remain in the soil for 2 to 3 years. Do not plant susceptible shrubs or trees in an area with a history of the disease.
SUSCEPTIBLE PLANTS: PERENNIALS; ROSES; MANY SHRUBS, INCLUDING EUONYMUS, FLOWERING QUINCE, FORSYTHIA, AND WEIGELA..

PROBLEM: Overnight, young seedlings suddenly topple over. Stems are rotted through at the soil line.

CAUSE: Damping-off is caused by various fungi in the soil that attack seeds and the roots of young seedlings at ground level. The problem often occurs in wet, poorly drained soil with a high nitrogen content.

SOLUTION: Use fresh or treated seeds. Plant in a sterile planting medium topped with a thin layer of sand or perlite to keep seedlings dry at the soil line. Plants in containers are more susceptible than those growing outdoors. Give them well-drained soil with plenty of light; avoid overcrowding and overwatering.
SUSCEPTIBLE PLANTS: ALL SEEDLINGS.

PROBLEM: Leaves turn yellow. Angular pale green or yellow blotches appear on the leaf's upper surface, with corresponding gray or tan fuzzy growths that resemble tufts of cotton forming on the underside. Leaves wilt, turn brown, and die.

CAUSE: Downy mildew, a disease caused by a fungus, thrives in cool, wet weather and appears most often in late summer and early fall.

SOLUTION: Grow resistant species and cultivars. Do not water plants overhead after morning. Space plants and thin stems to encourage air circulation. Remove and destroy blighted plant parts or the entire plant if the infection is severe. Mow lawn only when grass is dry since wet clippings on mowing tools can spread the disease. *SUSCEPTIBLE PLANTS: ALL TURF GRASSES; MANY PERENNIALS, INCLUDING ASTER, CINQUEFOIL, CONEFLOWER, CRANESBILL, DELPHINIUM, LUPINE, SPEEDWELL, AND WORMWOOD; ROSES, BOTH CULTIVATED AND WILD; SHRUBS, ESPECIALLY VIBURNUM.*

PROBLEM: Leaves and branches suddenly wilt, turn black, and appear to have been scorched by fire. Twigs may also turn black. Dark brown cankers several inches long develop on trunks and main branches. In warm, moist spring weather, drops of brown ooze appear on sunken bark. Young trees may die.

CAUSE: Fire blight is a bacterial disease that spreads in warm, wet conditions. It enters through blossoms and is spread by splashing water or pollinating insects.

SOLUTION: Prune out damaged branches when plants are dry or during dry weather, disinfecting pruning shears with alcohol after each cut. Cut several inches below the discolored area. When trees begin to bloom, begin spraying applications of the antibiotic streptomycin or Bordeaux mixture, a solution of copper sulfate and lime, to prevent the disease. *SUSCEPTIBLE PLANTS: ALL ROSES; SHRUBS, PARTICULARLY QUINCE, PYRACANTHA, AND COTONEASTER; HAWTHORN AND MOUNTAIN ASH TREES.*

PROBLEM: Leaves develop small yellow, brown, or black spots that are surrounded by a rim of discolored tissue. Spots often join to produce large, irregular blotches. Entire leaf may turn yellow, wilt, and drop. Spotting usually starts on lower leaves and moves upward.

CAUSE: Leaf-spot diseases are caused by a number of fungi or bacteria. All are particularly severe in wet weather because they are spread by splashing water.

SOLUTION: Clean up all fallen leaves before winter. Water overhead only in the morning, as damp foliage in cool night air encourages spreading of the diseases. Prune and destroy infected leaves of perennials and shrubs. A fungicide can protect healthy foliage but will not destroy fungus on infected leaves; begin applying when leaf buds start to open. *SUSCEPTIBLE PLANTS: TURF GRASSES; MANY PERENNIALS; ROSES, ESPECIALLY SHRUB VARIETIES; SHRUBS, ESPECIALLY AZALEA AND EUONYMUS; MANY TREES, INCLUDING ASH, BUCKEYE, DOGWOOD, ELM, MAPLE, OAK, AND POPLAR.*

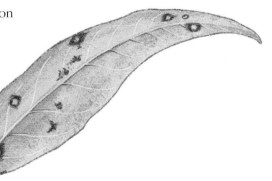

PROBLEM: Leaves or grass blades are covered with spots or a thin layer of grayish white powdery material. Infected parts may distort and curl, then turn yellow or purplish; leaves may finally drop off. Badly infected buds will not open properly.

CAUSE: Powdery mildews are fungus diseases that thrive when nights are cool and days are hot and humid. The diseases are most noticeable in late summer and fall.

SOLUTION: Plant mildew-resistant varieties. Susceptible plants should receive full sun with good air circulation. Water overhead only in the early morning. In the fall, cut infected perennials to the ground and discard. Fungicides may be used to prevent spreading. Also effective are summer oil sprays and antitranspirants, which decrease the amount of water lost through leaves. *SUSCEPTIBLE PLANTS: TURF GRASSES, ESPECIALLY BLUEGRASS; MANY PERENNIALS; YOUNG GROWTH OF MANY WOODY PLANTS, INCLUDING ROSES; SHRUBS, ESPECIALLY LILAC AND EUONYMUS.*

PROBLEM: Upper leaf surfaces have pale yellow or white spots, and undersides are covered with orange or yellow raised pustules. Leaves wilt and hang down along the stem. Pustules may become more numerous, destroying leaves and occasionally the entire plant. Plants may be stunted. Grass blades turn yellow, then are coated with orange. Lawns may thin out.

CAUSE: Rust, a fungus disease, is a problem in the late summer and early fall, and is most prevalent when nights are cool and humid. The orange or brown powder, which consists of fungus spores, spreads easily in wind.

SOLUTION: Buy rust-resistant varieties whenever possible. Water early in the day so plants can dry before nightfall. Avoid wetting leaves. Remove and destroy all infected leaves, including those on the ground. To prevent the disease, spray with an appropriate fungicide in cool, wet weather, especially in the late spring. *SUSCEPTIBLE PLANTS: TURF GRASSES, ESPECIALLY BLUEGRASS AND RYEGRASS; MANY PERENNIALS, INCLUDING ASTER, CHRYSANTHEMUM, COREOPSIS, DIANTHUS, AND HOLLYHOCK; ROSES, ESPECIALLY HYBRID TEAS, CLIMBERS, AND HYBRID PERPETUALS; SHRUBS, SUCH AS AZALEA AND RHODODENDRON; TREES, PARTICULARLY HAWTHORN, JUNIPER, PINE, POPLAR, AND RED CEDAR.*

PROBLEM: A side or branch of the plant wilts. Leaves turn yellow, then brown, wilt, and die. Wilt progresses upward and outward. A cross section of a tree branch reveals a dark ring or rings.

CAUSE: Verticillium wilt is a fungal disease that can be confirmed only by a laboratory test of a damaged branch. The fungus thrives in cool, moist soil but usually does not reveal its presence until warm, dry weather has stressed plants.

SOLUTION: There are no organic or chemical controls. Once soil is infected, plant only resistant varieties. If infection on a tree is detected early, fertilize and water to encourage natural recovery, and remove damaged parts. If infection is severe, the tree cannot be saved and must be removed. Do not replant with the same species. *SUSCEPTIBLE PLANTS: SOME PERENNIALS, SUCH AS ASTER AND CHRYSANTHEMUM; ALL ROSES; SHRUBS, INCLUDING AZALEA AND VIBURNUM; TREES, ESPECIALLY JAPANESE AND OTHER MAPLES.*

Plant Selection Guide

Organized by plant type, this chart provides information needed to select species and varieties that will thrive in the particular conditions of your garden. For additional information on each plant, refer to the Encyclopedia that begins on page 110.

	Zone 3	Zone 4	Zone 5	Zone 6	Zone 7	Zone 8	Zone 9	Zone 10	Zone 11	Dry	Moist	Full Sun	Partial Shade	Shade	Pests/Diseases	Drought	Pollution	Under 1	1-3	3-6	6-10	10-20	Over 20	Foliage	Flowers	Fruit	Form
GROUND COVERS																											
AJUGA REPTANS	✔	✔	✔	✔	✔	✔	✔			✔	✔	✔	✔	✔			✔							✔	✔		
ARCTOSTAPHYLOS UVA-URSI	✔	✔	✔	✔	✔					✔		✔	✔			✔	✔							✔	✔	✔	
CERATOSTIGMA PLUMBAGINOIDES			✔	✔	✔	✔	✔			✔		✔	✔		✔		✔							✔	✔		
CHRYSOGONUM VIRGINIANUM			✔	✔	✔	✔				✔		✔	✔	✔	✔		✔							✔	✔		
ECHEVERIA AGAVOIDES					✔	✔	✔	✔	✔	✔		✔				✔	✔							✔	✔		✔
EPIMEDIUM GRANDIFLORUM		✔	✔	✔	✔						✔		✔	✔	✔		✔							✔	✔		
GERANIUM MACRORRHIZUM		✔	✔	✔	✔					✔	✔	✔	✔			✔	✔							✔	✔		
HEDERA CANARIENSIS						✔	✔			✔	✔	✔	✔	✔			✔							✔			
HEDERA HELIX		✔	✔	✔	✔	✔	✔			✔	✔	✔	✔				✔							✔			
IBERIS SEMPERVIRENS		✔	✔	✔	✔					✔		✔					✔							✔	✔		✔
LAMIUM MACULATUM 'BEACON SILVER'		✔	✔	✔	✔	✔				✔	✔		✔	✔	✔		✔							✔	✔		
LIRIOPE MUSCARI 'MONROE'S WHITE'		✔	✔	✔	✔	✔	✔	✔		✔	✔	✔	✔	✔	✔				✔					✔	✔	✔	
LIRIOPE SPICATA	✔	✔	✔	✔	✔	✔	✔	✔		✔	✔	✔	✔	✔	✔		✔							✔	✔	✔	
OPHIOPOGON JAPONICUS			✔	✔	✔					✔	✔	✔	✔	✔			✔							✔	✔		
OSTEOSPERMUM FRUTICOSUM 'HYBRID WHITE'					✔	✔				✔		✔				✔	✔							✔	✔		
PACHYSANDRA PROCUMBENS			✔	✔	✔	✔					✔		✔	✔	✔		✔							✔	✔		
PHLOX STOLONIFERA	✔	✔	✔	✔	✔	✔					✔		✔				✔							✔	✔		
PHLOX SUBULATA	✔	✔	✔	✔	✔	✔				✔		✔					✔							✔	✔		
STACHYS BYZANTINA 'HELENE VON STEIN'		✔	✔	✔	✔	✔				✔		✔	✔			✔			✔					✔			
VINCA MINOR	✔	✔	✔	✔	✔	✔				✔	✔	✔	✔				✔							✔	✔		
PERENNIALS AND GRASSES																											
ACHILLEA MILLEFOLIUM 'ROSEA'	✔	✔	✔	✔	✔	✔	✔	✔		✔		✔				✔		✔						✔	✔		
ACONITUM NAPELLUS	✔	✔	✔	✔	✔						✔		✔							✔				✔	✔		
AEONIUM ARBOREUM 'SCHWARTZKOPF'					✔	✔				✔		✔				✔			✔					✔	✔		
AGAVE AMERICANA			✔	✔	✔	✔	✔			✔		✔				✔				✔				✔	✔		✔
ALOE STRIATA						✔	✔	✔	✔	✔		✔				✔		✔						✔	✔		✔
AMSONIA TABERNAEMONTANA	✔	✔	✔	✔	✔	✔	✔			✔	✔	✔	✔		✔				✔					✔	✔		
ANEMONE X HYBRIDA 'SEPTEMBER CHARM'		✔	✔	✔	✔	✔					✔		✔		✔				✔						✔		
AQUILEGIA CANADENSIS		✔	✔	✔	✔	✔	✔			✔	✔	✔	✔						✔					✔	✔		

PERENNIALS AND GRASSES

	ZONES									SOIL		LIGHT			RESISTANT TO			HEIGHT (IN FEET)						NOTED FOR			
	Zone 3	Zone 4	Zone 5	Zone 6	Zone 7	Zone 8	Zone 9	Zone 10	Zone 11	Dry	Moist	Full Sun	Partial Shade	Shade	Pests/Diseases	Drought	Pollution	Under 1	1-3	3-6	6-10	10-20	Over 20	Foliage	Flowers	Fruit	Form
ASCLEPIAS TUBEROSA		✓	✓	✓	✓	✓	✓	✓		✓		✓				✓		✓							✓		
ASTILBE TAQUETII 'SUPERBA'		✓	✓	✓	✓						✓	✓	✓						✓					✓	✓		✓
BAPTISIA AUSTRALIS	✓	✓	✓	✓	✓	✓	✓			✓	✓	✓	✓		✓				✓					✓	✓		
BERGENIA CORDIFOLIA	✓	✓	✓	✓	✓						✓	✓	✓		✓		✓							✓	✓		
BOLTONIA ASTEROIDES 'SNOW BANK'		✓	✓	✓	✓	✓					✓	✓	✓							✓					✓		
BRUNNERA MACROPHYLLA	✓	✓	✓	✓	✓						✓	✓		✓		✓			✓					✓	✓		
CALAMAGROSTIS X ACUTIFLORA 'KARL FOERSTER'		✓	✓	✓	✓	✓				✓	✓	✓			✓	✓			✓					✓	✓		✓
CAMPANULA PORTENSCHLAGIANA		✓	✓	✓	✓						✓	✓	✓		✓		✓	✓						✓	✓		✓
CAREX MORROWII		✓	✓	✓	✓	✓					✓	✓	✓	✓	✓			✓						✓			
CIMICIFUGA SIMPLEX		✓	✓	✓	✓						✓		✓		✓				✓					✓	✓		
COREOPSIS ROSEA		✓	✓	✓	✓	✓					✓	✓			✓			✓						✓	✓		
DICENTRA EXIMIA	✓	✓	✓	✓	✓						✓		✓		✓			✓						✓	✓		✓
DICTAMNUS ALBUS	✓	✓	✓	✓	✓	✓					✓	✓	✓		✓			✓						✓	✓	✓	
ECHINACEA PALLIDA	✓	✓	✓	✓	✓	✓				✓		✓				✓			✓						✓		
EUPATORIUM FISTULOSUM 'GATEWAY'	✓	✓	✓	✓	✓	✓	✓			✓	✓	✓								✓					✓		
EUPHORBIA COROLLATA		✓	✓	✓	✓	✓	✓	✓		✓		✓				✓	✓	✓						✓	✓		
EUPHORBIA EPITHYMOIDES		✓	✓	✓	✓	✓	✓			✓		✓				✓	✓	✓						✓	✓		✓
GAZANIA 'FIESTA RED'					✓	✓	✓			✓		✓				✓	✓	✓							✓		
GERBERA JAMESONII					✓	✓	✓	✓			✓	✓	✓			✓		✓							✓		
HELIANTHUS MAXIMILIANI	✓	✓	✓	✓	✓	✓				✓	✓	✓			✓						✓				✓		
HELICTOTRICHON SEMPERVIRENS		✓	✓	✓	✓					✓	✓	✓			✓				✓					✓	✓		
HELLEBORUS FOETIDUS			✓	✓	✓						✓		✓						✓					✓	✓		
HEMEROCALLIS 'EENIE WEENIE'	✓	✓	✓	✓	✓	✓	✓			✓	✓	✓	✓		✓		✓							✓	✓		
HEMEROCALLIS 'INCA TREASURE'	✓	✓	✓	✓	✓	✓	✓	✓		✓	✓	✓	✓		✓				✓					✓	✓		
HEUCHERA MICRANTHA 'PALACE PURPLE'		✓	✓	✓	✓	✓					✓	✓	✓		✓				✓					✓	✓		✓
HIBISCUS 'LADY BALTIMORE'		✓	✓	✓	✓	✓					✓	✓	✓							✓					✓		
HOSTA PLANTAGINEA	✓	✓	✓	✓	✓	✓	✓				✓		✓	✓					✓					✓	✓		✓
IMPERATA CYLINDRICA RUBRA 'RED BARON'			✓	✓	✓	✓				✓		✓	✓		✓				✓					✓			
IRIS SIBIRICA		✓	✓	✓	✓	✓					✓	✓	✓		✓					✓				✓	✓		
LAVANDULA ANGUSTIFOLIA			✓	✓	✓	✓				✓		✓							✓					✓	✓		
LAVANDULA STOECHAS					✓	✓	✓			✓		✓							✓					✓	✓		
LIATRIS SPICATA	✓	✓	✓	✓	✓	✓				✓	✓	✓	✓						✓						✓		

	ZONES									SOIL		LIGHT			RESISTANT TO			HEIGHT (IN FEET)						NOTED FOR			
	Z3	Z4	Z5	Z6	Z7	Z8	Z9	Z10	Z11	DRY	MOIST	FULL SUN	PARTIAL SHADE	SHADE	PESTS/DISEASES	DROUGHT	POLLUTION	UNDER 1	1-3	3-6	6-10	10-20	OVER 20	FOLIAGE	FLOWERS	FRUIT	FORM
PERENNIALS AND GRASSES																											
MISCANTHUS SINENSIS 'YAKU JIMA'			✓	✓	✓	✓	✓			✓		✓			✓	✓			✓					✓	✓		
PAEONIA 'KRINKLED WHITE'	✓	✓	✓	✓	✓	✓					✓	✓	✓						✓					✓	✓		
PAEONIA 'RASPBERRY SUNDAE'	✓	✓	✓	✓	✓	✓					✓	✓	✓						✓					✓	✓		
PANICUM VIRGATUM			✓	✓	✓	✓	✓			✓	✓	✓			✓	✓			✓					✓	✓		
PAPAVER ORIENTALE	✓	✓	✓	✓	✓	✓				✓		✓	✓						✓						✓		
PATRINIA SCABIOSIFOLIA			✓	✓	✓	✓	✓			✓		✓	✓						✓						✓	✓	
PENNISETUM ALOPECUROIDES			✓	✓	✓	✓	✓			✓		✓			✓	✓			✓					✓	✓		
PEROVSKIA ATRIPLICIFOLIA			✓	✓	✓	✓	✓			✓		✓				✓			✓					✓	✓		
PHLOX MACULATA 'MISS LINGARD'	✓	✓	✓	✓	✓	✓				✓	✓	✓							✓						✓		
PLATYCODON GRANDIFLORUS		✓	✓	✓	✓	✓	✓			✓	✓	✓	✓						✓						✓		
POLYGONATUM BIFLORUM	✓	✓	✓	✓	✓	✓					✓		✓	✓					✓					✓	✓	✓	
ROMNEYA COULTERI				✓	✓	✓	✓			✓		✓				✓				✓				✓	✓		
RUDBECKIA NITIDA 'HERBSTSONNE'		✓	✓	✓	✓	✓	✓			✓	✓	✓								✓				✓			
SALVIA GREGGII				✓	✓	✓	✓			✓		✓				✓			✓					✓	✓		
SANTOLINA CHAMAECYPARISSUS			✓	✓	✓					✓		✓			✓	✓			✓					✓	✓		✓
SEDUM X 'VERA JAMESON'	✓	✓	✓	✓	✓	✓	✓	✓		✓		✓	✓		✓	✓	✓							✓	✓		
SOLIDAGO 'GOLDEN FLEECE'	✓	✓	✓	✓	✓	✓	✓			✓		✓	✓						✓					✓			
SPIGELIA MARILANDICA			✓	✓	✓	✓					✓		✓						✓						✓		
VERONICA INCANA		✓	✓	✓	✓	✓				✓	✓	✓	✓			✓			✓					✓	✓		
ZANTEDESCHIA AETHIOPICA 'CROWBOROUGH'						✓	✓			✓	✓	✓	✓						✓					✓	✓		
DECIDUOUS SHRUBS																											
ABELIA X GRANDIFLORA 'FRANCIS MASON'			✓	✓	✓	✓				✓	✓	✓	✓							✓				✓	✓		
ABELIA X GRANDIFLORA 'PROSTRATA'			✓	✓	✓	✓				✓	✓	✓	✓						✓					✓	✓		
ACANTHOPANAX SIEBOLDIANUS 'VARIEGATUS'		✓	✓	✓	✓	✓				✓	✓	✓	✓	✓	✓	✓	✓				✓			✓			
ARONIA ARBUTIFOLIA 'BRILLIANTISSIMA'		✓	✓	✓	✓	✓				✓	✓	✓	✓								✓					✓	
BERBERIS THUNBERGII 'GOLDEN RING'		✓	✓	✓	✓	✓				✓	✓	✓	✓			✓	✓		✓					✓			
BERBERIS THUNBERGII 'ROSE GLOW'		✓	✓	✓	✓					✓	✓	✓	✓			✓	✓		✓					✓			
CALYCANTHUS FLORIDUS		✓	✓	✓	✓	✓				✓	✓	✓	✓			✓					✓			✓	✓		
CARYOPTERIS X CLANDONENSIS			✓	✓	✓	✓				✓		✓							✓						✓		
CERATOSTIGMA WILLMOTTIANUM					✓	✓	✓			✓	✓	✓	✓			✓			✓					✓	✓		
CHAENOMELES SPECIOSA 'TEXAS SCARLET'		✓	✓	✓	✓	✓				✓	✓	✓	✓						✓						✓		
CISTUS X PURPUREUS					✓	✓				✓		✓				✓			✓					✓	✓		
CISTUS SALVIIFOLIUS					✓	✓				✓		✓				✓		✓						✓	✓		

DECIDUOUS SHRUBS

	ZONE 3	ZONE 4	ZONE 5	ZONE 6	ZONE 7	ZONE 8	ZONE 9	ZONE 10	ZONE 11	DRY	MOIST	FULL SUN	PARTIAL SHADE	SHADE	PESTS/DISEASES	DROUGHT	POLLUTION	UNDER 1	1-3	3-6	6-10	10-20	OVER 20	FOLIAGE	FLOWERS	FRUIT	FORM
CLETHRA ALNIFOLIA	✔	✔	✔	✔	✔	✔	✔				✔	✔	✔	✔						✔				✔	✔		
CLETHRA BARBINERVIS			✔	✔	✔	✔					✔	✔	✔	✔						✔				✔	✔		
CORNUS ALBA 'SIBIRICA'	✔	✔	✔	✔	✔						✔	✔	✔							✔							✔
CORNUS MAS		✔	✔	✔	✔						✔	✔	✔								✔			✔	✔	✔	
COTINUS COGGYGRIA 'ROYAL PURPLE'		✔	✔	✔	✔	✔	✔			✔	✔										✔			✔	✔	✔	
DEUTZIA GRACILIS 'NIKKO'		✔	✔	✔	✔						✔	✔	✔				✔		✔					✔	✔		✔
ENKIANTHUS CAMPANULATUS		✔	✔	✔	✔	✔					✔	✔	✔		✔						✔			✔	✔		
FORSYTHIA X INTERMEDIA 'SPECTABILIS'			✔	✔	✔	✔				✔	✔	✔								✔					✔		
FORSYTHIA VIRIDISSIMA 'BRONXENSIS'			✔	✔	✔	✔				✔	✔	✔					✔								✔		✔
FOTHERGILLA GARDENII		✔	✔	✔	✔						✔	✔	✔		✔				✔					✔	✔		
FOTHERGILLA MAJOR		✔	✔	✔	✔						✔	✔	✔		✔					✔				✔	✔		
HAMAMELIS X INTERMEDIA		✔	✔	✔	✔						✔	✔	✔		✔							✔		✔	✔		
HIBISCUS SYRIACUS 'DIANA'			✔	✔	✔	✔					✔				✔					✔					✔		
HYDRANGEA ARBORESCENS 'GRANDIFLORA'	✔	✔	✔	✔	✔	✔					✔		✔						✔						✔		
HYDRANGEA PANICULATA	✔	✔	✔	✔	✔	✔					✔	✔	✔									✔		✔	✔		✔
HYDRANGEA QUERCIFOLIA			✔	✔	✔	✔	✔				✔	✔	✔						✔					✔	✔		✔
ILEX 'SPARKLEBERRY'	✔	✔	✔	✔	✔						✔	✔	✔								✔					✔	
ITEA VIRGINICA 'HENRY'S GARNET'			✔	✔	✔	✔	✔				✔	✔	✔	✔					✔					✔	✔		
KERRIA JAPONICA		✔	✔	✔	✔	✔	✔				✔		✔	✔					✔					✔	✔		
MALUS SARGENTII		✔	✔	✔	✔	✔				✔	✔	✔									✔				✔	✔	
MYRICA PENSYLVANICA	✔	✔	✔	✔						✔	✔	✔	✔			✔				✔				✔		✔	
NANDINA DOMESTICA				✔	✔	✔	✔				✔	✔	✔							✔				✔	✔	✔	✔
POTENTILLA FRUTICOSA	✔	✔	✔	✔	✔					✔	✔	✔	✔			✔			✔					✔	✔		
RHODODENDRON CALENDULACEUM			✔	✔	✔						✔	✔	✔						✔					✔	✔		
RHODODENDRON VASEYI 'WHITE FIND'	✔	✔	✔	✔	✔	✔					✔	✔	✔						✔					✔	✔		
ROSA ALBA 'INCARNATA'		✔	✔	✔	✔	✔	✔	✔			✔	✔			✔				✔					✔	✔	✔	
ROSA RUGOSA	✔	✔	✔	✔	✔	✔	✔	✔			✔	✔			✔				✔					✔	✔	✔	
ROSA VIRGINIANA	✔	✔	✔	✔	✔						✔	✔			✔				✔					✔	✔		
SPIRAEA X CINERA 'GREFSHEIM'	✔	✔	✔	✔	✔	✔					✔	✔							✔					✔	✔		
SPIRAEA NIPPONICA 'SNOWMOUND'	✔	✔	✔	✔	✔	✔					✔	✔							✔					✔	✔		
STEPHANANDRA INCISA 'CRISPA'	✔	✔	✔	✔	✔	✔					✔	✔	✔				✔							✔			
SYRINGA MICROPHYLLA 'SUPERBA'		✔	✔	✔	✔						✔	✔								✔				✔	✔		

105

	ZONES									SOIL		LIGHT			RESISTANT TO			HEIGHT (IN FEET)						NOTED FOR			
	Zone 3	Zone 4	Zone 5	Zone 6	Zone 7	Zone 8	Zone 9	Zone 10	Zone 11	Dry	Moist	Full Sun	Partial Shade	Shade	Pests/Diseases	Drought	Pollution	Under 1	1-3	3-6	6-10	10-20	Over 20	Foliage	Flowers	Fruit	Form
DECIDUOUS SHRUBS																											
SYRINGA PATULA 'MISS KIM'	✓	✓	✓	✓	✓	✓					✓	✓							✓					✓	✓		
VACCINIUM ANGUSTIFOLIUM	✓	✓	✓	✓							✓	✓	✓				✓							✓	✓	✓	
VIBURNUM CARLCEPHALUM			✓	✓	✓	✓					✓	✓	✓		✓						✓			✓	✓		
VIBURNUM DILATATUM			✓	✓	✓						✓	✓	✓		✓						✓			✓	✓		
VIBURNUM PLICATUM VAR. TOMENTOSUM 'ESKIMO'			✓	✓	✓						✓	✓	✓		✓					✓				✓	✓		
EVERGREEN SHRUBS																											
ARBUTUS UNEDO 'COMPACTA'					✓	✓	✓			✓	✓	✓	✓							✓				✓	✓	✓	
ARCTOSTAPHYLOS DENSIFLORA					✓	✓	✓	✓		✓		✓				✓				✓				✓			
BERBERIS JULIANAE			✓	✓	✓					✓	✓	✓	✓				✓			✓				✓			
BUXUS MICROPHYLLA 'WINTERGREEN'			✓	✓	✓	✓					✓	✓	✓				✓							✓			✓
BUXUS SEMPERVIRENS 'VARDAR VALLEY'		✓	✓	✓	✓	✓					✓	✓	✓				✓							✓			✓
CAMELLIA JAPONICA					✓	✓	✓				✓		✓								✓			✓	✓		
CAMELLIA SASANQUA					✓	✓	✓				✓		✓							✓				✓	✓		
CEANOTHUS 'DARK STAR'						✓	✓	✓	✓	✓		✓				✓			✓					✓	✓		
DAPHNE ODORA				✓	✓	✓					✓		✓						✓					✓	✓		
GREVILLEA ROSMARINIFOLIA						✓	✓	✓		✓		✓				✓			✓					✓	✓		
HETEROMELES ARBUTIFOLIA					✓	✓	✓			✓	✓	✓				✓						✓		✓		✓	
ILEX CRENATA 'HELLERI'			✓	✓	✓	✓					✓	✓	✓				✓							✓			✓
ILEX GLABRA 'COMPACTA'		✓	✓	✓	✓	✓					✓	✓	✓	✓					✓					✓			✓
ILEX VOMITORIA				✓	✓	✓	✓				✓	✓	✓								✓	✓	✓	✓		✓	
JUNIPERUS CHINENSIS 'GOLD COAST'	✓	✓	✓	✓	✓	✓	✓			✓		✓				✓		✓						✓			
KALMIA LATIFOLIA		✓	✓	✓	✓	✓					✓	✓	✓	✓							✓			✓	✓		
LEPTOSPERMUM SCOPARIUM						✓	✓				✓	✓	✓			✓					✓			✓	✓		
LEUCOTHOE FONTANESIANA		✓	✓	✓	✓	✓					✓		✓	✓						✓				✓	✓		✓
LONICERA PILEATA			✓	✓	✓						✓		✓	✓	✓			✓									✓
MAHONIA AQUIFOLIUM		✓	✓	✓	✓	✓					✓		✓							✓				✓	✓	✓	
MAHONIA BEALEI			✓	✓	✓	✓					✓		✓								✓			✓	✓	✓	
NERIUM OLEANDER 'LITTLE RED'					✓	✓	✓			✓	✓	✓	✓			✓	✓			✓				✓	✓		
OSMANTHUS HETEROPHYLLUS					✓	✓	✓				✓	✓	✓								✓			✓	✓		
PIERIS FLORIBUNDA		✓	✓	✓	✓						✓	✓	✓							✓				✓	✓		✓
PITTOSPORUM TOBIRA					✓	✓	✓			✓	✓	✓	✓	✓		✓					✓			✓	✓		
PLUMBAGO AURICULATA						✓	✓	✓	✓		✓	✓	✓				✓				✓			✓	✓		
PRUNUS LAUROCERASUS 'OTTO LUYKEN'			✓	✓	✓	✓					✓	✓	✓	✓	✓					✓				✓	✓		

Category	Plant	Zone 3	Zone 4	Zone 5	Zone 6	Zone 7	Zone 8	Zone 9	Zone 10	Zone 11	Dry	Moist	Full Sun	Partial Shade	Shade	Pests/Diseases	Drought	Pollution	Under 1	1-3	3-6	6-10	10-20	Over 20	Foliage	Flowers	Fruit	Form
EVERGREEN SHRUBS	PYRACANTHA COCCINEA 'MOJAVE'			✓	✓	✓	✓					✓	✓								✓				✓	✓	✓	
	RAPHIOLEPIS INDICA 'SNOW WHITE'					✓	✓	✓			✓	✓	✓				✓			✓					✓	✓		
	RHODODENDRON 'BOULE DE NEIGE'		✓	✓	✓	✓						✓	✓	✓						✓					✓	✓		
	RHODODENDRON YAKUSIMANUM		✓	✓	✓	✓						✓	✓							✓					✓	✓		✓
	TAXUS BACCATA 'REPANDENS'		✓	✓	✓							✓	✓	✓	✓					✓					✓		✓	✓
	TAXUS X MEDIA 'DENSIFORMIS'	✓	✓	✓	✓							✓	✓	✓						✓					✓		✓	
	YUCCA FILAMENTOSA 'GOLDEN SWORD'		✓	✓	✓	✓	✓				✓		✓	✓				✓							✓	✓		✓
DECIDUOUS TREES	ACER GRISEUM		✓	✓	✓	✓						✓	✓										✓		✓			✓
	ACER PALMATUM 'DISSECTUM ATROPURPUREUM'			✓	✓	✓						✓		✓									✓		✓			✓
	AMELANCHIER ARBOREA		✓	✓	✓	✓	✓					✓	✓	✓										✓	✓	✓	✓	
	CERCIS CANADENSIS		✓	✓	✓	✓	✓					✓	✓	✓											✓	✓	✓	
	CERCIS RENIFORMIS					✓	✓					✓	✓	✓									✓		✓	✓		
	CORNUS KOUSA			✓	✓	✓	✓					✓	✓	✓		✓								✓	✓	✓	✓	✓	
	CORNUS 'AURORA' CV. RUTBAN			✓	✓	✓						✓	✓			✓								✓	✓	✓		
	CRATAEGUS VIRIDIS 'WINTER KING'	✓	✓	✓	✓						✓	✓	✓											✓	✓	✓	✓	
	KOELREUTERIA PANICULATA		✓	✓	✓	✓	✓				✓	✓	✓				✓	✓	✓						✓	✓	✓	✓	
	LAGERSTROEMIA INDICA 'NATCHEZ'				✓	✓	✓					✓	✓				✓						✓			✓		✓
	MAGNOLIA X 'GALAXY'			✓	✓	✓	✓					✓	✓	✓										✓	✓	✓		
	MAGNOLIA 'RANDY'			✓	✓	✓	✓					✓	✓										✓		✓	✓	✓	
	MAGNOLIA VIRGINIANA			✓	✓	✓	✓					✓	✓	✓										✓	✓	✓	✓	
	MALUS X 'DONALD WYMAN'	✓	✓	✓	✓					✓	✓	✓											✓		✓	✓	✓	
	OXYDENDRUM ARBOREUM			✓	✓	✓	✓					✓	✓	✓		✓								✓	✓	✓		
	PRUNUS 'HALLY JOLIVETTE'			✓	✓	✓						✓	✓										✓		✓	✓		✓
	PRUNUS SARGENTII	✓	✓	✓	✓							✓	✓											✓	✓	✓		✓
	PYRUS CALLERYANA 'CAPITAL'			✓	✓	✓	✓				✓	✓	✓				✓	✓						✓	✓	✓		✓
EVERGREEN TREES	AGONIS FLEXUOSA								✓		✓		✓	✓			✓							✓	✓	✓		
	CHAMAECYPARIS OBTUSA 'CRIPPSII'		✓	✓	✓	✓	✓					✓	✓											✓	✓			✓
	ILEX X ATTENUATA 'FOSTER #2'				✓	✓	✓	✓				✓	✓	✓										✓	✓	✓	✓	✓
	JUNIPERUS SCOPULORUM 'SKYROCKET'	✓	✓	✓	✓	✓					✓		✓						✓						✓	✓			
	MAGNOLIA GRANDIFLORA 'LITTLE GEM'			✓	✓	✓	✓					✓	✓	✓									✓		✓	✓	✓	✓
	MYRICA CALIFORNICA				✓	✓	✓				✓	✓	✓	✓									✓	✓	✓		✓	
	PINUS BUNGEANA		✓	✓	✓	✓	✓				✓	✓	✓											✓	✓			✓

Column groups: ZONES (Zone 3–Zone 11) · SOIL (Dry, Moist) · LIGHT (Full Sun, Partial Shade, Shade) · RESISTANT TO (Pests/Diseases, Drought, Pollution) · HEIGHT (IN FEET) (Under 1, 1-3, 3-6, 6-10, 10-20, Over 20) · NOTED FOR (Foliage, Flowers, Fruit, Form)

A Zone Map of the United States

A plant's winter hardiness is critical in deciding whether it is suitable for your garden. The map below divides the United States into 11 climatic zones based on average minimum temperatures, as compiled by the United States Department of Agriculture. Find your zone and check the zone information in the Plant Selection Guide *(pages 102-107)* or the Encyclopedia entries *(pages 110-161)* to help you choose the plants most likely to flourish in your climate.

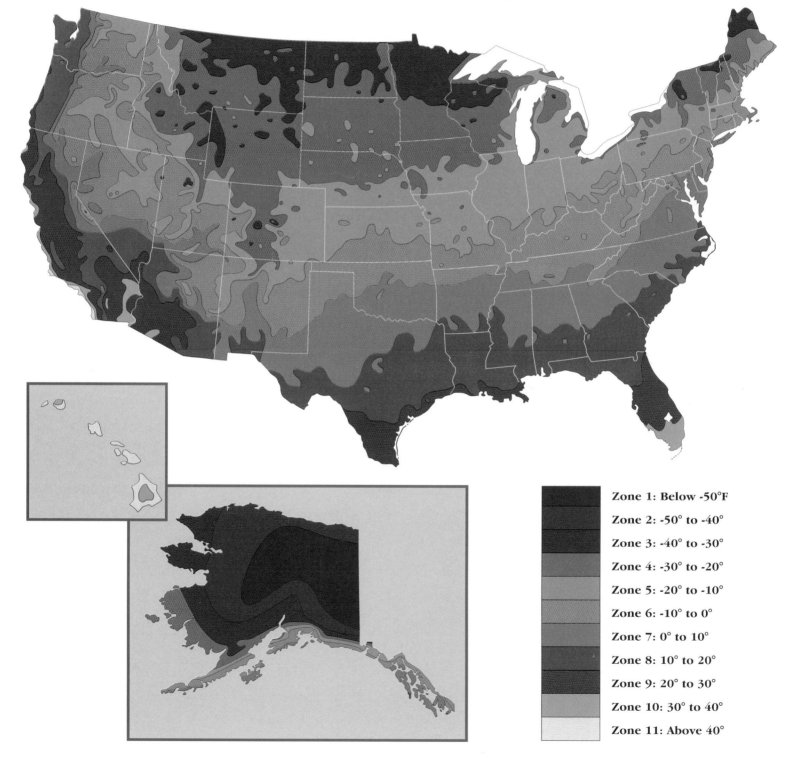

Zone 1: Below -50°F

Zone 2: -50° to -40°

Zone 3: -40° to -30°

Zone 4: -30° to -20°

Zone 5: -20° to -10°

Zone 6: -10° to 0°

Zone 7: 0° to 10°

Zone 8: 10° to 20°

Zone 9: 20° to 30°

Zone 10: 30° to 40°

Zone 11: Above 40°

Cross-Reference Guide to Plant Names

Adam's-needle—*Yucca filamentosa*
African daisy—*Osteospermum*
Alumroot—*Heuchera*
Andromeda—*Pieris japonica*
Azalea—*Rhododendron* species and hybrids
Balloon flower—*Platycodon grandiflorus*
Barberry—*Berberis*
Barrenwort—*Epimedium*
Bayberry—*Myrica*
Bearberry—*Arctostaphylos*
Bellflower—*Campanula*
Black cohosh—*Cimicifuga racemosa*
Blazing star—*Liatris*
Bleeding heart—*Dicentra* species
Bluebeard—*Caryopteris*
Blueberry—*Vaccinium*
Blue oat grass—*Helictotrichon*
Bluestar—*Amsonia*
Boneset—*Eupatorium*
Boxwood—*Buxus*
Bugbane—*Cimicifuga*
Bugleweed—*Ajuga*
Butterfly weed—*Asclepias tuberosa*
California holly—*Heteromeles*
California tree poppy—*Romneya*
Calla lily—*Zantedeschia aethiopica*
Callery pear—*Pyrus calleryana*
Candytuft—*Iberis*
Cape plumbago (Cape leadwort)—*Plumbago auriculata*
Carolina cherry laurel—*Prunus caroliniana*
Cedar—*Juniperus*
Century plant—*Agave*
Cherry laurel—*Prunus laurocerasus*
Chinese silver grass—*Miscanthus sinensis*
Chokeberry—*Aronia*
Cinquefoil—*Potentilla*
Columbine—*Aquilegia*

Coneflower—*Rudbeckia*
Coral bells—*Heuchera sanguinea*
Cornelian cherry—*Cornus mas*
Crabapple—*Malus* species
Cranesbill—*Geranium*
Crape myrtle—*Lagerstroemia indica*
Creeping phlox—*Phlox stolonifera*
Daylily—*Hemerocallis*
Dead nettle—*Lamium*
Dogwood—*Cornus*
Drooping leucothoe—*Leucothoe fontanesiana*
Eulalia—*Miscanthus*
False cypress—*Chamaecyparis*
False indigo—*Baptisia*
Five-finger—*Potentilla*
Flowering cherry—*Prunus* species
Flowering quince—*Chaenomeles*
Fountain grass—*Pennisetum*
Funkia—*Hosta*
Gas plant—*Dictamnus*
Gay-feather—*Liatris*
Golden rain tree—*Koelreuteria paniculata*
Goldenrod—*Solidago*
Goldenstar—*Chrysogonum*
Hardy ageratum—*Eupatorium coelestinum*
Hawthorn—*Crataegus*
Hellebore—*Helleborus*
Hens and chicks—*Echeveria*
Holly—*Ilex*
Honeysuckle—*Lonicera*
Indian hawthorn—*Raphiolepis indica*
Indian pink—*Spigelia marilandica*
Inkberry—*Ilex glabra*
Ivy—*Hedera*
Japanese andromeda—*Pieris floribunda*
Japanese blood grass—

Imperata cylindrica var. *rubra*
Japanese flowering cherry—*Prunus yedoensis*
Joe-Pye weed—*Eupatorium fistulosum*
Juniper—*Juniperus*
Lace-bark pine—*Pinus bungeana*
Lamb's ears—*Stachys byzantina*
Lavender—*Lavandula*
Lavender cotton—*Santolina*
Leadwort—*Ceratostigma*
Leatherleaf mahonia—*Mahonia bealei*
Lenten rose—*Helleborus orientalis*
Lilac—*Syringa*
Lilyturf—*Liriope*
Mallow—*Hibiscus*
Maple—*Acer*
Mondo grass—*Ophiopogon*
Monkshood—*Aconitum*
Moss phlox—*Phlox subulata*
Mountain laurel—*Kalmia latifolia*
Myrtle—*Vinca*
New Zealand tea tree—*Leptospermum scoparium*
Oleander—*Nerium oleander*
Oregon grape, Oregon grape holly—*Mahonia aquifolium*
Orrisroot—*Iris pallida*
Peony—*Paeonia*
Peppermint tree—*Agonis flexuosa*
Periwinkle—*Vinca*
Pinkroot—*Spigelia marilandica*
Plantain lily—*Hosta*
Plumbago—*Ceratostigma*
Poppy—*Papaver*
Purple coneflower—*Echinacea*
Redbud—*Cercis*
Reed grass—*Calamagrostis*
Rockrose—*Cistus*
Rose—*Rosa*

Rose of Sharon—*Hibiscus syriacus*
Russian sage—*Perovskia*
Sage—*Salvia*
Scarlet firethorn—*Pyracantha coccinea*
Sedge—*Carex*
Serviceberry—*Amelanchier*
Siberian bugloss—*Brunnera macrophylla*
Smoke tree (smokebush)—*Cotinus*
Soapweed—*Yucca glauca*
Solomon's-seal—*Polygonatum*
Sorrel tree (sourwood)—*Oxydendrum arboreum*
Southern magnolia—*Magnolia grandiflora*
Speedwell—*Veronica*
Spirea—*Spiraea*
Spotted phlox—*Phlox maculata*
Spurge—*Euphorbia*
Spurge—*Pachysandra*
Stonecrop—*Sedum*
Strawberry tree—*Arbutus unedo*
Summer-sweet—*Clethra*
Sunflower—*Helianthus*
Sweet bay magnolia (swamp magnolia)—*Magnolia virginiana*
Sweet shrub—*Calycanthus*
Sweetspire—*Itea*
Switch grass—*Panicum virgatum*
Tickseed—*Coreopsis*
Toyon—*Heteromeles*
Transvaal daisy—*Gerbera*
Wax myrtle—*Myrica*
Wild indigo—*Baptisia*
Wild lilac—*Ceanothus*
Windflower—*Anemone*
Winterberry—*Ilex verticillata*
Witch hazel—*Hamamelis*
Wolfsbane—*Aconitum*
Woodland phlox—*Phlox divaricata*
Yarrow—*Achillea*
Yew—*Taxus*

Encyclopedia of Low Maintenance Plants

Presented here is a selection of plants for gardens designed for easy care. The plants are listed alphabetically by their Latin botanical names; common names appear in bold type beneath the Latin. If you know a plant only by its common name, check the name against the chart on page 109 or in the index.

A botanical name consists first of the genus name, such as Achillea, which is usually printed in italics. Within a genus are one or more species, whose names are also in italics but are not capitalized, as in Achillea millefolium. Many species contain one or more varieties, either naturally occurring or cultivated; these names are enclosed in single quotation marks, as in Achillea millefolium 'Cerise Queen'. An "x" in a name, as in Achillea x 'Paprika', indicates a hybrid. "Zones" refers to the U.S. Department of Agriculture Plant Hardiness Zone Map (page 108). Plants grown outside recommended zones may do poorly or fail to survive.

Abelia
(a-BEE-li-a)
ABELIA

Abelia x grandiflora 'Francis Mason'

Hardiness: *Zones 6-9*
Plant type: *shrub*
Height: *1½ to 6 feet*
Interest: *foliage, flowers*
Soil: *well-drained, moist, acid*
Light: *full sun to partial shade*

The glossy dark green leaves of abelia turn a lovely bronze in the fall; they are evergreen in warmer zones, semi-evergreen in cooler areas. From summer through late fall, small, fragrant white flowers with a delicate pink blush appear in abundance. Abelia is useful as a specimen with a long season of interest, as a dense hedge, or combined with other shrubs in a mixed border.

Selected species and varieties: *A.* x *grandiflora* 'Francis Mason'—4 to 5 feet tall, with foliage variegated deep green and yellow; 'Prostrata' is 1½ to 2 feet tall with a spreading habit, is semi-evergreen even in mild climates, and is effective as a ground cover. *A.* x 'Edward Goucher'—3 to 5 feet tall, with lavender-pink flowers.

Growing conditions and maintenance: Plant abelia in soil amended with organic matter. It flowers best in full sun, but can handle up to half a day of shade. It needs occasional selective pruning to maintain a neat form. Do not shear. Remove cold-damaged stems in spring.

Acanthopanax
(a-kan-tho-PA-naks)
FIVE-LEAF ARALIA

Acanthopanax sieboldianus 'Variegatus'

Hardiness: *Zones 4-8*
Plant type: *deciduous shrub*
Height: *8 to 10 feet*
Interest: *foliage*
Soil: *well-drained*
Light: *full sun to full shade*

Acanthopanax is an excellent plant for difficult sites. The arching, wide-spreading stems form the plant into a broad, rounded shrub, but it can be sheared to produce a dense hedge. Its bright green compound leaves appear in early spring and persist late into fall. Slender prickles along the stems make acanthopanax an effective barrier.

Selected species and varieties: *A. sieboldianus*—an erect shrub with arching branches, five to seven leaflets per leaf, and light brown stems with slender prickles; 'Variegatus' stands 6 to 8 feet tall and has leaves with creamy white margins.

Growing conditions and maintenance: Acanthopanax is easy to transplant and adapts to nearly every site. It tolerates a wide range of soil types from acid to alkaline and from sandy to clay, and it stands up well to air pollution and drought. As a hedge, it can be heavily pruned or sheared to encourage compact growth and maintain the desired height. In an informal, mixed planting, little pruning is necessary.

Acer
(AY-ser)
MAPLE

Acer palmatum 'Dissectum Atropurpureum'

Hardiness: *Zones 4-8*

Plant type: *large shrub or small tree*

Height: *6 to 30 feet*

Interest: *foliage, bark*

Soil: *moist, well-drained*

Light: *full sun to partial shade*

The smaller species of maple provide year-round interest as understory plantings and specimens.

Selected species and varieties: *A. palmatum* 'Dissectum Atropurpureum'—6 to 12 feet tall, with deep red, finely cut leaves and a wide-spreading form with twisted branches that are attractive in winter; 'Bloodgood' grows 15 to 20 feet tall with reddish purple leaves; 'Senkaki', to 10 feet, with coral red branches that are outstanding in winter; Zones 5-8. *A. griseum* (paperbark maple)—20 to 30 feet tall, with leaves that turn orange in fall; its peeling bark is cinnamon brown, striking in winter; Zones 4-8. *A. japonicum* 'Aconitifolium'—8 to 10 feet tall, with an equal spread of soft green leaves that turn crimson in fall; 'Aureum' grows 10 to 20 feet tall with golden yellow leaves throughout summer; Zones 5-7.

Growing conditions and maintenance: Plant *A. griseum* in full sun; the others prefer light shade and some protection from winds and late frosts. All are slow-growing plants that benefit from liberal amounts of organic matter incorporated into the soil.

Achillea
(a-kil-EE-a)
YARROW

Achillea x 'Paprika'

Hardiness: *Zones 3-8*

Plant type: *herbaceous perennial*

Height: *1 to 3 feet*

Interest: *flowers, foliage*

Soil: *average to poor, well-drained*

Light: *full sun to full shade*

Yarrow is a summer-blooming, drought-tolerant perennial suitable for a sunny border or wildflower garden.

Selected species and varieties: *A.* 'Coronation Gold'—2½ to 3 feet tall, with yellow flowers blooming over a long season and gray-green fernlike leaves; 'Hoffnung' grows to 1½ feet with antique yellow flowers; 'Moonshine', to 2 feet, with pale yellow flowers good for cutting and gray leaves; *A.* x 'Paprika', to 1½ feet, with hot pink flowers fading to creamy yellow. *A. millefolium* 'Cerise Queen', cherry red flowers; 'Fire King', deep rose-red flowers; 'Rosea', to 2 feet, with dense pink flower heads from midsummer to fall; Zones 4-8.

Growing conditions and maintenance: Some yarrows are fast spreading and may become invasive. They tolerate considerable neglect and can withstand drought and infertile soils. When grown in rich soil with abundant moisture, they become weak-stemmed and produce poor-quality flowers. They are easily divided in spring or fall.

Aconitum
(ak-o-NY-tum)
MONKSHOOD

Aconitum napellus

Hardiness: *Zones 3-8*

Plant type: *herbaceous perennial*

Height: *2 to 4 feet*

Interest: *flowers, foliage*

Soil: *fertile, moist, well-drained, acid*

Light: *partial shade*

Monkshood produces lush, glossy green foliage that remains attractive throughout the growing season. Tall, upright stems of blue or purple helmet-shaped flowers appear from mid to late summer.

Selected species and varieties: *A. carmichaelii*—2 to 4 feet tall, with leathery, dark green leaves and deep blue flowers that bloom in late summer on strong stems. *A. napellus*—3 to 4 feet, with finely divided leaves and blue to violet flowers from mid to late summer. *A.* x *bicolor*—a hybrid between *A. napellus* and *A. variegatum* that has given rise to many attractive garden hybrids, including 'Spark's Variety', with deep violet-blue flowers.

Growing conditions and maintenance: Though it prefers partial shade, monkshood will tolerate full sun if it receives ample water. Plants should not be allowed to dry out. Taller types may need staking. They can remain undisturbed indefinitely. The leaves and roots are poisonous, so do not plant near a vegetable garden.

Aeonium
(ee-OH-nee-um)
AEONIUM

Aeonium arboreum 'Schwartzkopf'

Hardiness: *Zones 9-10*

Plant type: *succulent perennial*

Height: *1 to 3 feet*

Interest: *flowers, foliage*

Soil: *light, well-drained*

Light: *full sun*

Aeoniums bear fleshy leaves in attractive rosettes on succulent stems. Flowers in shades of yellow develop in terminal pyramidal clusters. Aeoniums are prized for their long season of interest in West Coast gardens, where they are often used as accents in rock gardens, dry borders, and containers.

Selected species and varieties: *A. arboreum* 'Schwartzkopf'—2 to 3 feet tall, upright and shrubby, with golden yellow flowers and dark, shiny, purple-black leaves appearing in 6- to 8-inch rosettes on branched stems. *A. tabuliforme*—12 inches, with leaves forming saucer-shaped, stemless rosettes 3 to 10 inches across and pale yellow flowers.

Growing conditions and maintenance: Aeoniums thrive in California coastal conditions, where their soil and light needs are best met and they enjoy high humidity and mild temperatures. They can be grown farther inland, but may require some shade for protection from midday heat. They do not tolerate frost.

Agave
(a-GAH-vay)
CENTURY PLANT

Agave americana

Hardiness: *Zones 9-10*

Plant type: *succulent perennial*

Height: *5 to 6 feet*

Interest: *foliage, flowers*

Soil: *sandy, well-drained*

Light: *full sun*

The century plant is an effective accent or barrier in warm, dry climates. Planted in groups, it will naturalize on dry banks.

Selected species and varieties: *A. americana*—leaves up to 6 feet long in a basal rosette; the leaves are gray-green, succulent, stiff, evergreen, and armed with spines along margin and tip. When plants reach 6 to 10 years of age, a branched flower stalk rises from the rosette and may grow to 15 to 40 feet. The fragrant, yellow-green flowers appear in summer, and last 1 to 2 months.

Growing conditions and maintenance: Good drainage is essential for the century plant. Though it is very drought tolerant, its leaves may shrivel under extremely dry conditions, but will recover as soon as water is supplied. After flowering, the plant dies, leaving dozens of small plantlets around the base of the original rosette. These should be transplanted to separate locations when small.

Agonis
(a-GO-nis)
PEPPERMINT TREE

Agonis flexuosa

Hardiness: *Zone 10*

Plant type: *evergreen tree*

Height: *25 to 35 feet*

Interest: *foliage, bark, flowers*

Soil: *well-drained to dry*

Light: *full sun to partial shade*

The peppermint tree is a fast-growing evergreen for warm climates. Its leaves are willowlike and are borne on graceful, arching branches. It is a good choice for a wide-spreading lawn tree, street tree, or large container plant.

Selected species and varieties: *A. flexuosa*—to 35 feet, with an equal spread of deep green leaves that grow 3 to 6 inches long and are aromatic when crushed; small white, fragrant flowers appear in early summer, followed by woody capsules; attractive reddish brown, vertically fissured bark.

Growing conditions and maintenance: The peppermint tree requires a nearly frost-free location; it will die back to the ground if temperatures fall below 25° F. It thrives in warm coastal locations and is tolerant of most soils and moisture conditions.

Ajuga
(a-JOO-ga)
BUGLEWEED

Ajuga reptans

Hardiness: *Zones 3-9*

Plant type: *herbaceous perennial*

Height: *6 to 9 inches*

Interest: *foliage, flowers, form*

Soil: *well-drained, acid*

Light: *full sun to partial shade*

Ajuga is an effective ground cover for growing under trees where grass will not grow. Its colorful foliage is effective year round, making it an excellent choice for the foreground of a shrub border or rock garden. The flowers are usually blue and are borne on short, erect stems from spring to early summer.

Selected species and varieties: *A. pyramidalis*—4 to 6 inches tall with blue flowers, it forms a neat clump and is slower spreading than other species; 'Metallica Crispa' grows 6 inches tall, with deep green to purple leaves of wrinkled texture. *A. reptans*—6 to 9 inches tall, it spreads fast to form a dense mat of deep green leaves, with violet-blue flowers; 'Bronze Beauty' has bronze leaves; 'Catlan's Giant' reaches 8 inches tall, with large green leaves; 'Silver Beauty', green-and-white variegated leaves.

Growing conditions and maintenance: Ajuga is adaptable to moist or dry soils. *A. reptans* spreads rapidly by stolons and may become invasive. Divide plants in spring or fall to prevent overcrowding.

Aloe
(AL-oh)
ALOE

Aloe striata

Hardiness: *Zones 10-11*

Plant type: *succulent perennial*

Height: *1½ to 3 feet*

Interest: *foliage, form*

Soil: *dry to well-drained*

Light: *full sun*

Aloes thrive in warm, dry climates. Although they are primarily grown for their attractive rosette-forming leaves, some species produce exotic flowers as well. They can be effectively used as specimens, ground covers, container plants, or in a rock garden.

Selected species and varieties: *A. striata* (coral aloe)—1½ to 3 feet tall, forming large clumps; grows thick, succulent, sword-shaped gray-green leaves 15 to 20 inches long with pink margins, 12 to 20 per rosette; its flowers are tubular, coral red on well-branched stems; numerous hybrids are available.

Growing conditions and maintenance: Aloes tolerate seaside conditions, poor soil, and drought; excess water promotes root rot. They prefer a frost-free location; serious injury occurs at temperatures below 25° F. Once aloes are established, the only care they require is occasional deep watering.

Amelanchier
(am-el-ANG-kee-er)
SERVICEBERRY

Amelanchier arborea

Hardiness: *Zones 4-9*

Plant type: *large shrub or tree*

Height: *15 to 40 feet*

Interest: *foliage, flowers, fruit, bark*

Soil: *moist, well-drained, acid*

Light: *full sun to partial shade*

Serviceberry provides year-round landscape interest. White flower clusters appear in early spring; leaves emerge purplish gray and change to deep green in summer and to shades from yellow to apricot and red in fall. The smooth gray bark is attractive all winter.

Selected species and varieties: *A. arborea*—30 to 40 feet in the wild, rarely above 20 feet in cultivation, its leaves grow 1 to 3 inches long, its flowers form 2- to 4-inch pendulous clusters, and its fruit is blueberry-like and attracts birds; it is useful in naturalized areas, woodland gardens, and mixed-shrub borders.

Growing conditions and maintenance: Serviceberry is often found growing wild beside stream banks, at the edge of woodlands, or along fence rows. In the garden, it tolerates a broad range of moisture conditions. Pruning is generally not necessary other than to remove damaged wood.

Amsonia
(am-SO-nee-a)
BLUESTAR

Amsonia tabernaemontana

Hardiness: *Zones 3-9*

Plant type: *herbaceous perennial*

Height: *2 to 3 feet*

Interest: *foliage, flowers*

Soil: *moderately fertile, well-drained*

Light: *full sun to partial shade*

Amsonia produces pale blue star-shaped blossoms. Blooming in late spring and early summer, they are particularly effective combined with more brightly colored flowers. Its densely mounded willowlike leaves remain attractive throughout the growing season, providing a lovely foil for later-blooming perennials.

Selected species and varieties: *A. tabernaemontana*—produces steel blue flowers in terminal clusters on 2- to 3-foot-tall stiff, erect stems with densely occurring leaves 3 to 6 inches long that turn yellow in fall; *A. t.* var. *salicifolia* has longer and thinner leaves and blooms slightly later than the species.

Growing conditions and maintenance: Amsonias grown in shade will have a more open habit than those grown in sun. In poor to moderately fertile soil, amsonia stems rarely need staking; avoid highly fertile soil, which produces rank, floppy growth. Other than for propagating, division is usually not necessary.

Anemone
(a-NEM-o-ne)
WINDFLOWER

Anemone blanda

Hardiness: *Zones 3-8*

Plant type: *herbaceous perennial*

Height: *3 inches to 4 feet*

Interest: *flowers*

Soil: *fertile, moist, well-drained*

Light: *partial shade to full sun*

Anemones vary in habit, height, flowering season, and color. Spring-blooming species are short, suited for the front of a border or rock garden. Fall-flowering anemones are taller, more upright, and useful for the middle or back of a border.

Selected species and varieties: *A.* x *hybrida*—stems 2 to 4 feet tall, with fall-blooming pink or white single, semidouble, or double flowers, Zones 4-8; 'Honorine Jobert' grows to 3 feet with white flowers; 'Margarete', 2 to 3 feet tall with semidouble pink blooms; 'September Charm', 2½ feet, with single silvery pink flowers. *A. hupehensis* var. *japonica*—similar to *A.* x *hybrida*, with pink to purple flowers; Zones 6-8. *A. vitifolia* 'Robustissima'—3 to 4 feet tall, with pink flowers in late summer and fall. *A. blanda*—3- to 8-inch midspring flowers in blue, red, white, or pink; Zones 5-8.

Growing conditions and maintenance: Although they prefer partial shade, anemones will tolerate full sun with adequate water. Incorporate generous amounts of organic matter into soil. *A. blanda* is grown from tubers planted in fall. Fall-blooming types may need staking.

Aquilegia
(ak-wil-EE-jee-a)
COLUMBINE

Aquilegia canadensis

Hardiness: *Zones 3-9*

Plant type: *herbaceous perennial*

Height: *2 to 3 feet*

Interest: *flowers, foliage*

Soil: *moist, well-drained, acid*

Light: *full sun to partial shade*

Columbines are dainty plants bearing unusual spurred flowers and fernlike leaves. They are useful in the border, naturalized areas, and rock gardens.

Selected species and varieties: *A. canadensis*—2 to 3 feet tall, forming a rounded clump of finely divided leaves and producing several yellow-and-red flowers per nodding stem in spring and early summer that attract hummingbirds and stay in bloom longer than many species with larger flowers; 'Corbett' has yellow flowers.

Growing conditions and maintenance: Columbine does not do well in dry soil; add organic matter to the soil before planting to help retain moisture. Though plants are generally short-lived (2 or 3 years), *A. canadensis* self-sows readily. Leaf miners often infest plantings; infected leaves should be removed.

Arbutus
(ar-BEW-tus)
STRAWBERRY TREE

Arbutus unedo

Hardiness: *Zones 7-9*

Plant type: *large shrub or small tree*

Height: *8 to 12 feet*

Interest: *foliage, bark, flowers, fruit*

Soil: *well-drained, acid*

Light: *full sun to partial shade*

The strawberry tree provides interest to southern and West Coast gardens throughout the year. The leaves are evergreen, the bark is deep reddish brown and exfoliates, and the branches become attractively gnarled with age. Small urn-shaped flowers grow in 2-inch clusters in the fall, and the orange-red berrylike fruit ripens the following season.

Selected species and varieties: *A. unedo* 'Compacta'—a slow-growing dwarf variety that eventually reaches 8 to 12 feet in height, it produces leaves of dark green, flowers, and fruit almost continuously; useful as a hedge, as a specimen, or in a mixed-shrub border.

Growing conditions and maintenance: Plant where leaves will be protected from drying winds. The strawberry tree tolerates a wide range of soil conditions as long as drainage is good. It requires watering only during periods of drought. It is also tolerant of seaside conditions.

Arctostaphylos
(ark-toh-STAF-i-los)
BEARBERRY

Arctostaphylos densiflora

Hardiness: *Zones 2-10*

Plant type: *ground cover or shrub*

Height: *6 inches to 8 feet*

Interest: *foliage, flowers, fruit, bark*

Soil: *poor, sandy, acid*

Light: *full sun to partial shade*

Bearberry is a site-tolerant evergreen bearing tiny urn-shaped spring-blooming flowers.

Selected species and varieties: *A. uva-ursi*—a ground cover that grows 6 to 12 inches high with trailing stems up to 15 feet long and leathery, dark green leaves; it produces white flowers with a pink blush and, in late summer, bright red fruit that attracts birds; Zones 2-7. *A. densiflora*—grows 4 to 6 feet tall and equally wide, with mahogany red bark and pink or white flowers in early spring; it serves well in a mixed-shrub border or as a specimen; Zones 7-10.

Growing conditions and maintenance: Both species require well-drained soil. They are drought resistant, though periodic deep watering is suggested during droughts. They are difficult to transplant except from containers. *A. uva-ursi* requires no pruning. *A. densiflora* is primarily grown along the West Coast. It may be pruned to reveal attractive bark and a branching habit.

Aronia
(a-RO-nee-a)
CHOKEBERRY

Aronia arbutifolia 'Brilliantissima'

Hardiness: *Zones 4-9*

Plant type: *deciduous shrub*

Height: *6 to 10 feet*

Interest: *fruit*

Soil: *well-drained*

Light: *full sun to partial shade*

Chokeberry bears a profusion of bright red berries in the fall that persist into winter and attract birds. It is an effective plant for massing or combining with other shrubs in a mixed border.

Selected species and varieties: *A. arbutifolia* 'Brilliantissima'—has dark green, lustrous leaves that turn scarlet in fall; flowers appear in spring in clusters 1 to 1½ inches in diameter; its flowers and fruit grow more abundantly than those of the species.

Growing conditions and maintenance: Chokeberry is easy to transplant and tolerant of almost any soil, but it will produce more fruit and better fall color in sun than in shade. Suckers growing from the base may become a nuisance.

Asclepias
(as-KLEE-pee-as)
BUTTERFLY WEED

Asclepias tuberosa

Hardiness: *Zones 3-9*

Plant type: *herbaceous perennial*

Height: *18 to 36 inches*

Interest: *flowers*

Soil: *dry, poor*

Light: *full sun*

Butterfly weed is a long-lived perennial that requires minimal care. Its flowers are usually vivid orange, though yellow and red flowers occasionally occur both in the wild and in cultivation. Flowering begins in late spring and may continue until late summer.

Selected species and varieties: *A. tuberosa*—stems erect, to 3 feet, with thin pointed leaves along the entire length; individual flowers grow ¼ inch across in terminal clusters and are excellent for fresh or dried arrangements; the milkweedlike pods are also useful for dried arrangements.

Growing conditions and maintenance: Butterfly weed does not grow well in wet areas or where it must compete with tree roots. A taproot makes transplanting difficult, so once established the plant should be left alone; it will not spread invasively. It emerges late in the spring, so mark its location to avoid planting something on top of it.

Astilbe
(a-STIL-be)
ASTILBE, FALSE SPIREA

Astilbe x arendsii 'Fanal'

Hardiness: *Zones 4-8*

Plant type: *herbaceous perennial*

Height: *8 inches to 4 feet*

Interest: *flowers, foliage*

Soil: *fertile, moist, well-drained*

Light: *full sun to partial shade*

Astilbes grace a garden with their mounds of fernlike foliage that range in color from deep green to bronze. Their plumelike flowers rise above the leaves in early to late summer. Astilbes are an excellent choice for the edge of a woodland garden, the front or middle of a border, or on the bank of a stream or garden pond.

Selected species and varieties: *A. taquetii* 'Superba'—to 4 feet tall, with pinkish purple flowers in late summer. *A. chinensis* 'Pumila'—8 to 15 inches tall, with a spreading habit and mauve pink flowers in mid to late summer. *A. x arendsii* 'Fanal'—2 feet tall, with bronze leaves and carmine red flowers in early to midsummer.

Growing conditions and maintenance: Add generous amounts of organic matter to the soil before planting astilbes to aid moisture retention. Foliage will shrivel and turn brown if allowed to dry out. Astilbe is a heavy feeder, and should be divided every 3 to 4 years to maintain vigor and prolific flowering.

Baptisia
(bap-TIZ-ee-a)
WILD INDIGO

Baptisia australis

Hardiness: *Zones 3-9*

Plant type: *herbaceous perennial*

Height: *3 to 4 feet*

Interest: *flowers, foliage*

Soil: *well-drained to dry, sandy*

Light: *full sun*

Wild (false) indigo produces dainty blue pealike flowers from midspring to early summer. Its blue-green leaves are an attractive foil for both its own blooms and those of surrounding plants. The leaves remain handsome throughout the growing season. The plant is useful for the background of a border or as a specimen; its pods are often used in dried arrangements.

Selected species and varieties: *B. australis*—erect stems to 4 feet in height, producing compound leaves with three leaflets, each 1½ to 3 inches long, and indigo blue flowers in long, terminal racemes, good for cutting. *B. alba*—to 3 feet tall with white flowers; Zones 5-8.

Growing conditions and maintenance: Wild indigo adapts to almost any well-drained soil. It is slow growing and noninvasive. Tall selections may require staking. Remove faded flowers to extend the blooming season.

Berberis
(BER-ber-is)
BARBERRY

Berberis thunbergii 'Crimson Pigmy'

Hardiness: *Zones 4-8*

Plant type: *shrub*

Height: *3 to 10 feet*

Interest: *foliage, fruit*

Soil: *moist, well-drained, acid*

Light: *full sun to light shade*

Barberries are useful as foundation plantings, barriers, hedges, or specimens. Varieties with yellow or red foliage provide dramatic color contrast to the landscape and are good candidates for shrub borders and for combining with perennials. This genus includes both deciduous and evergreen species, which vary in height, form, and foliage color. All of the barberries produce spines along their stems, are adaptable to a wide range of growing conditions, and are extremely easy to cultivate.

Selected species and varieties: *B. thunbergii* 'Aurea'—deciduous, 3 to 4 feet tall, and slow growing, with bright yellow leaves when grown in full sun, yellow-green in shade; excellent for foliage contrast in mixed-shrub plantings; Zones 4-8. *B. thunbergii* 'Atropurpurea'—4 to 6 feet tall with an equal or greater spread, a dense, rounded habit, burgundy red foliage all season, yellow flowers in spring, small, bright red berries in fall persisting into winter and keeping the plant interesting after leaves fall; 'Crimson Pigmy' grows 1½ to 2 feet tall by 3 to 5 feet wide with a dense, moundlike habit; 'Golden Ring', 4 to 6 feet tall with equal or greater spread, purplish red leaves with a green or yellow-green margin; 'Rose Glow', 4 to 5 feet tall with equal spread and leaves that emerge rose pink and become marbled with deeper pink and burgundy red as they mature; Zones 4-8. *B. julianae* (wintergreen barberry)—evergreen; forming a dense mound that becomes 6 to 10 feet tall and equally wide, it produces narrow, 2- to 3-inch-long leaves that are a lustrous dark green above and pale green below with spiny, serrated margins. Clusters of yellow flowers bloom in early spring and are followed by blue-black fruit in summer that persist into fall; wintergreen barberry makes an impenetrable hedge or dense screen; Zones 5-8.

Growing conditions and maintenance: Barberries are tolerant of most soil conditions as long as good drainage is provided; they do not adapt well in a soil that is very moist. They withstand dry

Berberis thunbergii 'Aurea'

soils and urban conditions such as air pollution. Foliage color is best when they are grown in full sun. Pruning is generally unnecessary except to remove damaged branches.

Bergenia
(ber-JEN-ee-a)
BERGENIA

Bergenia cordifolia

Hardiness: *Zones 3-8*

Plant type: *herbaceous perennial*

Height: *8 to 18 inches*

Interest: *foliage, flowers*

Soil: *moist, well-drained, poor*

Light: *full sun to partial shade*

The shiny evergreen leaves of bergenia, in their basal clumps, provide textural contrast to more delicately proportioned plants at the front of a herbaceous border or rock garden. They also create an interesting ground cover in front of shrubs. Their spring flowers are usually pink and are of secondary interest to the leaves.

Selected species and varieties: *B. cordifolia*—12 to 18 inches in height, with heart-shaped leaves and pink flowers. *B.* 'Abendglut'—9 inches tall, with maroon leaves and deep magenta flowers. *B.* 'Morgenrote'—grows 8 to 12 inches in height, with deep green foliage and carmine red blooms. *B.* 'Silberlicht'—produces white flowers that turn pink later in the season.

Growing conditions and maintenance: Though bergenias prefer a soil with abundant organic matter, they are tolerant of most other soil conditions. They spread by rhizomes, and in fertile sites must be divided every 3 or 4 years, after flowering. In drier, less fertile situations, they can remain undisturbed for many years.

117

Boltonia
(bowl-TO-nee-a)
BOLTONIA

Boltonia asteroides 'Snowbank'

Hardiness: *Zones 4-8*

Plant type: *herbaceous perennial*

Height: *3 to 4 feet*

Interest: *flowers*

Soil: *well-drained to moist*

Light: *full sun*

Boltonia flowers from midsummer through fall, providing an extended display for the back of a mixed border or center of an island bed. Its daisylike blossoms appear above tall stems of narrow, gray-green willowlike leaves.

Selected species and varieties: *B. asteroides* 'Snowbank'—3 to 4 feet tall, with a compact, self-supporting habit; it produces white flowers ¾ to 1 inch across, borne profusely on branched stems.

Growing conditions and maintenance: Boltonia is adaptable to most sunny sites. In loose, moist soil it tends to spread more rapidly than in dry soil, but it is not generally invasive. Pinching off the tops of plants in late spring encourages bushy, compact growth. It can be divided in spring or fall.

Brunnera
(BRUN-er-a)
BRUNNERA

Brunnera macrophylla

Hardiness: *Zones 3-8*

Plant type: *herbaceous perennial*

Height: *12 to 18 inches*

Interest: *flowers, foliage*

Soil: *moist, well-drained*

Light: *partial shade*

Brunnera is a richly colored foreground plant or ground cover for a shady, moist area. Its dark green foliage contrasts well with the tiny deep blue flowers that are borne in branched clusters in spring and early summer.

Selected species and varieties: *B. macrophylla*—rounded habit, 12 to 18 inches tall and wide, with heart-shaped leaves up to 8 inches across and blue star-shaped flowers ⅛ to ¼ inch across.

Growing conditions and maintenance: Although brunnera prefers moist soil, it will tolerate dry soil as long as there is shade. For use as a ground cover, space plants 15 inches apart. When the clump shows signs of deterioration at the center, usually after several years of growth, dig it up and divide off the vigorous, outer portions for replanting, discarding the center.

Buxus
(BUK-sus)
BOXWOOD

Buxus sempervirens

Hardiness: *Zones 4-9*

Plant type: *shrub*

Height: *2 to 20 feet*

Interest: *foliage*

Soil: *well-drained*

Light: *full sun to light shade*

Boxwood is an elegant long-lived evergreen shrub whose tiny leaves impart a fine texture to any planting. It is well suited for use as a hedge, an edging, or a foundation planting.

Selected species and varieties: *B. microphylla koreana*—to 2½ feet tall and twice as wide, hardy to Zone 4; 'Wintergreen' grows 2 feet tall and 4 feet wide, retains bright green leaf color throughout winter when many other varieties fade to brownish green, and is hardy to Zone 6. *B. sempervirens*—to 20 feet tall with equal spread, moundlike habit, hardy to Zone 5 or 6 depending on variety; 'Handsworthiensis' has dark green leaves and takes a large, upright form, good for hedges; 'Suffruticosa' is a dwarf form, extremely slow growing to just 3 feet; 'Vardar Valley' also grows to 3 feet tall and spreads to 5 feet wide, with a flat-topped habit and dark blue-green leaves.

Growing conditions and maintenance: Plant boxwood in well-drained soil amended with organic matter in a site protected from drying winds. Mulch to help retain moisture. In warm climates, partial shade is beneficial.

Calamagrostis
(kal-a-ma-GROS-tis)
REED GRASS

Calamagrostis x acutiflora 'Karl Foerster'

Hardiness: *Zones 6-9*

Plant type: *ornamental grass*

Height: *4 to 7 feet*

Interest: *flowers, foliage*

Soil: *well-drained, acid*

Light: *full sun to partial shade*

Reed grass has a slender, erect habit that provides a vertical accent in the border. As one of the first grasses to bloom, it offers a long season of interest.

Selected species and varieties: *C.* x *acutiflora* 'Karl Foerster'—4 to 6 feet tall, with pink flowers maturing to golden tan from early summer to fall; 'Stricta', 5 to 7 feet tall, with greenish pink flowers appearing about 2 weeks later than those of 'Karl Foerster' and lasting through fall.

Growing conditions and maintenance: Reed grass is adaptable to a wide range of conditions, tolerating both heavy soils and poor, dry soils. It withstands moist to wet areas as well as drought. It is effective used as a garden accent, as a specimen, or massed beside ponds or streams.

Calycanthus
(kal-i-KAN-thus)
SWEET SHRUB

Calycanthus floridus 'Athens'

Hardiness: *Zones 4-9*

Plant type: *shrub*

Height: *6 to 9 feet*

Interest: *flowers, fragrance*

Soil: *moist, well-drained*

Light: *full sun to partial shade*

Sweet shrub is an adaptable plant that blends well with other shrubs in many garden settings. Its summer flowers are unusual looking and produce a delightfully fruity fragrance.

Selected species and varieties: *C. floridus*—6 to 9 feet tall and up to 12 feet wide, with long, dark green aromatic leaves that are deciduous but persist late into fall; rounded, fragrant, dark burgundy flowers with spreading, straplike petals blooming from late spring through early summer; and urn-shaped fruit persisting into winter; 'Athens' is a cultivar with highly fragrant yellow flowers.

Growing conditions and maintenance: Although it prefers moist, deep, well-drained soil, sweet shrub tolerates other soil conditions. It is easily transplanted. Suckers sometimes present a problem in beds.

Camellia
(kah-MEEL-ee-a)
CAMELLIA

Camellia japonica

Hardiness: *Zones 8-10*

Plant type: *shrub or small tree*

Height: *6 to 25 feet*

Interest: *flowers, foliage*

Soil: *moist, well-drained, acid*

Light: *partial shade*

Camellias are dense evergreens that produce very showy flowers in shades of pink, rose, white, and red. The flowers bloom from fall through spring and may be single, semidouble, or double.

Selected species and varieties: *C. japonica* (Japanese camellia)—grows 10 to 25 feet tall as a large shrub or a small tree, with a dense, upright habit, dark glossy evergreen leaves, and flowers 3 to 5 inches across from late winter through spring. *C. sasanqua* (sasanqua camellia)—6 to 10 feet tall, with a pyramidal habit, dark glossy evergreen leaves, and flowers 2 to 3 inches across blooming from fall to winter; varieties with increased cold hardiness include 'Polar Ice', 'Snow Flurry', 'Winter's Charm', 'Winter's Dream', 'Winter's Hope', 'Winter's Interlude', 'Winter's Rose', 'Winter's Star', and 'Winter's Waterlily'.

Growing conditions and maintenance: Camellias require protection from winter winds. They benefit from the addition of generous amounts of organic matter to the soil. Keep them continuously mulched, and do not overfertilize.

Campanula
(kam-PAN-ew-la)
BELLFLOWER

Campanula portenschlagiana

Hardiness: *Zones 3-9*

Plant type: *herbaceous perennial*

Height: *4 to 12 inches*

Interest: *flowers, foliage*

Soil: *moist, well-drained*

Light: *full sun to partial shade*

The Dalmatian and Serbian bellflowers, which are small with delicate blue flowers, are actually quite vigorous and well suited for rock gardens, dry walls, or the front of a border. They have a creeping, spreading habit and form attractive clumps of neat foliage. The flowers appear in sprays above the leaves.

Selected species and varieties: *C. portenschlagiana* (Dalmatian bellflower)—4 to 8 inches tall, spreading, with rounded, sharply serrated leaves and star-shaped, lilac-blue flowers that bloom late spring to early summer; hardy to Zone 5. *C. poscharskyana* (Serbian bellflower)—8 to 12 inches tall, up to 18 inches wide, with midsummer-blooming lilac flowers and roots that may become invasive; hardy to Zone 4.

Growing conditions and maintenance: Both species thrive when growing among rocks or cascading over walls. In warmer zones, they benefit from partial shade and supplemental moisture.

Carex
(KAY-reks)
SEDGE

Carex morrowii 'Variegata'

Hardiness: *Zones 5-9*

Plant type: *ornamental grass*

Height: *6 to 18 inches*

Interest: *foliage*

Soil: *moist, well-drained*

Light: *full sun to full shade*

Sedge is a clump-forming plant with grasslike leaves. Unlike most ornamental grasses, it can grow in the shade, making it a good choice for massing in the front of a shady border or edging a shady walk. Its leaves are arching and often unusually colored; the flowers are insignificant.

Selected species and varieties: *C. glauca*—6 inches tall, with blue-green leaves; good for rock gardens, massing, or containers. *C. morrowii* 'Variegata'—12 to 18 inches tall; the semi-evergreen leaves have a white stripe down the center; it makes an excellent ground cover or edging.

Growing conditions and maintenance: Although sedge thrives in shade, it adapts to full sun as long as it receives sufficient water. It produces such dense mounds of growth that few weeds are able to penetrate. The clumps can be divided in the spring.

Caryopteris
(kar-i-OP-ter-is)
BLUEBEARD

Caryopteris x clandonensis 'Dark Knight'

Hardiness: *Zones 6-9*

Plant type: *shrub*

Height: *1½ to 4 feet*

Interest: *flowers, foliage*

Soil: *light, well-drained*

Light: *full sun*

Bluebeard is a small deciduous shrub with pleasantly aromatic flowers, stems, and leaves. The slender, upright stems form a rounded mound of gray-green foliage that is topped with blue flowers from mid to late summer.

Selected species and varieties: *C.* x *clandonensis* 'Blue Mist'—2 feet tall, with powder blue flowers; 'Dark Knight', 2 feet tall, deep purple flowers; 'Longwood Blue'—1½ to 2 feet tall, violet-blue flowers with dark stamens.

Growing conditions and maintenance: Although it produces woody stems, bluebeard is best treated as a herbaceous perennial; cut it back to the ground in the winter. When flower production tails off in the summer, a light pruning will often stimulate a second flush of blooms.

Ceanothus
(see-a-NO-thus)
WILD LILAC

Ceanothus 'Dark Star'

Hardiness: *Zones 9-11*

Plant type: *shrub*

Height: *4 to 15 feet*

Interest: *flowers, foliage*

Soil: *light, well-drained*

Light: *full sun*

The wild lilac is a free-flowering plant well adapted to the rugged coastal conditions of the West. It is useful planted in a mass on dry, sunny slopes or as a screen. Individual plants make fine garden accents or specimens.

Selected species and varieties: *C.* 'Dark Star'—4 to 6 feet tall, 5 to 6 feet wide, with evergreen leaves ¼ to ½ inch long and cobalt blue flowers borne prolifically in spring; 'Gloire de Versailles' is deciduous and flowers late in the growing season; 'Ray Hartman' reaches 15 feet tall and 10 to 20 feet wide, and can be trained as a small tree, with dark, glossy, evergreen leaves 1 to 2 inches long and spring-blooming medium blue flowers in 3- to 5-inch clusters.

Growing conditions and maintenance: Wild lilacs thrive in hot, dry conditions and can withstand winds and drought. They do not tolerate heavy soils or overwatering. Plant them in fall and water occasionally, allowing soil to dry out well between waterings. Once established, the plants generally require no supplemental moisture.

Ceratostigma
(ser-at-o-STIG-ma)
PLUMBAGO, LEADWORT

Ceratostigma plumbaginoides

Hardiness: *Zones 5-10*

Plant type: *herbaceous perennial or shrub*

Height: *8 to 48 inches*

Interest: *flowers, foliage*

Soil: *well-drained*

Light: *full sun to partial shade*

Plumbago develops shiny leaves and blue flowers that bloom late in the season. Low-growing species are effectively used as a ground cover for shrub borders, an edging for a garden walk, or creeping among stones in a rock garden. Taller types make attractive additions to a mixed-shrub border.

Selected species and varieties: *C. plumbaginoides*—8 to 12 inches tall and 18 inches wide, leaves to 3 inches, turning bronze in fall in cool climates, flowers dark blue, saucer shaped, in summer to late fall; hardy to Zone 6. *C. willmottianum*—to 4 feet, upright, deciduous, 2 inch leaves, bears 1-inch bright blue flowers continuously from midsummer through fall; hardy to Zone 8.

Growing conditions and maintenance: Plumbago requires good drainage but is otherwise tolerant of most soils. It will die out in soils that remain wet over the winter, and it does not compete well with tree roots. Mark location of *C. plumbaginoides* because it is slow to emerge in spring.

Cercis
(SER-sis)
REDBUD

Cercis occidentalis

Hardiness: *Zones 4-10*

Plant type: *tree*

Height: *10 to 35 feet*

Interest: *flowers, foliage*

Soil: *moist, well-drained*

Light: *full sun to light shade*

The redbud's early-season flowers signal the start of spring. It is effective as a specimen, in small groups, or in a woodland garden. Trees begin blooming when they are very young.

Selected species and varieties: *C. canadensis* (Eastern redbud)—20 to 30 feet tall with 25- to 35-foot spread, trunk often divided close to ground to produce interesting branching habit, leaves heart shaped, 3 to 5 inches across, flower buds reddish purple, opening to pink in early spring, Zones 4-9; 'Forest Pansy'—purple foliage. *C. occidentalis* (California redbud)—10 to 15 feet; Zones 8-10. *C. reniformis* (Texas redbud)—to 35 feet; Zones 8-9.

Growing conditions and maintenance: Redbuds tolerate most soils as long as they are well drained. They thrive in full sun or as understory trees in a woodland garden. They require occasional pruning to remove injured wood. Redbuds are short-lived, often surviving no longer than 10 to 15 years.

Chaenomeles
(kee-NOM-e-lees)
FLOWERING QUINCE

Chaenomeles speciosa 'Texas Scarlet'

Hardiness: *Zones 4-8*

Plant type: *shrub*

Height: *3 to 10 feet*

Interest: *flowers*

Soil: *light to heavy, acid*

Light: *full sun to partial shade*

Flowering quince produces brightly colored flowers in early spring. Its dense growth habit makes it useful as a hedge or barrier.

Selected species and varieties: *C. speciosa* 'Cameo'—compact form, 3 to 5 feet, produces abundant, double, apricot pink flowers; 'Nivalis'—vigorous, large upright form with white flowers; 'Texas Scarlet'—3 to 5 feet tall, low-spreading habit, intense tomato red flowers.

Growing conditions and maintenance: Flowering quince is extremely easy to grow and will tolerate most soil and light conditions. It may become chlorotic in alkaline soil and require supplemental iron. When plants become leggy or flowering is reduced, remove largest stems back to the ground, or cut entire plant back to 6 inches immediately after flowering in the spring. Because they have a short flowering season and lose their leaves early in the fall, they are best used as a background plant, or in combination with other flowering shrubs.

Chamaecyparis
(kam-ee-SIP-a-ris)
FALSE CYPRESS

Chamaecyparis obtusa 'Crippsii'

Hardiness: *Zones 4-8*

Plant type: *tree or shrub*

Height: *3 to 60 feet or more*

Interest: *foliage*

Soil: *rich, moist, well-drained*

Light: *full sun*

False cypresses are evergreens that offer a wide range of growth habits, foliage colors, and garden uses. Juvenile plants display needlelike leaves; adult foliage is scalelike. Smaller varieties are useful as specimens in beds or rock gardens; taller ones make attractive screens or specimens.

Selected species and varieties: *C. lawsoniana*—40 to 60 or more feet tall, with a pyramidal outline, horizontal drooping branches, and a massive trunk; Zones 5-7. *C. obtusa* 'Compacta'—3 to 5 feet tall, with blue-green leaves; 'Crippsii' grows to 30 feet tall with yellow-green leaves; 'Nana Gracilis', 4 to 6 feet with dark green leaves; Zones 4-8.

Growing conditions and maintenance: Although they prefer full sun, false cypresses will tolerate light shade. They thrive in humid areas and should be protected from hot, drying winds.

Chrysogonum
(kris-AHG-o-num)
GOLDENSTAR

Chrysogonum virginianum var. virginianum

Hardiness: *Zones 5-9*

Plant type: *herbaceous perennial*

Height: *4 to 9 inches*

Interest: *flowers, foliage*

Soil: *well-drained*

Light: *full sun to full shade*

The deep green foliage of goldenstar provides a lush background for its bright yellow, star-shaped flowers, which appear from late spring into summer. Its low-growing, spreading habit makes it useful as a ground cover, for edging at the front of a border, or in a rock garden.

Selected species and varieties: *C. virginianum* var. *virginianum*—6 to 9 inches, with dark green leaves that are bluntly serrated along upright spreading stems and flowers 1½ inches across that bloom throughout the spring in warm areas, well into summer in cooler zones; var. *australe* is similar to var. *virginianum* but more prostrate.

Growing conditions and maintenance: Goldenstar grows well in most soils with average fertility. For use as a ground cover, space plants 12 inches apart. Divide every other year in spring.

Cimicifuga
(si-mi-SIFF-yew-ga)
BUGBANE

Cimicifuga simplex 'White Pearl'

Hardiness: *Zones 3-9*

Plant type: *herbaceous perennial*

Height: *3 to 8 feet*

Interest: *flowers, foliage*

Soil: *rich, moist, well-drained*

Light: *full sun to partial shade*

Bugbane is a graceful perennial for the rear of a shady border or wildflower garden. Its tall spires of white flowers, borne well above handsome dark green leaves, are a welcome sight in late summer and fall. It is also a fine choice to plant alongside a pond or stream.

Selected species and varieties: *C. racemosa*—4 to 8 feet tall, with deep green compound leaves and white flowers in 3-foot wandlike clusters on branched stems, blooming in midsummer; 'Atropurpurea' has purple foliage; Zones 3-9. *C. simplex*—3 to 4 feet tall, with attractive light green buds that open in fall to reveal 1- to 2-foot white flower spires; 'White Pearl' grows 3 to 4 feet tall, with a compact habit and pure white flowers; Zones 4-8.

Growing conditions and maintenance: Bugbane will tolerate full sun in cooler areas provided there is ample moisture. Incorporate generous amounts of organic matter into soil prior to planting.

Cistus
(SIS-tus)
ROCKROSE

Cistus x purpureus

Hardiness: *Zones 9-10*

Plant type: *shrub*

Height: *18 inches to 4 feet*

Interest: *flowers, foliage*

Soil: *dry to well-drained*

Light: *full sun*

Rockrose is well suited to dry areas of the West Coast. It adds a long season of color to mixed-shrub borders, rock gardens, and dry banks. Its leaves are aromatic and nearly evergreen. The flowers, which resemble roses, last only one day but are prolific, so that flowering continues over several weeks in the spring and early summer.

Selected species and varieties: *C. x purpureus*—3 to 4 feet tall and equally wide, with attractive 2-inch-long leaves that are dark green on top, gray-green below, and reddish purple flowers with a red spot at the base in early summer. *C. salviifolius*—18 to 24 inches tall, to 6 feet wide, with gray-green textured leaves and white flowers with a yellow spot at the base in late spring.

Growing conditions and maintenance: Rockroses grow well in dry, windy areas, tolerating drought, seaside conditions, and poor soil. They are useful as a fire retardant.

Clethra
(KLETH-ra)
SUMMER-SWEET

Clethra barbinervis

Hardiness: *Zones 3-9*

Plant type: *shrub*

Height: *3 to 20 feet*

Interest: *flowers, fragrance, foliage*

Soil: *moist, acid*

Light: *full sun to full shade*

Summer-sweet is well named; its pink or white flowers appear in midsummer and are delightfully fragrant. With its wide tolerance for growing conditions, this deciduous shrub can easily be sited in any mixed border or moist woodland garden.

Selected species and varieties: *C. alnifolia*—3 to 8 feet tall and 4 to 6 feet wide, it produces deep green leaves that turn gold in fall and very fragrant white flowers in 2- to 6-inch-long clusters; 'Hummingbird' grows to 4 feet with a dense habit; 'Pink Spires' has deep pink buds that open to soft pink flowers. *C. barbinervis*—10 to 20 feet tall, with dark green leaves in clusters at branch tips, fragrant white late-summer flowers in 4- to 6-inch-long clusters and beautiful gray to brown smooth, exfoliating bark; Zones 5-8.

Growing conditions and maintenance: Summer-sweet tolerates most soil types as well as coastal conditions. It thrives in both sun and shade. Incorporate organic matter into soil prior to planting. Prune in early spring.

Coreopsis
(ko-ree-OP-sis)
TICKSEED

Coreopsis verticillata 'Zagreb'

Hardiness: *Zones 4-9*

Plant type: *herbaceous perennial*

Height: *6 inches to 3 feet*

Interest: *flowers, foliage*

Soil: *well-drained*

Light: *full sun*

Coreopsis provides a long season of flowers both for the garden and indoor arrangements. The delicate appearance of the blossoms belies the sturdiness and dependability of the plant.

Selected species and varieties: *C. auriculata*—12 to 24 inches tall, with 2-inch yellow-orange flowers, useful as ground cover or edging. *C. rosea*—15 to 24 inches, with needlelike leaves and pink flowers with yellow centers. *C. verticillata*—2 to 3 feet, with lacy, threadlike leaves and yellow flowers 1 to 2 inches across; 'Moonbeam' grows 18 to 24 inches tall, with a compact habit and pale yellow flowers; 'Zagreb', 12 to 18 inches, bright yellow flowers.

Growing conditions and maintenance: Coreopsis thrives in nearly any well-drained soil and can tolerate drought. *C. rosea* is an exception, however, preferring a heavier, moister soil. Continuous flowering throughout the summer can be encouraged by removing faded blossoms. For massing or for use as a ground cover, space plants 12 to 18 inches apart.

Cornus
(KOR-nus)
DOGWOOD

Cornus mas

Hardiness: *Zones 2-8*

Plant type: *tree or shrub*

Height: *5 to 30 feet*

Interest: *flowers, foliage, fruit, bark*

Soil: *moist, well-drained, acid*

Light: *full sun to partial shade*

Dogwoods are extremely ornamental and adaptable deciduous trees and shrubs. Some are best known for their flowers, others for their bark or twig color. Many sport vibrant fall foliage and colorful fruit. Most offer year-round interest in the garden and are useful as specimens, understory trees or shrubs, or mixed in a shrub border.

Selected species and varieties: *C. alba* 'Sibirica'—an 8- to 10-foot-tall shrub, growing 5 to 10 feet wide, with an erect, open habit, green stems that take on a red tinge in summer and turn coral red in winter, leaves that go reddish purple in fall, and modest-looking yellowish white flowers in late spring, followed by white to bluish fruit; Zones 2-8. *C. kousa*—a tree growing 20 to 30 feet tall with an equal spread, exfoliating bark mottled gray, tan, and brown on older specimens, leaves that often turn red in fall, small yellow-green flowers surrounded by showy white bracts that appear in late spring to early summer and that persist for several weeks, and raspberry-like red fruit in fall; Zones 5-8. *C.* x *rutgersensis* hybrids (crosses between *C. kousa* and

native Eastern dogwood, *C. florida*, which is susceptible to pests and diseases)—*C.* 'Aurora' (cv. Rutban) has white flowers in late spring, resists leaf spot, canker, borer, and anthracnose; *C.* 'Ruth Ellen' (cv. Rutlan) a low-spreading tree that blooms slightly earlier than 'Aurora'; hardy to Zone 6. *C. mas*—a small tree or large shrub, 10 to 25 feet tall, 15 to 20 feet wide, with exfoliating gray-and-brown bark, bright yellow flowers in very early spring, and red fruit in late summer; Zones 4-8. *C. sericea*—a shrub, 7 to 9 feet tall, with a 10-foot spread, multiple bright red stems that arise from the crown, leaves that turn red in fall, and modest white flowers in late spring followed by white fruit; 'Flaviramea' has yellow stems; Zones 2-8.

Growing conditions and maintenance: Dogwoods prefer a soil with generous amounts of organic matter added prior to planting. *C. kousa* prefers full sun. Thin lower branches of *C. kousa* to reveal attractive exfoliating bark. Occasionally prune the oldest stems of red-

Cornus kousa

stemmed dogwoods to 6 inches above the ground in late winter to encourage vigorous growth.

Cotinus
(ko-TI-nus)
SMOKE TREE

Cotinus coggygria

Hardiness: *Zones 5-8*

Plant type: *tree or shrub*

Height: *10 to 15 feet*

Interest: *foliage, flowers*

Soil: *well-drained*

Light: *full sun*

The smoke tree is valued for its attractive foliage and the unusual, wispy flower stalks that create a smokelike appearance and are effective throughout the summer. It can be grown as a large shrub with a width equal to its height, or pruned to a multiple-stemmed, small tree. It offers a colorful contrast with a green lawn when planted as a specimen or can be effectively combined with other shrubs in a mixed border.

Selected species and varieties: *C. coggygria* 'Royal Purple'—compact form, with oval, very dark, maroon red leaves 2 to 3 inches long that maintain color through fall and unusual feathery, dark pink to purplish red 8-inch fruiting stalks.

Growing conditions and maintenance: The smoke tree prefers a soil that is not too rich. It can be cut back to the ground in winter to encourage vigorous shoot growth. To grow it as a tree, remove all but three or four branches from the base and lower laterals.

Crataegus
(kra-TEE-gus)
HAWTHORN

Crataegus viridis 'Winter King'

Hardiness: *Zones 4-7*

Plant type: *tree*

Height: *20 to 35 feet*

Interest: *foliage, flowers, fruit*

Soil: *well-drained*

Light: *full sun*

Hawthorns are small, broad trees, often bearing sharp thorns, that produce a lovely spring flower display and an equally attractive show of fall fruit. They are useful as individual specimens, in small groupings, or as large barrier plantings, where their thorns discourage intrusion.

Selected species and varieties: *C. viridis* 'Winter King' (green hawthorn)—to 35 feet tall and equally wide, dense and wide spreading, with lustrous green leaves in summer that turn purple to red in fall, white flowers in 2-inch clusters in late spring, and red fruit, ½ inch in diameter, persisting into winter.

Growing conditions and maintenance: The green hawthorn tolerates a wide range of soils, provided they are well drained. Its dense foliage makes growing grass beneath it difficult. Prune as necessary in winter or early spring.

Daphne
(DAF-nee)
DAPHNE

Daphne odora 'Aureo-marginata'

Hardiness: *Zones 7-9*

Plant type: *shrub*

Height: *3 to 4 feet*

Interest: *flowers*

Soil: *well-drained, alkaline*

Light: *full sun to partial shade*

Winter daphne is a small evergreen shrub whose intensely fragrant flowers appear in late winter. The flowers last for weeks and if brought indoors fill a room with sweet scent.

Selected species and varieties: *D. odora* (winter daphne)—to 4 feet tall and wide, with a mounded habit, dark green leaves 1½ to 3½ inches long, and extremely fragrant pinkish purple flowers in 1-inch terminal clusters that bloom from late winter to early spring; 'Aureo-marginata' has leaves with yellow margins and flowers that are reddish purple toward the outside of cluster, light pink on the inside, and is slightly hardier than the species; 'Alba' has white flowers.

Growing conditions and maintenance: Winter daphne is probably the least fussy of its genus. It tolerates most soils, though it prefers one that is slightly alkaline to neutral. Prune if necessary immediately after flowering. Daphnes often thrive with little or no care, but they sometimes die for no apparent reason.

Deutzia
(DEWT-see-a)
SLENDER DEUTZIA

Deutzia gracilis

Hardiness: *Zones 4-8*

Plant type: *shrub*

Height: *2 to 5 feet*

Interest: *flowers*

Soil: *moist, well-drained*

Light: *full sun to partial shade*

Slender deutzia is a graceful deciduous shrub bearing pure white flowers in midspring. Like forsythia, it has a relatively short season of interest but is easy to grow and adaptable to most sites. Deutzia can be effectively used as a hedge, as a background for perennials, or in a mixed-shrub border.

Selected species and varieties: *D. gracilis*—to 5 feet tall and an equal width, with slender arching stems in a broad mounding habit, serrated leaves 1 to 3 inches long, and white flowers in erect clusters in spring that are effective for 2 weeks; 'Nikko'—compact cultivar 2 feet tall and 5 feet wide with leaves that turn burgundy in fall.

Growing conditions and maintenance: Planted in spring, deutzia is easy to transplant and grow and is tolerant of most soils. Encourage vigorous growth and abundant flowers by cutting the oldest stems back to the ground after flowering.

Dicentra
(dy-SEN-tra)
BLEEDING HEART

Dicentra formosa 'Luxuriant'

Hardiness: *Zones 3-8*

Plant type: *herbaceous perennial*

Height: *1 to 3 feet*

Interest: *flowers, foliage*

Soil: *moist, well-drained*

Light: *partial shade*

Bleeding heart bears unusual, drooping flowers along arched stems. The leaves are distinctly fernlike, and their soft colors and mounded form add grace to any shady garden.

Selected species and varieties: *D. eximia*—12 to 18 inches tall, with blue-green leaves that form a neat mound and pink to purple teardrop-shaped flowers that bloom throughout summer; 'Alba' has white flowers. *D.* hybrids—12 inches tall, similar to *D. eximia* in habit and culture; 'Adrian Bloom' has red flowers and blue-green foliage; 'Bountiful', deep pink flowers, blue-green foliage; 'Luxuriant', cherry red flowers, green foliage; 'Zestful', rose pink flowers, gray-green foliage. *D. spectabilis*—2 to 3 feet tall, with blue-green leaves and large pink-and-white heart-shaped blossoms in spring; 'Alba' has white flowers.

Growing conditions and maintenance: Although they thrive in partial shade, bleeding hearts will tolerate full shade. Add organic matter to the soil prior to planting. Leaves of *D. spectabilis* die back in midsummer, so place near plants that will minimize the resulting void.

Dictamnus
(dik-TAM-nus)
GAS PLANT, DITTANY

Dictamnus albus 'Purpureus'

Hardiness: *Zones 3-8*

Plant type: *herbaceous perennial*

Height: *2 to 3 feet*

Interest: *flowers, foliage, seed pods*

Soil: *moist, well-drained*

Light: *full sun to light shade*

Gas plant is easy to grow and long-lived, with soft-colored blossoms and shiny, aromatic dark green leaves. It adds lasting charm to a perennial border. The common name refers to the flammable gas that is secreted by the plant's leaves, stems, and roots.

Selected species and varieties: *D. albus*—leathery, lemon-scented leaves, white flowers 1½ to 2 inches across that bloom in early summer on erect stems held a foot above foliage, and seed pods that are attractive and useful in dried arrangements; *D. a.* 'Purpureus' has pale mauve purple flowers with darker purple veins.

Growing conditions and maintenance: Select your site for gas plants carefully, because once planted, they do not like to be disturbed. Add organic matter to soil prior to planting. It often takes a full season or more before plants bloom, but once established, they are reliable garden performers.

Echeveria
(ek-ee-VEER-ee-a)
HENS AND CHICKS

Echeveria agavoides

Hardiness: *Zones 9-11*

Plant type: *succulent perennial*

Height: *3 inches to 3 feet*

Interest: *foliage, flowers*

Soil: *well-drained to dry*

Light: *full sun*

Hens and chicks makes an interesting, attractive ground cover or rock-garden plant for warm, dry climates. It is grown primarily for the beauty of its fleshy, succulent, often colorful leaves that form compact rosettes. Bell-shaped nodding flowers develop on slender stems that rise well above the foliage.

Selected species and varieties: *E. agavoides*—6- to 8-inch rosettes of bright green leaves with reddish margins, topped in summer by red-and-yellow flowers. *E. crenulata*—loose rosettes of pale green leaves with wavy margins, growing up to 1 foot long and covered with white powder, and red to orange flowers on stems up to 3 feet tall. *E. imbricata*—4- to 6-inch rosettes of gray-green leaves, loose stems of orange, red, and yellow flowers; develops many offsets around the base.

Growing conditions and maintenance: Hens and chicks thrives in warm locations and is quite tolerant of drought and coastal conditions. It is easily propagated from offsets.

Echinacea
(ek-i-NAY-see-a)
CONEFLOWER

Echinacea purpurea

Hardiness: *Zones 3-9*

Plant type: *herbaceous perennial*

Height: *2 to 4 feet*

Interest: *flowers*

Soil: *well-drained*

Light: *full sun to light shade*

Coneflowers are reliable performers for a sunny border or wildflower garden. They produce durable, long-lasting, daisylike blossoms throughout the summer, followed by stiff brown seed cones that are lovely in dried arrangements.

Selected species and varieties: *E. pallida*—3 to 4 feet tall, with rosy purple or white flowers up to 3½ inches across. *E. purpurea*—2 to 4 feet tall, with pinkish purple or white flowers up to 3 inches across; 'Bright Star' has rosy pink flowers with maroon centers; 'Robert Bloom', carmine purple flowers with orange centers in a freely branching habit; 'White Lustre', prolific white flowers with bronze cones.

Growing conditions and maintenance: Coneflowers tolerate heat, drought, and wind. Their flowers are borne on sturdy stems that do not require staking. Flower colors are often deeper when plants are grown in partial shade.

Enkianthus
(en-kee-AN-thus)
ENKIANTHUS

Enkianthus campanulatus

Hardiness: *Zones 4-9*

Plant type: *shrub or small tree*

Height: *6 to 30 feet*

Interest: *flowers, foliage*

Soil: *moist, well-drained, acid*

Light: *full sun to partial shade*

Enkianthus bears delicate bell-shaped blossoms in pendulous clusters in spring. Its green leaves turn to brilliant shades of yellow, orange, and red in fall. This tall, erect shrub is an ideal companion to azaleas, rhododendrons, and similar acid-loving plants.

Selected species and varieties: *E. campanulatus* (red-veined enkianthus)—6 to 8 feet tall in cooler climates, to 30 feet in warmer zones, with a stiff, upright habit, leaves 1 to 3 inches long, mostly in tufts at ends of branches, and pale yellow or orange individual flowers with red veins that open before new leaves emerge in spring and may persist for several weeks.

Growing conditions and maintenance: Incorporate a generous quantity of organic matter into the soil before planting red-veined enkianthus. Mulch to maintain even moisture. Pruning is almost never necessary.

Epimedium
(ep-i-MEE-dee-um)
BARRENWORT

Epimedium grandiflorum 'Rose Queen'

Hardiness: *Zones 5-8*

Plant type: *herbaceous perennial*

Height: *6 to 12 inches*

Interest: *foliage, flowers*

Soil: *moist, well-drained*

Light: *partial to full shade*

The small, heart-shaped leaves of barrenwort are reddish bronze when they first emerge in spring. They soon turn deep green, providing a lush ground cover for shady gardens before turning bronze again in fall. Red, pink, yellow, or white flowers rise above the foliage on delicate, wiry stems in spring.

Selected species and varieties: *E. grandiflorum*—9 to 12 inches tall, forming dense clumps; 'Rose Queen' has deep pink flowers with white-tipped spurs. *E.* x *rubrum*—6 to 12 inches tall, with very showy bright red flowers flushed with white or yellow. *E.* x *youngianum* 'Niveum'—7 to 8 inches tall, compact, with white flowers.

Growing conditions and maintenance: Barrenwort is a rugged plant that grows in a clump and increases in size without becoming invasive. It can be left undisturbed indefinitely, or can be easily divided to increase the number of plants. Cut it back to the ground in late winter.

Eupatorium
(yew-pa-TO-ree-um)
BONESET

Eupatorium coelestinum

Hardiness: *Zones 5-10*

Plant type: *herbaceous perennial*

Height: *1 to 5 feet*

Interest: *flowers, foliage*

Soil: *moist, well-drained*

Light: *full sun to partial shade*

Boneset flowers late in the season, bearing fluffy blue, white, mauve, pink, or purple blooms on erect stems. It is well suited to an informal border or wildflower garden in sun or shade.

Selected species and varieties: *E. coelestinum*—1 to 2 feet tall, with blue to violet flowers in flat, fuzzy clusters, good for cutting; Zones 6-9. *E. fistulosum* 'Gateway'—erect stems 5 feet tall, topped with huge arcs of purplish flowers in summer and fall; Zones 3-9.

Growing conditions and maintenance: Boneset is extremely easy to grow and provides a long season of bloom. Care must be given in selecting the site, because it can spread rapidly. *E. coelestinum* advances by underground runners; it is the more invasive species and should be divided frequently to prevent its taking over a garden. *E. fistulosum* 'Gateway' can be cut back nearly to the ground in late spring to produce somewhat stockier plants.

Euphorbia
(yew-FOR-bee-a)
SPURGE

Euphorbia griffithii 'Fireglow'

Hardiness: *Zones 3-10*

Plant type: *herbaceous perennial*

Height: *6 inches to 3 feet*

Interest: *flowers, foliage*

Soil: *light, well-drained*

Light: *full sun to partial shade*

Euphorbia is a large, diverse genus that includes many interesting low-maintenance perennials well suited for rock gardens, dry herbaceous borders, south-facing slopes, and dry walls. As with another member of this genus, the poinsettia, euphorbia produces flowers that are actually quite small but are surrounded by showy bracts that create colorful effects both in the garden and in indoor arrangements. Many species produce attractive foliage with intense fall color.

Selected species and varieties: *E. corollata*—1 to 3 feet tall, with slender green leaves 1 to 2 inches in length that turn red in the fall. In mid to late summer flowering spurge bears clusters of flowers that are surrounded by small white bracts that resemble baby's-breath and impart an airy, lacy quality to a mixed border or indoor arrangement; hardy in Zones 3-10. *E. epithymoides* (cushion spurge)—forms a neat, very symmetrical mound 12 to 18 inches high, with green leaves that turn dark red in fall. In spring it produces numerous small green flowers that are surrounded by showy, inch-wide chartreuse-yellow bracts. Cushion spurge should be planted in partial shade in the South. It performs best in soil that is on the dry side; in moist, fertile soil it may become invasive. A long-lived plant, cushion spurge should be allowed to grow undisturbed since it may not respond well to transplanting; hardy to Zones 4-8. *E. griffithii* 'Fireglow'—2 to 3 feet tall, with green leaves that turn yellow and red in fall and brick red flower bracts in late spring and early summer; Zones 4-8. *E. myrsinites* (myrtle euphorbia)—6 to 8 inches high with 12- to 18-inch-long trailing stems; closely set fleshy evergreen blue-green leaves ½ inch long that grow in a dense spiral around the stem and remain handsome throughout winter if the plant is sheltered from wind and sun. Small spring-blooming green flowers surrounded by attractive pale yellow bracts measuring 2 to 4 inches across appear in clusters at the ends of the stems. Performing well in the hot, humid summers of the southeastern states, myrtle euphorbia is hardy to Zones 5-9.

Growing conditions and maintenance: Spurges require a sunny, dry location and soil that is not too rich. In moist, fertile locations, growth may become rank, un-

Euphorbia epithymoides

attractive, and invasive. These plants do not like to be transplanted. Use gloves when handling them, as they exude a milky sap that can cause skin irritations. When cutting for indoor arrangements, put a flame to the cut end of the stem.

Forsythia
(for-SITH-ee-a)
FORSYTHIA

Forsythia x intermedia 'Lynwood'

Hardiness: *Zones 5-8*

Plant type: *shrub*

Height: *1 to 10 feet*

Interest: *flowers*

Soil: *loose, well-drained*

Light: *full sun*

The bright yellow flowers of forsythia mark the onset of spring in many areas. Flowers are arranged along the entire length of the arching stems that grow from the base.

Selected species and varieties: *F.* x *intermedia* 'Spectabilis'—8 to 10 feet tall and equally wide, with leaves 3 to 4 inches long and bright yellow tapered flowers 1½ inches across; 'Lynwood' has lighter yellow flowers than 'Spectabilis' and grows 6 to 7 feet tall with a more upright habit, making it useful for mixed-shrub borders, when massed on sunny banks, or in small groupings. *F. viridissima* 'Bronxensis'—12 inches tall with a 2- to 3-foot spread, compact and flat-topped, it has bright green stems and yellow flowers that bloom slightly later and are less showy than those of other species.

Growing conditions and maintenance: Forsythias can adapt to partial shade, although flowering will be reduced. Prune immediately after flowering by removing the oldest stems back to the ground. Do not shear.

Fothergilla
(faw-ther-GIL-a)
FOTHERGILLA

Fothergilla major

Hardiness: *Zones 4-8*

Plant type: *shrub*

Height: *2 to 10 feet*

Interest: *flowers, foliage*

Soil: *moist, well-drained, acid*

Light: *full sun to partial shade*

Fothergilla is a deciduous shrub that provides two seasons of garden interest. In spring, it is covered with small, fragrant, white bottlebrush-type flowers, and in fall the leaves turn shades of yellow, orange, and scarlet; all colors may appear on a single leaf. It is a useful shrub for a mixed border, a mass planting, or a small grouping. It makes an attractive companion to azaleas and rhododendrons.

Selected species and varieties: *F. gardenii*—2 to 3 feet tall with an equal or greater spread, dark blue-green leaves 1 to 2½ inches long, and petalless flowers with a showy stamen growing in 1- to 2-inch-long clusters in spring. *F. major*—6 to 10 feet tall with a slightly smaller spread and leaves 2 to 4 inches long, but otherwise similar to *F. gardenii.*

Growing conditions and maintenance: Fothergilla is easy to grow in soil with generous amounts of organic matter.

Gazania
(ga-ZAY-nee-a)
GAZANIA

Gazania x hybrida 'Aztec Red'

Hardiness: *Zones 8-10*

Plant type: *herbaceous perennial*

Height: *6 to 12 inches*

Interest: *flowers*

Soil: *well-drained*

Light: *full sun*

Gazanias are valued for their daisylike blooms in shades of white, yellow, orange, red, lavender, and pink. Their main season of bloom is early spring to early summer, but they often flower year round in mild climates.

Selected species and varieties: Gazanias fall into two distinct types—clumping and trailing. Both types have been extensively hybridized. Clumping gazanias grow 6 to 12 inches high with a 12- to 18-inch spread; *G.* x *hybrida* 'Aztec Red' and 'Fiesta Red' are two outstanding clumping varieties. Trailing gazanias have long, spreading stems and are well suited for growing on banks as a ground cover; varieties include *G.* x *hybrida* 'Sunburst' and 'Sunrise Yellow'.

Growing conditions and maintenance: Although gazanias require good drainage and full sun to look their best, they tolerate drought, coastal conditions, and poor soil. Too much water and fertilizer will weaken them. They spread naturally, and after several years may require thinning.

Geranium
(jer-AY-nee-um)
CRANESBILL

Geranium sanguineum 'Album'

Hardiness: *Zones 4-8*

Plant type: *herbaceous perennial*

Height: *8 to 12 inches*

Interest: *flowers, foliage*

Soil: *moist, well-drained*

Light: *full sun to partial shade*

Cranesbill is valued both for the profusion of flowers that appear in spring and summer and for its mounds of dense, lush green foliage that turns red or yellow in the fall.

Selected species and varieties: *G. macrorrhizum*—forms a wide-spreading mound 8 to 12 inches high, with aromatic leaves and magenta, pink, or white flowers that emerge in clusters in late spring and early summer; 'Ingwersen's Variety' has lilac-pink flowers; 'Spessart', pink flowers. *G. sanguineum*—forms a deep green mound of foliage 9 to 12 inches tall and 24 inches across that turns red in fall and bears magenta flowers; 'Album' has white flowers. *G. s.* var. *striatum* (also known as *G. s.* var. *lancastriense*)—light pink flowers with dark red veins.

Growing conditions and maintenance: In the warmer zones, cranesbill prefers partial shade. Do not overfertilize, as it produces rank growth and weakened plants. Divide in spring when clumps show signs of crowding—approximately every 4 years.

Gerbera
(GER-be-ra)
TRANSVAAL DAISY

Gerbera jamesonii

Hardiness: *Zones 8-11*

Plant type: *herbaceous perennial*

Height: *12 to 18 inches*

Interest: *flowers*

Soil: *well-drained*

Light: *full sun to partial shade*

Transvaal daisies produce spectacular 4-inch flowers on sturdy stems, providing a fine display in the garden, in containers, or as cut flowers for indoor arrangements. Although they are hardy only to Zone 8, in cooler areas they can be planted as annuals or dug up in the fall and planted in containers to grow indoors as houseplants.

Selected species and varieties: *G. jamesonii*—has gray-green, deeply lobed leaves 5 to 10 inches long growing in the form of a basal rosette, erect flower stems 12 to 18 inches tall, and flowers 2 to 4 inches across with strap-shaped petals in yellow, salmon, cream, pink, rose, or red.

Growing conditions and maintenance: Incorporate organic matter into the soil before planting Transvaal daisies, and fertilize regularly. For massing, space plants 2 feet apart. Water deeply, allowing soil to dry before watering again. Protect plants over the winter in Zone 8 with a nonmatting mulch.

Grevillea
(gre-VIL-ee-a)
GREVILLEA

Grevillea rosmarinifolia

Hardiness: *Zones 10-11*

Plant type: *shrub*

Height: *4 to 6 feet*

Interest: *flowers, foliage*

Soil: *well-drained, acid*

Light: *full sun*

Rosemary grevillea is a tender evergreen shrub with dark, needle-shaped leaves. It produces dense clusters of red-and-cream flowers that cover the entire plant. The flowers attract hummingbirds.

Selected species and varieties. *G. rosmarinifolia*—has a rounded, well-branched form, 1-inch-long narrow leaves that are dark green on top and white below with silky hairs, and flowers 1 inch across.

Growing conditions and maintenance: Rosemary grevillea tolerates heat, drought, and wind. It can be grown in containers to be moved indoors in areas where it is not hardy. Water container-grown plants sparingly in winter.

Hamamelis
(ha-ma-MEL-lis)
WITCH HAZEL

Hamamelis x intermedia 'Jelena'

Hardiness: *Zones 5-8*

Plant type: *large shrub or small tree*

Height: *15 to 20 feet*

Interest: *flowers, foliage*

Soil: *moist, well-drained*

Light: *full sun to light shade*

Witch hazel is a deciduous plant with interesting fragrant flowers and vivid fall leaf color. It is a valuable addition to mixed-shrub borders or woodland gardens, and it also performs effectively as a specimen or a screen.

Selected species and varieties: *H.* x *intermedia*—vigorous plants with an upright, spreading habit, broadly oval leaves 3 to 4 inches long that turn yellow to red in fall, and flowers that emerge on bare twigs in late winter and early spring with strap-shaped petals ranging in color from yellow to red; 'Jelena' produces copper-colored flowers and orange-red fall foliage; 'Arnold Promise', very fragrant, clear yellow flowers.

Growing conditions and maintenance: Witch hazel thrives in deciduous wooded areas, but performs well in full sun with adequate moisture. Sun-grown plants are usually more dense than those grown in shade. Incorporate organic matter into soil before planting.

Hedera
(HED-er-a)
IVY

Hedera canariensis

Hardiness: *Zones 4-10*

Plant type: *woody vine or shrub*

Height: *6 inches to 90 feet*

Interest: *foliage*

Soil: *moist, well-drained*

Light: *full sun to full shade*

Ivy produces a dense mat of dark, evergreen leaves that are effective for covering sunny banks, or trailing along the woodland floor in dense shade. Its deep roots help prevent erosion on banks.

Selected species and varieties: *H. helix* (English ivy)—6 to 8 inches high as trailing ground cover, to 90 feet tall as a climbing vine, Zones 4-9; 'Glacier' and 'Gold Heart' are two of many variegated varieties; 'Needlepoint' has small leaves, compact form. *H. canariensis* (Algerian ivy)—produces glossy leaves to 8 inches across, tolerates coastal conditions; Zones 9-10. *H. colchica* (Persian ivy)—to 10 inches high, with leaves 5 to 8 inches across; Zones 6-9.

Growing conditions and maintenance: Ivy prefers a rich soil and benefits from a generous helping of organic matter incorporated into the soil. Prune to encourage compact growth and to prevent unwanted spread.

Helianthus
(hee-li-AN-thus)
SUNFLOWER

Helianthus angustifolius

Hardiness: *Zones 3-9*

Plant type: *herbaceous perennial*

Height: *5 to 12 feet*

Interest: *flowers*

Soil: *moist, well-drained*

Light: *full sun*

Perennial sunflowers are tall, stately plants that put on a dramatic flower show in late summer and fall. They are well suited to the back of a sunny border or the center of an island bed. Their flowers are excellent for indoor arrangements.

Selected species and varieties: *H. angustifolius*—5 to 7 feet tall, 4 feet wide, with yellow petals around dark brown or purple centers forming flowers 2 to 3 inches across in midsummer to late fall; Zones 6-9. *H. maximiliani*—3 to 12 feet tall, with yellow flowers growing in leaf axils along the entire length of stems, emerging in midsummer in the warmer zones, late summer in the cooler areas, and continuing through fall; Zones 3-9.

Growing conditions and maintenance: Plant sunflowers in soil rich in organic matter. The plants will grow in shade but will develop a more open habit than in sun and will require staking. Cutting back stems by a third in late spring produces bushier plants. *H. maximiliani* tolerates dry conditions.

Helictotrichon
(he-lik-toh-TRY-kon)
BLUE OAT GRASS

Helictotrichon sempervirens

Hardiness: *Zones 4-8*

Plant type: *ornamental grass*

Height: *2 to 3 feet*

Interest: *foliage, flowers*

Soil: *well-drained*

Light: *full sun*

Blue oat grass produces a dense clump of stiff, steel blue foliage and is a valuable addition to a rock garden or a herbaceous border for both color and form. It contrasts well with perennials having green or silvery white foliage. The color is also a lovely complement to the burgundy leaves of shrubs such as barberry 'Crimson Pigmy' or smoke bush 'Royal Purple'. The flowers are buff-colored and appear in graceful sprays above the leaves.

Selected species and varieties: *H. sempervirens*—forms a dense mound 2 to 3 feet high and equally wide, with light blue-gray leaves and flowers arrayed in drooping, one-sided 4- to 6-inch clusters on slender stems held above the foliage.

Growing conditions and maintenance: Blue oat grass is easy to grow in most soils, including dry, infertile ones. It requires good air circulation to prevent disease. Cut back foliage in early spring, before new growth begins.

Helleborus
(hell-e-BOR-us)
HELLEBORE

Helleborus orientalis

Hardiness: *Zones 4-9*

Plant type: *herbaceous perennial*

Height: *1 to 2 feet*

Interest: *flowers, foliage*

Soil: *moist, well-drained*

Light: *partial shade*

Hellebores should be placed where their flowers can be viewed at close range. The flowers, which appear very early in the growing season, are also good for indoor arrangements, except for those of the aptly named stinking hellebore.

Selected species and varieties: *H. argutifolius* ssp. *corsicus* (also known as *H. lividus*)—1½ to 2 feet tall, producing glossy, evergreen leaves with toothed margins and long-lasting, saucer-shaped green flowers 2 inches across that appear in early spring; Zones 6-8. *H. foetidus* (stinking hellebore)—18 to 24 inches tall, with dark, leathery, evergreen, compact leaves and light green flowers that bloom in late winter and spring; Zones 6-9. *H. orientalis*—to 18 inches tall, with medium green, toothed, usually evergreen leaves and flowers 2 to 3 inches across that bloom in shades of white, green, purple, and brown from early to late spring; Zones 4-9.

Growing conditions and maintenance: Plant hellebores in spring in soil that is rich in organic matter and able to retain moisture. Apply a mulch in summer.

Hemerocallis
(hem-er-o-KAL-lis)
DAYLILY

Hemerocallis 'Stella de Oro'

Hardiness: *Zones 3-10*

Plant type: *herbaceous perennial*

Height: *7 inches to 4 feet*

Interest: *flowers, foliage*

Soil: *moist, well-drained*

Light: *full sun to partial shade*

Daylilies produce colorful rewards with minimal care. Planted in groups, they become a vigorous, soil-stabilizing ground cover that can outgrow most weeds. Their grasslike, arching leaves are attractive throughout the growing season, providing a lush foil for their blossoms. The flowers are borne on stout, branched stems called scapes, and while most blooms last only a day, there are many buds on each scape, so the flowering season continues for weeks. Additionally, breeders have achieved a wide range of flowering times, colors, and sizes, so with care in selection, you can have daylilies blooming in your yard from late spring until frost.

Selected species and varieties: The following are just a few of the hundreds of daylily varieties available; they are generally distinguished by their height, flower color, and season. 'Bountiful Valley' grows 28 inches tall and produces prolific, durable, lemon yellow flowers with lime throats that bloom in midseason; 'Catherine Woodbury', 30 inches, pale pink flowers 4 inches across with lavender undertones and yellow throats

blooming in midseason; 'Ed Murray', 30 inches, deep maroon red flowers of medium size with green throats, midseason; 'Eenie Weenie', a 7-inch-tall dwarf with yellow flowers over an extended season; 'Inca Treasure', 34 inches, large, deep orange, midseason flowers; 'Kindly Light', yellow spider-type flowers 6 inches wide, midseason; 'Mary Todd', 26 inches, early-blooming deep yellow flowers with ruffled edges; 'Oriental Ruby', 34 inches tall, with deep carmine red flowers in late midseason; 'Peach Fairy', a 26-inch-tall miniature producing 2½-inch-wide melon pink, midseason flowers; 'Ruffled Apricot', 30 inches, very large and showy apricot melon flowers with lavender-pink midribs, blooming in early midseason; 'Singing Sixteen', 20 inches tall with late-season apricot blend flowers; 'Stella de Oro', the most popular variety of daylily, a 12-inch-tall miniature with fragrant 2- to 3-inch

Hemerocallis 'Cherry Cheeks'

golden yellow flowers emerging mid to late season.

Growing conditions and maintenance: Plant daylilies in spring or fall. In light shade they will produce fewer blooms than in full sun. The flowers of light-colored varieties often show up better when given a little shade. Daylilies compete well with tree roots and tolerate poor soil. They thrive in soil amended with organic matter. Avoid overfertilizing, which causes rank growth and reduced flowers.

Heteromeles
(het-er-oh-MEE-leez)
TOYON

Heteromeles arbutifolia

Hardiness: *Zones 8-10*

Plant type: *shrub or small tree*

Height: *12 to 25 feet*

Interest: *foliage, fruit*

Soil: *well-drained*

Light: *full sun to partial shade*

The California holly has glossy, dark, evergreen leaves. In late summer it produces large clusters of orange-to-red berries that attract birds and other wildlife to the garden. You can cut the prolific berry clusters for indoor arrangements and holiday decorations.

Selected species and varieties: *H. arbutifolia*—to 25 feet tall and equally wide, with leathery, sharply toothed leaves and inconspicuous white flowers that bloom in spring and are followed by showy clusters of fruit.

Growing conditions and maintenance: Although California holly prefers a fertile, well-drained soil and full sun, it tolerates a wide range of conditions, including drought and partial shade. It can be pruned to reveal its attractive branching habit.

Heuchera
(HEW-ker-a)
ALUMROOT

Heuchera micrantha 'Palace Purple'

Hardiness: *Zones 4-10*

Plant type: *herbaceous perennial*

Height: *12 to 24 inches*

Interest: *flowers, foliage*

Soil: *rich, moist, well-drained*

Light: *partial shade to full sun*

Alumroot produces a neat mound of leaves that make an attractive addition to the front of a perennial border. In late spring and summer, a slender stalk of tiny bell-shaped flowers rises well above the leaves. The flowers are very long-lasting.

Selected species and varieties: *H. micrantha* 'Palace Purple'—15 to 18 inches tall, with purple bronze leaves and white flowers. *H. sanguinea* (coral bells)—12 to 24 inches tall, with dark green, lobed leaves and flowers ¼ to ½ inch long on wiry stems, Zones 4-8; 'Chatterbox' grows 18 inches tall with deep pink flowers; 'June Bride', 15 inches, white flowers; 'Pluie de Feu', 18 inches, red flowers. *H.* x 'Santa Ana Cardinal'—18 to 24 inches tall in clumps 3 to 4 feet across, with rose red flowers that appear over a 3- to 5-month period; Zones 7-10.

Growing conditions and maintenance: Plant alumroot in spring in soil amended with organic matter. In warm areas, it performs best in partial shade. Remove spent blooms to prolong flowering.

Hibiscus
(hy-BIS-kus)
MALLOW

Hibiscus syriacus 'Diana'

Hardiness: *Zones 5-9*

Plant type: *shrub or herbaceous perennial*

Height: *3 to 12 feet*

Interest: *flowers*

Soil: *damp to moist, well-drained*

Light: *full sun to light shade*

The genus *Hibiscus* includes both woody shrubs and herbaceous perennials. All are grown for their large, showy flowers that appear from midsummer until frost. They can be used effectively as a specimen, part of a mixed-shrub or herbaceous border, a hedge, or to dress up a fence or bare wall.

Selected species and varieties: *H. syriacus* 'Diana' (rose of Sharon)—a dense, upright shrub, 6 to 8 feet tall, narrow when young but more wide spreading with age, with medium green three-lobed leaves that appear late in spring and drop late in fall and pure white, single flowers 6 inches across with red eyes that grow prolifically throughout the summer and make the plant exceptional as a specimen or for a hedge; Zones 5-8. *H. coccineus* (scarlet rose mallow)—a narrow, upright herbaceous perennial, 6 to 8 feet tall, with deeply lobed leaves 5 to 6 inches wide, and funnel-shaped red flowers 5 to 6 inches across blooming from mid to late summer; Zones 5-9. Two outstanding hybrids are *H.* 'Lady Baltimore', which grows pink flowers with crimson eyes, and *H.* 'Lord Balti-

more', with deep crimson flowers. *H. moscheutos* (swamp mallow)—a herbaceous perennial, 3 to 8 feet tall, with multiple stems from the base, bright green leaves to 8 inches long, and single flowers 6 to 12 inches across from midsummer until frost; Zones 4-9; 'Cotton Candy' has soft pink flowers; 'Satan', deep crimson flowers.

Growing conditions and maintenance: Both rose mallow and rose of Sharon prefer full sun and an evenly moist soil amended with organic matter. They tolerate light shade, but will produce fewer flowers and a less compact habit than those grown in full sun. 'Diana' rose of Sharon is adaptable to most soils, except those that are extremely wet or dry. It tolerates air pollution and can be grown alongside parking lots. Pruning is not necessary for a natural look and plentiful, medium-size flowers. The natural habitats of rose and swamp mallows is

Hibiscus coccineus

swamps and wetlands, so they will thrive in damp locations and are a good choice for wet spots in the landscape or beside a pond or stream. These mallows can also be grown in moist soil. For use as a summer hedge, plant rose or swamp mallows 3 feet apart.

Hosta
(HOS-ta)
PLANTAIN LILY, FUNKIA

Hosta sieboldiana 'Elegans'

Hardiness: *Zones 3-9*

Plant type: *herbaceous perennial*

Height: *8 inches to 3 feet*

Interest: *foliage, flowers*

Soil: *rich, moist, well drained, acid*

Light: *partial to dense shade*

Although grown primarily for their luxuriant foliage, many hostas produce graceful spires of lilylike flowers during the summer. They are valuable additions to a woodland garden or at the front of a shady border.

Selected species and varieties: *H. fortunei* 'Albopicta'—15 inches tall, with leaves having yellow-green centers and dark green margins. *H. plantaginea*—forms a large mound of broad bright green leaves, with fragrant white flowers on 2½-foot stems. *H.* 'Honeybells'—fragrant lavender flowers with blue stripes on 2-foot stems. *H. sieboldiana* 'Elegans'—large blue-gray leaves and white flowers; 'Frances Williams', large blue-green leaves with broad yellow margins; other fine varieties include 'Gold Standard', 'Blue Cadet', and 'Hyacintha'.

Growing conditions and maintenance: Hostas prefer shade, but will tolerate a sunny location in cooler areas with abundant moisture. Good drainage, especially during the winter, is critical.

Hydrangea
(hy-DRAN-jee-a)
HYDRANGEA

Hydrangea arborescens 'Annabelle'

Hardiness: *Zones 3-9*

Plant type: *shrub, tree, or vine*

Height: *3 to 50 feet*

Interest: *flowers, foliage, bark*

Soil: *moist, well-drained*

Light: *full sun to partial shade*

Hydrangeas are valued for their large clusters of summer flowers. The genus includes deciduous shrubs that go well in mixed borders or mass plantings, small trees that make excellent specimens, and a climbing vine that can grow to 80 feet or more if supported. All have relatively coarse leaves, are easy to grow, and produce long-lasting blossoms that are used in both fresh and dried arrangements.

Selected species and varieties: *H. anomala* ssp. *petiolaris* (climbing hydrangea)—a vine capable of reaching 60 to 80 feet in height but maintainable at a much lower height with pruning, having very attractive cinnamon brown bark in winter, glossy dark green leaves 2 to 4 inches long, and white flowers in 6- to 10-inch flat-topped clusters emerging early to midsummer; excellent for growing on brick or stone walls, arbors, trellises, or trees; Zones 4-7. *H. arborescens* 'Grandiflora' (hills-of-snow hydrangea)—3 feet tall and equally wide, with 6- to 8-inch clusters of white flowers in mid to late summer, useful as a foundation planting or an informal hedge, Zones 3-9; 'Annabelle' produces flower clusters up to 10 inches across that bloom about 2 weeks later than those of 'Grandiflora'. *H. paniculata*—10 to 25 feet tall, 10 to 20 feet wide, an upright, spreading, large shrub or small tree with dark green leaves 3 to 6 inches long and white flowers maturing to dusty pink in grapelike clusters 6 to 8 inches long in midsummer, Zones 3-8; 'Grandiflora' (peegee hydrangea) grows flower clusters up to 18 inches long and makes a spectacular specimen. *H. quercifolia* (oakleaf hydrangea)—4 to 6 feet tall and more than 6 feet wide, with coarse, deeply lobed leaves 3 to 8 inches long that are deep green in summer and turn a brilliant dark reddish bronze in fall and white flowers turning dusty pink,

Hydrangea quercifolia

then brown in erect clusters up to 12 inches long, Zones 5-9, 'Snowflake' grows flowers in clusters to 15 inches long with layered bracts that give the flowers the appearance of double blooms; 'Snow Queen' has wine red fall leaf color and flowers larger and denser than those of the species.

Growing conditions and maintenance: Hydrangeas thrive in fertile soil; incorporate abundant amounts of organic matter into the soil before planting. *H. arborescens* prefers partial shade; other species adapt well to sun or light shade. Climbing hydrangea requires several years to adjust after transplanting, but once established will grow rapidly.

Iberis
(eye-BEER-is)
CANDYTUFT

Iberis sempervirens 'Snowmantle'

Hardiness: *Zones 4-8*

Plant type: *perennial*

Height: *6 to 12 inches*

Interest: *flowers, foliage*

Soil: *moist, well-drained*

Light: *full sun*

The dark green leaves of candytuft are effective year round covering the ground before a perennial border, edging a walkway, or cascading over a stone wall. The delicate white flowers that cover the plant in spring are a delightful bonus.

Selected species and varieties: *I. sempervirens*—to 12 inches high and 24 inches wide, with a low, mounded habit, linear evergreen leaves 1 inch long, semiwoody stems, and very showy white flowers in dense clusters 1 inch across; 'Snowflake' grows 10 inches high, with 2- to 3-inch flower clusters; 'Snowmantle', 8 inches high, with a dense, compact habit.

Growing conditions and maintenance: Incorporate organic matter into the soil before planting candytuft. Protect the plant from severe winter weather with a loose mulch in colder zones. Cut it back at least 2 inches after it flowers to maintain vigorous growth.

Ilex
(EYE-leks)
HOLLY

Ilex 'Sparkleberry'

Hardiness: *Zones 3-10*

Plant type: *shrub or tree*

Height: *3 to 50 feet*

Interest: *foliage, fruit*

Soil: *moist, well-drained, acid*

Light: *full sun to partial shade*

Hollies are a diverse group of plants that includes both evergreen and deciduous trees and shrubs. Female hollies produce fruit in the fall that is often highly ornamental, but most require male plants located within 100 feet for pollination to assure fruit set. From low-growing foundation plants to tall, pyramidal specimen trees, there is a holly suitable to nearly every landscape.

Selected species and varieties: *I. aquifolium* (English holly)—to 70 feet, pyramidal form, dark, glossy, evergreen leaves with spines, bright red fruit in fall ¼ inch in diameter, well suited to Pacific Northwest and mid-Atlantic regions; several outstanding cultivars display leaf variegation or heavy fruit production; Zones 6-9. *I.* x *attenuata* 'Foster #2'—20 to 25 feet, narrow, conical, compact form, neat, small, evergreen leaves with spiny margins, fruit deep red, persists through winter; Zones 6-9. *I. cornuta* 'Burfordii' (Burford holly)—to 25 feet, but may be maintained at 8 to 10 feet with pruning, wider than tall, leaves rectangular, shiny, dark, evergreen with terminal spine, fruit red, abundant, no pollination required

for fruit set, persists through winter; Zones 6-9. *I. crenata* 'Convexa'—4 to 9 feet, broader than tall, small, oval, convex, evergreen leaves, boxwoodlike appearance, can be sheared, fruit black, Zones 5-8; 'Helleri'—3 feet tall, 5-foot spread, mounded form, Zones 5-8; 'Hetzii'—dwarf form of 'Convexa'. *I. glabra* 'Compacta' (dwarf inkberry)—4 to 6 feet with equal or greater spread, dense, rounded form, leaves evergreen, smooth, to 2 inches long, fruit black, excellent as foundation plant or hedge; Zones 4-9. *I. meserveae* 'Blue Prince'—8 to 12 feet, compact and broadly pyramidal, dark blue-green leaves (evergreen), male clone, Zones 4-9; 'Blue Princess'—12 feet tall by 9 feet wide, leaves evergreen, glossy, blue-green, all female clone, fruit dark red; Zones 4-9. *I. opaca* (American holly)—usually 10 to 15 feet, may reach 40 feet with age, evergreen, pyramidal form, Zones 5-9; 'Cardi-

Ilex aquifolium cultivar

nal'—compact form of species, small dark green leaves, light red fruit; 'Goldie'—leaves dull green, fruit yellow, prolific; 'Old Heavy Berry'—leaves large, dark green, pea-size red fruit, prolific, vigorous. *I. pedunculosa* (long-stalk holly)—usually 15 feet, may reach 30 feet with age, large, pyramidal shrub or small tree, leaves spineless, 1 to 3 inches, lustrous, dark green turning yellow-green in winter, fruit bright red, ¼ inch in diameter, on 1- to 1½-inch stems, very attractive in fall; Zones 5-8; *I.* 'Sparkleberry'—to 12 feet, upright deciduous shrub, leaves to 3 inches, deep green, fruit bright red, ⅜ inch in diameter, prolific, ripens in late summer, persists into winter; Zones 4-8. *I. verticillata* 'Winter Red'—8 feet, rounded form, leaves deciduous, dark green, fruit bright red, ⅜-inch diameter, extremely prolific, dramatic after leaves drop in fall; Zones 3-9. *I. vomitoria* (yaupon holly)—15 to 25 feet, upright shrub or small tree, leaves evergreen, dark, fruit translucent, scarlet red, ¼-inch diameter, persists throughout winter,

Ilex cornuta 'Burfordii'

useful as hedge, screen, foundation plant, topiary, takes pruning well.

Growing conditions and maintenance: Hollies perform well in sun or partial shade, though shade-grown plants will produce less fruit. They are tolerant of a wide range of soils as long as drainage is good. They benefit from organic matter added to the soil prior to planting as well as annual late-winter applications of a complete fertilizer. Be sure hollies have plenty of water throughout the growing season. Since male and female flowers are borne on separate plants, it is usually necessary to have both types for berries, even though only the females bear the fruit. (Burford holly is an exception—the all-female plants require no pollen for fruit production.) Not all hollies produce pollen at the same time, so plant a pollinator of the same species. Generally, 1 male plant is sufficient to pollinate 10 to 20 females.

Imperata
(im-per-AY-ta)
JAPANESE BLOOD GRASS

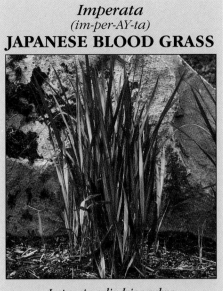

Imperata cylindrica rubra

Hardiness: *Zones 6-9*

Plant type: *ornamental grass*

Height: *12 to 18 inches*

Interest: *foliage*

Soil: *well-drained*

Light: *full sun to partial shade*

Japanese blood grass produces clumps of leaves whose top half turns a rich blood red. It is very effective planted in small groups or large masses at the front of a border. The flowers of this grass are ornamentally insignificant, but its vivid foliage, which provides color from summer through fall, makes it well worth including in a garden.

Selected species and varieties: *I. cylindrica rubra* 'Red Baron'—leaves are 12 to 18 inches long and ¼ inch wide, beginning to turn red in early summer; color increases in intensity in fall. Outstanding for long-season color contrast.

Growing conditions and maintenance: Japanese blood grass grows in sun or partial shade in nearly any well-drained soil. It is particularly showy when viewed with the sun shining through the colorful leaves. It is completely dormant in the winter, and old leaves should be cut back before new growth emerges in spring. *Note:* If any part of 'Red Baron' reverts to green, it should be removed at once. The green form is highly aggressive and is listed in the United States as a noxious weed.

Iris
(EYE-ris)
IRIS

Iris cristata 'Alba'

Hardiness: *Zones 4-9*

Plant type: *herbaceous perennial*

Height: *2 inches to 4 feet*

Interest: *flowers, foliage*

Soil: *well-drained to moist*

Light: *full sun to light shade*

Irises bear unique flowers that present an elegant display in both the garden and cut-flower arrangements. Their blooms are available in a range of colors, and species vary widely in cultural requirements, height, and flower size and type. All iris varieties produce sword-shaped leaves, and all share a distinct flower structure composed of three drooping petallike sepals called falls, three usually erect petals called standards, and three narrow petallike "styles."

Selected species and varieties: *I. cristata* (crested iris)—6 to 9 inches tall, flowers bloom early to mid spring and have two yellow or white crested ridges along falls, effective in the front of a border or woodland garden, hardy to Zone 4; 'Alba'—white flowers; 'Shenandoah Sky'—pale blue flowers; 'Summer Storm'—deep blue flowers. *I. danfordiae* (Danford iris)—4 to 6 inches tall, grown from bulbs, yellow to gold flowers in early spring, hardy to Zone 5. *I. pallida* 'Dalmatica' (orrisroot)—3 feet tall, rigid and erect habit, 24-inch-long gray-green leaves, fragrant bluish purple flowers, blooming late spring or early summer, Zones 4-8; 'Aureo-Variegata'—yellow-striped foliage, dramatic accent to border. *I. reticulata* (netted iris)—3 to 9 inches tall, grown from bulbs, erect habit, purple and yellow fragrant flowers, plants are excellent for rock garden, front of border, or near water, hardy to Zone 5. *I. sibirica* (Siberian iris)—2 to 4 feet tall, foliage grows in dense, erect clumps, attractive throughout growing season, flowers in early summer, good choice for perennial borders, hardy to Zone 4; 'Caesar's Brother'—36 inches tall, blue-black flowers; 'Dewful'—24 inches tall, blue flowers with pale blue styles; 'White Swirl'—40 inches tall, white flowers with touch of yellow.

Growing conditions and maintenance: Iris species vary considerably in their cultural requirements. Crested iris prefers

Iris reticulata

partial shade and a well-drained, not too fertile soil. Other species perform better in the sun, though they will tolerate some shade. Siberian iris thrives in a moist, fertile, slightly acid soil, while netted iris prefers a well-drained, alkaline site. Netted irises can be left undisturbed for many years before division is necessary.

Itea
(IT-ee-a)
SWEETSPIRE

Itea virginica

Hardiness:	*Zones 5-9*
Plant type:	*shrub*
Height:	*2 to 5 feet*
Interest:	*flowers, foliage*
Soil:	*fertile, moist*
Light:	*full sun to partial shade*

Sweetspire offers a fine garden display in both summer and fall. Its flowers appear in midsummer, well after most shrubs have finished blooming. In fall its leaves put on a show, turning reddish purple to scarlet and persisting for several weeks.

Selected species and varieties: *I. japonica* 'Beppu'—2 to 5 feet tall with spreading, moundlike habit, plants spread by suckers, leaves are rich green in summer, red in fall, flowers are white and fragrant, useful as a ground cover. *I. virginica* 'Henry's Garnet'—3 to 4 feet tall, 4 to 6 feet wide, green leaves turn purple-red in fall, fragrant white flowers in clusters up to 6 inches long, excellent addition to mixed-shrub border.

Growing conditions and maintenance: Sweetspire is easily transplanted, and new plants can be obtained by dividing an existing specimen. It prefers a rich, moist to wet site. In mild climates it is semi-evergreen.

Juniperus
(joo-NIP-per-us)
JUNIPER

Juniperus scopulorum 'Skyrocket'

Hardiness:	*Zones 2-9*
Plant type:	*tree or shrub*
Height:	*2 to 60 feet*
Interest:	*foliage*
Soil:	*light, well-drained*
Light:	*full sun*

Junipers vary widely in their height and form, from low-spreading ground covers to tall, columnar trees. All are evergreen with scale-like leaves that range in color from dark green to silvery blue to yellow.

Selected species and varieties: *J. chinensis* 'Gold Coast'—2 to 3 feet tall, up to 5 feet wide, gracefully mounded habit, foliage soft-textured, golden yellow; Zones 3-9. *J. scopulorum* 'Blue Heaven'—20 to 30 feet, neat pyramidal form, foliage very blue throughout the year, Zones 3-7; 'Sky Rocket'—15 to 30 feet tall, 2 to 3 feet wide, form is extremely narrow and columnar, bluish green foliage, dramatic vertical accent; Zones 3-7. *J. virginiana*—40 to 50 feet tall, highly variable spread of 8 to 20 feet, foliage medium green in summer, brownish green in winter' Zones 2-9.

Growing conditions and maintenance: Junipers thrive in open, sunny locations and prefer a sandy soil but tolerate most soils if drainage is good. They tolerate air pollution, and taller types make effective windbreaks.

Kalmia (KAL-mee-a) **MOUNTAIN LAUREL**	*Kerria* (KER-ee-a) **JAPANESE KERRIA**	*Koelreuteria* (kol-roo-TEER-ee-a) **GOLDEN RAIN TREE**

Kalmia latifolia 'Ostbo Red'

Kerria japonica 'Plentiflora'

Koelreuteria paniculata

Hardiness: *Zones 4-9*

Plant type: *shrub*

Height: *7 to 15 feet*

Interest: *flowers, foliage*

Soil: *moist, well-drained, acid*

Light: *full sun to full shade*

In early summer, mountain laurel bears white, pink, or rose-colored blossoms, set off by a background of dark, leathery leaves. It is equally at home as a foundation plant, within a mixed-shrub border, or in a naturalized, woodland garden.

Selected species and varieties: *K. latifolia*—variable height, usually to 15 feet with equal spread, leaves 2 to 5 inches long, evergreen, flower buds are deep pink or red and crimped, flowers are ¾ to 1 inch across in 4- to 6-inch rounded, terminal clusters; 'Nipmuck'—red buds, flowers are creamy white to light pink on inside and dark pink on outside; 'Ostbo Red'—red buds, soft pink flowers; 'Pink Charm'—deep pink buds, pink flowers with red ring on inside near base.

Growing conditions and maintenance: Mountain laurel is easy to grow and virtually maintenance free as long as its cultural conditions are met. While it adapts to sun or shade, it requires a moist, acid soil, to which generous amounts of organic matter have been added. Mulch to maintain moisture.

Hardiness: *Zones 4-9*

Plant type: *shrub*

Height: *3 to 8 feet*

Interest: *flowers, stems*

Soil: *fertile, loamy, well-drained*

Light: *partial to full shade*

Japanese kerria produces masses of bright yellow spring flowers on arched, lime green stems. It is a lively addition to the mixed-shrub border or a woodland garden. Its green stems add color to the winter landscape.

Selected species and varieties: *K. japonica*—3 to 6 feet tall, spreading to 9 feet across, arching green stems zigzag from one node to the next, deciduous, bright green leaves are 1½ to 4 inches long, bright yellow five-petaled flowers, 1½ inches across; 'Picta'—leaves with attractive white margin; 'Pleniflora'—up to 8 feet, habit more erect than species, flowers are double, rounded, golden yellow.

Growing conditions and maintenance: Japanese kerria performs better with some shade; too much sun causes flowers to fade quickly. Prune to remove dead branches whenever they appear, and remove green shoots that arise among the variegated foliage of 'Picta'. Do not overfertilize, as this causes rank growth and reduces flowering.

Hardiness: *Zones 5-9*

Plant type: *tree*

Height: *30 to 40 feet*

Interest: *flowers, fruit, foliage*

Soil: *well-drained*

Light: *full sun*

The golden rain tree is valued for its summer display of yellow flowers and attractive seed pods in the fall. It is an excellent choice for a lawn tree.

Selected species and varieties: *K. paniculata*—30 to 40 feet tall with equal to greater spread, deciduous, leaves are compound, 9 to 18 inches long, bright green, turning yellow in fall, flowers in midsummer are bright yellow, blooming in loose, showy clusters 12 to 15 inches long, papery seed pods are 2 inches long, changing from green to yellow-tan to brown from summer to fall; 'September'—less hardy than the species, flowers appear several weeks later.

Growing conditions and maintenance: The golden rain tree adapts to a wide range of soils, from light to heavy and from acid to alkaline. It tolerates wind, drought, heat, and air pollution, and adapts well to city conditions. Prune in winter to promote high branching and to remove crowded or crossing branches.

Lagerstroemia
(la-gur-STREE-mee-a)
CRAPE MYRTLE

Lagerstroemia indica 'Natchez'

Hardiness: *Zones 7-9*

Plant type: *large shrub or small tree*

Height: *15 to 25 feet*

Interest: *flowers, bark*

Soil: *moist, well-drained*

Light: *full sun*

Crape myrtles can be grown as large shrubs or small trees. They add interest to the landscape during summer with their vibrantly colored flower clusters and during winter with their smooth, multicolored bark.

Selected species and varieties: While the species is subject to powdery mildew, the following are among the newer varieties that are resistant: *L. indica* 'Choctaw'—dark green leaves turn maroon in fall, long-lasting bright pink flowers in mid to late summer; 'Natchez'—fast growing, dark green leaves turn orange-red in fall, white flowers; 'Tuskegee'—strong, horizontal growth habit, leaves are glossy, dark green, and leathery, turning orange-red in fall, flowers are dark pink.

Growing conditions and maintenance: Crape myrtles grow best in hot, sunny locations. To expose the ornamental bark, restrict growth to one to four branches from the base, pruning out others that arise. Also prune to remove winter-injured branches, but wait until late spring because they are slow to leaf out.

Lamium
(LAY-mee-um)
DEAD NETTLE

Lamium maculatum 'Beacon Silver'

Hardiness: *Zones 4-8*

Plant type: *herbaceous perennial*

Height: *8 to 12 inches*

Interest: *foliage, flowers*

Soil: *well-drained*

Light: *partial to full shade*

The spreading, trailing habit of dead nettle makes it useful as a ground cover among shrubs or trees or in the front of a shady border. It helps hide the fading foliage of early spring bulbs and fills in bare spots, and is also well suited for trailing over a stone wall or cascading from a container.

Selected species and varieties: *L. maculatum* 'Beacon Silver'—effective for brightening a shady part of the garden, silver 1- to 2-inch leaves with narrow green margins, pink flowers in late spring bloom in whorls at the ends of stems; 'Chequers'—green leaves with a wide stripe down the center, pink flowers in late spring through summer.

Growing conditions and maintenance: Dead nettle tolerates a wide range of soils as long as they are well drained. Bare patches may appear if the plant is allowed to dry out too often. It prefers shade but will tolerate sun if sufficient moisture is supplied. To contain its aggressive, spreading habit and to promote compact growth, shear dead nettle in midsummer.

Lavandula
(la-VAN-dew-la)
LAVENDER

Lavandula angustifolia 'Hidcote'

Hardiness: *Zones 5-9*

Plant type: *perennial*

Height: *10 inches to 3 feet*

Interest: *foliage, flowers, fragrance*

Soil: *well-drained*

Light: *full sun*

Lavender is an evergreen perennial with a woody base. Both leaves and flowers are extremely fragrant. Its soft colors and fine texture show up well when combined with more brightly colored perennials.

Selected species and varieties: *L. angustifolia* (English lavender), Zones 5-9; 'Hidcote'—15 to 20 inches, silvery gray foliage, purple flowers; 'Jean Davis'—15 inches, blue-green foliage, pale pink flowers; 'Munstead'—10 to 12 inches, 18 inches in flower, wide-spreading, gray-green foliage, purple flowers, very fragrant. *L. stoechas* (French lavender)—3 feet tall, shrublike, gray-green leaves, purple or white flowers; Zones 8-10.

Growing conditions and maintenance: Lavender prefers a soil with very good drainage that is not too rich. In areas subject to freezing, French lavender should be grown in a container and brought indoors for the winter. Cut lavender stems back to 8 inches in early spring to encourage compact growth and to remove old woody stems that produce few flowers.

Leptospermum
(lep-toh-SPER-mum)
NEW ZEALAND TEA TREE

Leptospermum scoparium

Hardiness: *Zones 9-10*

Plant type: *shrub*

Height: *6 to 10 feet*

Interest: *flowers, foliage*

Soil: *fertile, moist, well-drained, acid*

Light: *full sun to light shade*

The New Zealand tea tree is a fine-textured evergreen shrub with a dense branching habit and small leaves. Its flowers are borne in winter, spring, or summer, and though blossoms of the species are white, varieties are available with pink or red flowers.

Selected species and varieties: *L. scoparium*—6 to 10 feet, slightly smaller in spread, rounded form, compact, leaves are dark gray-green and aromatic, profuse white flowers are ½ inch across.

Growing conditions and maintenance: The New Zealand tea tree is easy to grow in mild climates in a well-drained acid to neutral soil. It prefers full sun, except in hot dry areas, where it benefits from partial shade, and thrives under humid, coastal conditions. Though it is somewhat drought tolerant, supplemental water should be supplied moderately, especially where the climate is hot. Prune in early spring.

Leucothoe
(loo-KO-tho-ee)
DROOPING LEUCOTHOE

Leucothoe fontanesiana 'Nana'

Hardiness: *Zones 5-9*

Plant type: *shrub*

Height: *2 to 6 feet*

Interest: *foliage, flowers*

Soil: *moist, well-drained, acid*

Light: *partial to full shade*

Drooping leucothoe is a graceful evergreen shrub whose arching branches support chains of fragrant white flowers in the spring. Branches and leaves extend to the ground, making it a good choice to plant in front of leggy shrubs. It combines well with azaleas and rhododendrons in woodland settings.

Selected species and varieties: *L. fontanesiana*—fountainlike, arching habit, leaves are 2 to 5 inches long, bronze when young, dark green in summer, turning bronze to purple in fall and winter, flowers are white and fragrant, borne in 2- to 3-inch drooping clusters in late spring; 'Nana'—2 feet tall, 6 feet wide; 'Girard's Rainbow'—new leaves emerge variegated white and pink and mature to yellow, copper, and green.

Growing conditions and maintenance: Plant drooping leucothoe in a shady location, adding generous amounts of organic matter to the soil. It will tolerate full sun if abundant moisture is supplied.

Liatris
(ly-AY-tris)
SPIKE GAY-FEATHER

Liatris spicata 'Kobold'

Hardiness: *Zones 3-9*

Plant type: *herbaceous perennial*

Height: *18 inches to 5 feet*

Interest: *flowers*

Soil: *sandy, well-drained*

Light: *full sun to light shade*

The flowers of spike gay-feather are borne on erect stems, and unlike most spike flowers the top buds open first and proceed downward. The effect is that of a feathery bottle brush. It provides a striking vertical accent in both the garden and indoor arrangements.

Selected species and varieties: *L. spicata*—usually 2 to 3 feet tall and 2 feet wide but may reach 5 feet tall, leaves are narrow and tapered, up to 5 inches long, on erect, stout stems, flowers are purple or rose, borne closely along top of stem in mid to late summer; 'Kobold'—18- to 24-inch dwarf form, bright purple flowers, good for front or middle of herbaceous border.

Growing conditions and maintenance: Spike gay-feather prefers a light, well-drained soil and full sun but adapts to light shade and tolerates wet conditions better than other species of liatris. Tall types often need support; however, 'Kobold', with its stout habit, rarely requires staking.

Liriope
(li-RYE-o-pee)
LILYTURF

Liriope muscari 'Variegata'

Hardiness:	*Zones 4-10*
Plant type:	*herbaceous perennial*
Height:	*8 to 18 inches*
Interest:	*foliage, flowers*
Soil:	*fertile, moist to dry*
Light:	*full sun to full shade*

Lilyturf produces evergreen grasslike leaves that make an almost impenetrable ground cover. In summer, spikes of blue, violet, or white flowers arise from the clumps of foliage and are followed by dark blue-black berrylike fruit.

Selected species and varieties: *L. spicata*—8 to 12 inches tall, spreads by underground stems, leaves up to 18 inches long and ¼ inch wide, pale violet to white flowers in loose clusters. *L. muscari*—up to 18 inches tall, leaves 12 to 18 inches long and 1 inch wide, lilac-purple flowers, Zones 6-10; 'Big Blue'—larger leaves and flower spikes than species; 'Christmas Tree'—lilac flowers on tapered spikes; 'John Burch'—variegated leaves and crested lavender flowers; 'Majestic'—large violet-blue flowers; 'Monroe's White'—large white flowers.

Growing conditions and maintenance: Lilyturf thrives in sun or shade, though plants grown in the sun produce more flowers. It prefers a moist soil but adapts well to drier conditions. Mow or cut back old growth in late winter.

Lonicera
(lon-ISS-e-ra)
HONEYSUCKLE

Lonicera heckrottii

Hardiness:	*Zones 4-9*
Plant type:	*woody vine or shrub*
Height:	*20 feet or more*
Interest:	*flowers, foliage*
Soil:	*moist, well-drained*
Light:	*full sun to partial shade*

Honeysuckles include both vines and shrubs. These species have discrete growth habits and adorn the garden with their abundant flowers in spring without taking over.

Selected species and varieties: *L. flava* (yellow honeysuckle)—vine, leaves are bright green above, bluish green below, yellow-orange flowers in midspring, Zones 6-8; *L. heckrottii* (goldflame honeysuckle)—vine, blue-green leaves, red flower buds open to yellow on inside and pink outside in spring to early summer, Zones 4-9; *L. pileata*—evergreen or semi-evergreen shrub, up to 3 feet tall, low, spreading branches with small, lustrous, dark green leaves, Zones 6-9; *L. sempervirens* (trumpet honeysuckle)—dark blue-green leaves, flowers are tubular, orange-red to red, spring-blooming, Zones 4-9.

Growing conditions and maintenance: Plant honeysuckles in moist, well-drained soil amended with organic matter. They thrive in sun or shade, but sun-grown plants flower more heavily. Provide support for twining stems. Prune after flowering to maintain size.

Magnolia
(mag-NO-lee-a)
MAGNOLIA

Magnolia virginiana

Hardiness:	*Zones 5-9*
Plant type:	*tree or shrub*
Height:	*10 to 80 feet*
Interest:	*flowers, foliage, fruit*
Soil:	*moist, well-drained, loamy, acid*
Light:	*full sun to partial shade*

Magnolias include both deciduous and evergreen large shrubs and trees. They vary greatly in size and form, but all produce large, lovely flowers in shades from pink and purple to pure white. The fruit of magnolias is a conelike pod, which splits to reveal bright pink or red seeds.

Selected species and varieties: *M. grandiflora* (southern magnolia)—60 to 80 feet tall, 30 to 50 feet wide, low branching, pyramidal, evergreen or semi-evergreen to deciduous, leaves are 5 to 10 inches long, tops are dark green and shiny, undersides are light green, brown, or rust-colored, flowers are creamy white and richly textured, 8 to 12 inches across, blooming in late spring and sporadically throughout summer, 3- to 5-inch cone-shaped fruit pods open to reveal scarlet seeds in fall; Zones 6-9. 'Bracken's Brown Beauty'—up to 30 feet, compact habit, small leaves are 6 inches long and dark brown on undersides, flowers are 5 to 6 inches; 'Edith Bogue'—tight pyramidal form, leaves are narrow and deep green, flowers are large and fragrant, probably the hardiest southern magnolia variety; 'Goliath'—large flowers up to 12 inches across; 'Little Gem'—10 to 20 feet tall, shrublike habit, small leaves are 4 inches with bronze undersides, flowers bloom in spring and fall, well suited for small landscapes; 'St. Mary'—20 feet tall with equal spread, compact habit, produces flowers at a young age. *M.* x 'Galaxy' —30- to 40-foot deciduous tree with stout branches, pyramidal habit, medium green leaves, reddish purple flowers up to 10 inches in diameter; Zones 5-9. *M.* x 'Nimbus'—up to 40 feet, single- or multiple-trunk tree, leaves are dark and

Magnolia grandiflora 'Little Gem'

shiny green, flowers are creamy white, very fragrant, blooming in late spring; Zones 5-9. Several hybrids have been developed from crosses of *M. liliiflora* (lily magnolia) and *M. stellata* 'Rosea': They are deciduous with a shrublike habit, 10 to 15 feet tall at maturity, bark is light gray, flower buds are furry and attractive in winter, flowers appear before leaves in spring but later than star magnolia's so they are less susceptible to damage by late frosts, flowering continues sporadically through summer, Zones 5-9; 'Ann'—10 feet tall with equal or greater spread, blooms earliest among these hybrids, deep purple-red flowers; 'Judy'— 10 to 15 feet tall, erect habit, flowers are deep purple-red on outside, white on inside; 'Randy'—narrow habit to 15 feet, flowers are purple outside, white inside; 'Ricky'—similar to 'Randy' with flowers deep purple on outside and white to purple on inside. *M. virginiana* (sweet bay or swamp magnolia)—size and form vary with growing conditions, 10 to 20 feet tall, large multiple-stem deciduous shrub in colder zones, in warmer climates may reach 60 feet as semi-ever-

green to evergreen pyramidal tree, 3- to 5-inch-long dark green leaves, creamy white flowers, 2 to 3 inches across, blooms late spring and early summer and continues sporadically until fall, 2-inch fruit opens to show bright red seeds; Zones 5-9.

Growing conditions and maintenance: Transplant magnolias in early spring. The southern magnolia often drops many of its leaves when it is transplanted but usually recovers quickly. All require moist, rich, acid soils and grow well in woodland areas with the protection of nearby trees, as long as they are not too close. The southern magnolia prefers a well-drained, sandy soil, while the hybrids and sweet bay magnolias tolerate heavier, poorly drained soils; the sweet bay magnolia thrives even in swampy conditions. The southern magnolia, with its broad evergreen leaves, requires protection from winter winds and sun, espe-

Magnolia 'Ricky'

cially in colder areas; leaves exposed to winter stress look ragged and scorched. Deciduous magnolia flowers can be damaged by late spring frosts. Give plants a northern exposure to delay flowering, thus reducing possible frost damage.

Mahonia
(ma-HO-nee-a)
MAHONIA

Mahonia bealei

Hardiness:	*Zones 4-9*
Plant type:	*shrub*
Height:	*3 to 12 feet*
Interest:	*foliage, flowers, fruit*
Soil:	*moist, well-drained, acid*
Light:	*partial shade*

Mahonias bear large clusters of yellow flowers in spring, followed by showy blue berries. They are attractive year round as foundation plants and border shrubs, or in a woodland garden.

Selected species and varieties: *M. aquifolium* (Oregon grape)—3 to 6 feet tall, 3 to 5 feet wide, spreads by suckers, compound leaves are evergreen, 6 to 12 inches long, each hollylike leaflet is dark green, turning purplish in winter, flowers are yellow in terminal clusters in early spring, grapelike berries are dark blue in late summer; Zones 4-8. *M. bealei* (leatherleaf mahonia)—6 to 12 feet, upright habit, compound leaves are evergreen and leathery, blue-green leaflets have prominent spines, fragrant yellow flowers in showy clusters in very early spring, steel blue berries appear midsummer; Zones 6-9.

Growing conditions and maintenance: Mahonias prefer partial shade. They perform well under trees but tolerate full sun if adequate moisture is supplied. Protect them from drying winter winds.

Malus
(MAY-lus)
CRABAPPLE

Malus sargentii

Hardiness: *Zones 4-8*

Plant type: *tree or shrub*

Height: *6 to 20 feet*

Interest: *flowers, fruit*

Soil: *moist, well-drained, acid*

Light: *full sun*

Crabapples are small deciduous trees or large shrubs that bear many flowers in spring before leaves are fully expanded. In summer and fall, the small, brightly colored fruit provide color and interest.

Selected species and varieties: *M.* x 'Donald Wyman'—20 feet tall, 25 feet wide, wide-spreading and rounded tree, lustrous dark green leaves, pink buds open to white, single flowers, fruit is bright red, ⅜ inch in diameter, persists into winter. *M. sargentii*—6 to 8 feet tall, 8 to 16 feet wide, densely branched, mounded shrub form, red flower buds open to white, single flowers, fruit is bright red, ¼ inch in diameter, attracts birds.

Growing conditions and maintenance: Crabapples tolerate a wide range of soil conditions. They are easy to transplant and should be pruned while young to establish desired shape and to remove suckers. Prune lightly to avoid the development of water sprouts. Pruning should be done immediately after flowering.

Miscanthus
(mis-KAN-thus)
EULALIA

Miscanthus sinensis 'Zebrinus'

Hardiness: *Zones 5-9*

Plant type: *ornamental grass*

Height: *3 to 10 feet*

Interest: *foliage, flowers*

Soil: *well-drained*

Light: *full sun*

The tall flower plumes of eulalia arise in summer and add graceful movement and soft colors to the garden. Both the flowers and the foliage remain attractive throughout the winter and are useful as specimens and screens. They add drama to rock gardens and herbaceous borders.

Selected species and varieties: *M. sinensis*—5 to 10 feet tall, narrow leaves 3 to 4 feet long with prominent white midrib, flowers are feathery, fan-shaped, blooming in late summer to fall; 'Morning Light'—5 feet, variegated leaves with silver midrib and white margins, reddish bronze flowers; 'Purpurascens'—3 to 4 feet, orange-red in fall; 'Variegatus'—5 to 7 feet, leaves have cream-colored stripes; 'Yaku Jima'—3- to 4-foot dwarf; 'Zebrinus'—6 to 7 feet, horizontal yellow stripes on leaves.

Growing conditions and maintenance: Transplant eulalia in spring, selecting a sunny site. It tolerates nearly any well-drained soil. Cut back old foliage in late winter 2 to 6 inches above the ground.

Myrica
(mi-RYE-ka)
BAYBERRY, WAX MYRTLE

Myrica cerifera

Hardiness: *Zones 2-9*

Plant type: *shrub or tree*

Height: *5 to 25 feet*

Interest: *foliage, fruit*

Soil: *adaptable*

Light: *full sun to partial shade*

Bayberries are irregularly shaped shrubs or small trees that serve well as hedges or foundation plants. Their blue-gray fruit, borne on female plants only, is covered with a waxy coating that is used to make bayberry candles.

Selected species and varieties: *M. californica* (California bayberry)—15 to 35 feet tall, 15 feet wide, bronze-colored evergreen leaves, purple fruit in fall and winter; Zones 7-8. *M. cerifera* (southern wax myrtle)—10 to 20 feet tall, equally wide, leaves are semi-evergreen or evergreen and aromatic, gray fruit clusters along stem of previous season's growth; Zones 7-9. *M. pensylvanica* (northern bayberry)—5 to 12 feet tall with equal spread, suckers help form dense thickets, aromatic deciduous or semi-evergreen leaves, gray fruit; Zones 2-6.

Growing conditions and maintenance: Bayberries adapt to a wide range of soil conditions. They thrive in sandy, sterile soil and tolerate heavy clay soils. They take pruning well and make attractive, dense hedges.

Nandina
(nan-DEE-na)
HEAVENLY BAMBOO

Nandina domestica 'Gulfstream'

Hardiness:	*Zones 6-9*
Plant type:	*shrub*
Height:	*1 to 8 feet*
Interest:	*foliage, flowers, fruit*
Soil:	*fertile, moist*
Light:	*full sun to partial shade*

Nandina is an upright shrub with extremely ornamental foliage. New leaves emerge bronze or pink in spring, become dark green in summer, and turn deep red in fall. In warmer zones nandina is evergreen; in the northern limits of its range it is deciduous. In late spring, it produces loose, drooping clusters of white flowers followed by bright red berries.

Selected species and varieties: *N. domestica*—6 to 8 feet tall, upright with multiple stems from base, compound leaves are 12 to 20 inches long, flowers are white in loose 8- to 15-inch clusters, fruit is bright red, ⅓-inch diameter in grapelike clusters, effective fall into winter; 'Gulfstream'—2 to 3 feet tall, compact, mounded form; 'Harbour Dwarf'—1 to 2 feet tall with greater spread, mounding habit.

Growing conditions and maintenance: Nandina prefers a moist, fertile soil but adapts to drier conditions. Add organic matter to soil prior to planting. Prune by removing one-third of the stems (the oldest canes) at ground level in late winter to maintain dense habit.

Nerium
(NEE-ri-um)
OLEANDER

Nerium oleander

Hardiness:	*Zones 8-10*
Plant type:	*shrub*
Height:	*6 to 20 feet*
Interest:	*flowers, foliage*
Soil:	*moist, well-drained*
Light:	*full sun to partial shade*

Oleander is a tough, easy-to-grow evergreen for warm climates. It bears attractive leaves that resemble bamboo as well as clusters of fragrant flowers from spring through fall. All parts of the oleander are poisonous.

Selected species and varieties: *N. oleander*—usually 6 to 12 feet with equal spread, may reach 20 feet, upright stems, bushy, rounded form, leaves are 3 to 5 inches long, leathery, and dark green throughout year, fragrant flowers form in terminal clusters, are pink, white, or red and very showy, long blooming season; 'Casablanca'—3 to 4 feet, single white flowers; 'Little Red'—red flowers; 'Mrs. Roeddling'—6 feet, smaller leaves result in finer texture, flowers are double and salmon pink.

Growing conditions and maintenance: Oleanders prefer a moist, well-drained soil but adapt to drier conditions. They tolerate drought, wind, salt spray, and air pollution. Prune in early spring to desired height and shape and to maintain dense habit.

Ophiopogon
(o-fi-o-PO-gon)
DWARF MONDO GRASS

Ophiopogon japonicus

Hardiness:	*Zones 7-9*
Plant type:	*herbaceous perennial*
Height:	*6 to 12 inches*
Interest:	*foliage, flowers, fruit*
Soil:	*moist, well-drained*
Light:	*full sun to partial shade*

Dense clumps of grasslike leaves make dwarf mondo grass an excellent ground cover or edging for a bed. It is similar in appearance to liriope but smaller and less hardy. Stems of light blue flowers are produced in the summer, followed by metallic blue berries, though both flowers and fruit are somewhat hidden among the leaves.

Selected species and varieties: *O. japonicus*—6 to 12 inches tall, leaves are dark, evergreen, arching, 8 to 16 inches long, plant spreads by underground runners, tiny individual flowers are lilac-blue and grow in clusters on short stems, steel blue fruit is pea-size.

Growing conditions and maintenance: Dwarf mondo grass is adaptable to sun or partial shade, though it prefers some protection from hot afternoon sun. It can be grown under trees and is useful for controlling erosion on slopes. Cut back foliage in early spring before new growth begins. It is easily propagated by division of clumps.

Osmanthus
(oz-MAN-thus)
HOLLY OSMANTHUS

Osmanthus x fortunei

Hardiness:	*Zones 7-9*
Plant type:	*shrub*
Height:	*8 to 20 feet*
Interest:	*foliage, flowers, fragrance*
Soil:	*moist, well-drained, acid*
Light:	*full sun to partial shade*

Holly osmanthus is a large, fragrant, evergreen shrub. Two distinctly different leaves are often present on the same plant; the juvenile leaves are hollylike, with spiny margins, while the adult leaves have smooth margins with a single spine at the tip. In the late summer or fall it bears tiny white flowers. Although they are largely hidden by the foliage, their presence is unmistakable because they are extremely fragrant. The plant takes shearing well and makes an excellent formal or informal hedge or barrier.

Selected species and varieties: *O. heterophyllus* 'Gulftide'—8 to 10 feet tall, compact, upright habit, leaves are 1 to 2½ inches long, toothed, glossy. *O.* x *fortunei*—15 to 20 feet tall, oval to rounded form, leaves are 2½ to 4 inches long.

Growing conditions and maintenance: Holly osmanthus performs best in a moist, well-drained soil that has been amended with organic matter, but it tolerates drier conditions if grown in partial shade. Plants can be heavily pruned to maintain desired size and shape.

Osteospermum
(os-ti-o-SPER-mum)
AFRICAN DAISY

Osteospermum fruticosum

Hardiness:	*Zones 9-10*
Plant type:	*herbaceous perennial*
Height:	*6 to 12 inches*
Interest:	*flowers, foliage*
Soil:	*well-drained*
Light:	*full sun*

The African daisy is a flowering ground cover for warm zones. It has a trailing habit and spreads rapidly to create a dense mat. Flowers bloom most heavily in late winter and early spring, and intermittently throughout the rest of the year. It makes a lovely show in containers or behind stone walls where it can spill over the edges.

Selected species and varieties: *O. fruticosum*—6 to 12 inches tall with 3-foot spread, stems root where they touch the ground, oval leaves are 1 to 2 inches long, flowers are lavender with purple centers, fading to white, 2 inches across; 'Hybrid White'—more upright habit, white flowers; 'African Queen'—deep purple flowers.

Growing conditions and maintenance: Because the stems root as they grow along the ground, the African daisy is well suited to covering large areas. It thrives in full sun and, once established, tolerates drought. Cut back old plants occasionally to encourage branching and to prevent stems from becoming straggly.

Oxydendrum
(ok-si-DEN-drum)
SORREL TREE

Oxydendrum arboreum

Hardiness:	*Zones 5-9*
Plant type:	*tree*
Height:	*25 to 30 feet*
Interest:	*foliage, flowers*
Soil:	*moist, well-drained, acid*
Light:	*full sun to partial shade*

The sorrel tree provides landscape interest throughout the year. In spring its leaves emerge a lustrous dark green. White, urn-shaped flowers hang in clusters from slender branches in midsummer. The fruit, which appears light green and pendulous in fall, creates a stunning display against the leaves, which turn a brilliant scarlet. The fruit turns brown and persists into winter.

Selected species and varieties: *O. arboreum*—25 to 30 feet tall and 20 feet wide in cultivation, pyramidal tree with rounded crown and drooping branches, leaves 3 to 8 inches long, fragrant white flowers form in drooping clusters 4 to 10 inches long.

Growing conditions and maintenance: Incorporate generous amounts of organic matter into soil prior to planting. The trees are slow growing but attractive even when young. Though they thrive in sun or partial shade, plants grown in the sun produce more flowers and better fall color.

Pachysandra
(pak-i-SAN-dra)
PACHYSANDRA

Pachysandra terminalis

Hardiness: *Zones 5-9*

Plant type: *herbaceous perennial*

Height: *6 to 12 inches*

Interest: *foliage, flowers*

Soil: *moist, well-drained, acid*

Light: *partial to full shade*

Pachysandra is a spreading ground cover whose dark green leaves provide a lush carpet beneath trees and shrubs. In early spring short flower spikes rise from the center of each whorl of leaves.

Selected species and varieties: *P. pro cumbens* (Allegheny pachysandra, Allegheny spurge)—6 to 12 inches tall, 12 inches wide, leaves are deciduous in cooler zones and semi-evergreen to evergreen in mild areas, 2 to 4 inches long, prominently toothed, blue-green, often with gray or purple mottling, flowers are white or pink on 2- to 4-inch spikes. *P. terminalis* (Japanese pachysandra)—6 to 8 inches tall, 12 to 18 inches wide, leaves are evergreen, dark, 2 to 4 inches long, flowers are white on 1- to 2-inch spikes.

Growing conditions and maintenance: Pachysandra thrives in the shade; given too much sun, leaves will yellow. It grows well beneath trees. Incorporate organic matter into the soil prior to planting. Space plants 8 to 10 inches apart for a ground cover, and keep new plantings uniformly moist.

Paeonia
(pee-O-nee-a)
PEONY

Paeonia 'Sword Dance'

Hardiness: *Zones 3-8*

Plant type: *herbaceous perennial*

Height: *18 to 36 inches*

Interest: *flowers, foliage*

Soil: *fertile, well-drained*

Light: *full sun to light shade*

Peonies are long-lived plants whose spectacular flowers are set off by mounds of neat foliage. New leaves bear a rosy tint as they emerge in spring, deepening to dark green and remaining attractive throughout the summer until frost. Leaves are compound and form a rounded mound of growth about 3 feet tall and equally wide. Flowers are large, 3 to 6 inches across, and extremely showy. Many are fragrant. Flowers are classified by season (early, mid, late) and form (single, Japanese, anemone, semidouble, and double). The single-flowered form is composed of one row of petals surrounding bright yellow stamens at the center. Japanese and anemone types have a single row of petals surrounding modified stamens that look like finely cut petals. Semidouble peonies have several rows of petals and conspicuous pollen-bearing stamens. Double-flowering forms have a huge, fluffy appearance created by several rows of petals and petallike stamens.

Selected species and varieties: Hundreds of peony varieties offer a selection of height, flower type, season, and color.

'Krinkled White'—27 inches, early-season, single, white; 'Sea Shell'—midseason, single, shell pink; 'Mrs. Franklin D. Roosevelt'—early midseason, double, light pink, fragrant; 'Raspberry Sundae' —27 inches, midseason, double, raspberry pink inner petals, pale pink outer petals, fragrant; 'Therese'—early mid season, double, light pink; 'Gay Paree'—anemone form, midseason, pink with white center; 'Sword Dance'—Japanese form, mid to late season, dark red.

Growing conditions and maintenance: The site for peonies should be well prepared because plants are heavy feeders and prefer to remain undisturbed indefinitely. Incorporate generous amounts of organic matter into the soil, but do not allow manure to come in contact with the fleshy roots. Peonies are best planted in the fall. Place the buds (eyes) 1 to 2 inches below the soil surface; if planted too deep, flowering will be delayed. Full sun will generally produce

Paeonia 'Seashell'

the most vigorous growth, but pastel flowers are often seen to best advantage in light shade.

Panicum
(PAN-i-kum)
SWITCH GRASS

Panicum virgatum 'Heavy Metal'

Hardiness: *Zones 5-9*

Plant type: *ornamental grass*

Height: *3 to 6 feet*

Interest: *foliage, flowers*

Soil: *moist, well-drained*

Light: *full sun*

Switch grass is excellent for massing as a tall ground cover or screen. Unlike clump-forming grasses, it spreads to cover large areas. In mid to late summer, fine-textured flowers arise from the arching leaves. Both foliage and flowers fade to a soft beige as the weather turns cold, remaining attractive well into winter.

Selected species and varieties: *P. virgatum*—4 to 6 feet tall, leaves are 2 to 3 feet long and ⅜ inch wide, green in summer, turning yellow and red in fall, flowers bloom on large branched stems and are dark red to purple; 'Haense Herms'—3 to 3½ feet, more compact and upright habit, leaves are red from midsummer through frost, seed heads are white-gray; 'Heavy Metal'—3 to 4 feet tall and 2 feet wide, upright, leaves are bluish gray, turning bright yellow in fall, tiny flowers are pinkish tan.

Growing conditions and maintenance: Grow switch grass in full sun. It thrives in moist soil but tolerates much drier conditions, including drought, though it will spread much more slowly. Cut it back to just above the ground in early spring before new growth begins.

Papaver
(pap-AY-ver)
POPPY

Papaver orientale 'Glowing Rose'

Hardiness: *Zones 3-8*

Plant type: *herbaceous perennial*

Height: *2 to 4 feet*

Interest: *flowers*

Soil: *well-drained*

Light: *full sun to partial shade*

The silky textured flowers of Oriental poppies are magnificent though short-lived. They appear in vivid shades of pink, red, salmon, orange, and white in late spring and early summer and last for about 2 weeks.

Selected species and varieties: *P. orientale*—2 to 4 feet, leaves up to 12 inches long, coarse, hairy, toothed, in clumps, flowers on erect stems stand well above foliage; 'Carousel'—28 inches, compact, petals are white with orange edges; 'China Boy'—flowers are orange and highlighted with white toward inside, maroon center; 'Dubloon'—clear orange double flowers; 'Glowing Rose'—large watermelon pink flowers; 'Helen Elizabeth'—salmon pink flowers with ruffled edges, early bloomers; 'Snow Queen'—white flowers with black spots.

Growing conditions and maintenance: Plant poppies in well-drained soil; excess winter moisture is often lethal. Foliage dies back after flowering and can leave a void in the garden, so plant among leafy perennials that will fill in the space.

Patrinia
(pat-RIN-ee-a)
PATRINIA

Patrinia scabiosifolia

Hardiness: *Zones 5-9*

Plant type: *herbaceous perennial*

Height: *2 to 6 feet*

Interest: *flowers, seed pods*

Soil: *moist, well-drained*

Light: *full sun to light shade*

Patrinia produces large, airy sprays of flowers late in the summer and fall. These are followed by bright yellow seed pods on orange stems. It is well suited to the middle or rear of a perennial border or a natural garden, where it combines particularly well with ornamental grasses. Patrinia flowers can be cut for long-lasting indoor arrangements.

Selected species and varieties: *P. scabiosifolia*—3 to 6 feet tall, leaves are ruffled, pinnately divided, 6 to 10 inches, and form a large, basal mound, yellow flowers form 2-inch clusters held well above foliage, long-lasting, late summer and fall bloom; 'Nagoya'—2 to 3 feet, compact habit, flowers are almost fluorescent yellow.

Growing conditions and maintenance: Plant patrinias in moist, well-drained soil in sun or light shade. Taller types often require staking. Once established, patrinias are long-lived perennials. They self-sow; to avoid an excess of plants, remove fading flowers before seed is released. They rarely need to be divided.

Pennisetum
(pen-i-SEE-tum)
FOUNTAIN GRASS

Pennisetum alopecuroides 'Hameln'

Hardiness: *Zones 5-9*

Plant type: *ornamental grass*

Height: *1 to 5 feet*

Interest: *foliage, flowers*

Soil: *well-drained*

Light: *full sun*

Fountain grass forms large clumps of slender, arching leaves. In mid to late summer numerous flower stalks arise from the clump, topped with spikes that resemble bottle brushes. Fountain grass is excellent in small groupings or for massing. It can be used in a herbaceous border, alongside a stream or garden pond, or as an edging along a path.

Selected species and varieties: *P. alopecuroides* (Chinese fountain grass)—3 to 4 feet tall, leaves are 2 to 3 feet long, ¼ inch wide, forming large arching mound, turning a bright almond color in winter, flowers are silvery mauve, 5 to 7 inches long, on erect stems up to 5 feet; 'Hameln'—1 to 2 feet, similar to species with smaller size, finer foliage, and flower heads.

Growing conditions and maintenance: Fountain grass thrives in full sun in nearly any well-drained soil. It tolerates wind and coastal conditions. Cut plants back to 6 inches above the ground before new growth begins in the spring.

Perovskia
(per-OV-skee-a)
RUSSIAN SAGE

Perovskia atriplicifolia

Hardiness: *Zones 5-9*

Plant type: *herbaceous perennial*

Height: *3 to 4 feet*

Interest: *flowers, foliage*

Soil: *well-drained*

Light: *full sun*

Russian sage adds cool colors, pleasing fragrance, and soft texture to any bed in which it is grown. Its leaves are silvery white and aromatic. The flowers are lavender-blue and appear for several weeks in the summer. It is lovely used as a filler among more boldly colored and textured plants in a herbaceous border.

Selected species and varieties: *P. atriplicifolia*—3 to 4 feet tall with equal spread, silver-white leaves and stems have a sagelike aroma when bruised, leaves are 1½ inches long, flowers are pale lavender-blue, two-lipped, growing in branched, spikelike clusters in summer.

Growing conditions and maintenance: Plant Russian sage in full sun; shade causes floppy, sprawling growth. It needs a well-drained soil, and established plants will withstand some drought. Though the lower stems become woody, cut the plant back to within several inches of the ground in early spring to promote bushy growth.

Phlox
(flox)
PHLOX

Phlox maculata 'Miss Lingard'

Hardiness: *Zones 3-9*

Plant type: *herbaceous perennial*

Height: *3 inches to 3 feet*

Interest: *flowers, foliage*

Soil: *dry to moist, sandy to fertile*

Light: *full sun to full shade*

Species of phlox vary widely in their heights, habits, uses, and cultural requirements. Some are low-growing spreaders; others are tall, erect border flowers. While some like full sun, others need shade. Some need abundant moisture; others prefer to be dry. Phlox flowers, which are borne singly or in clusters, all have five flat petals and often a conspicuous eye in the center.

Selected species and varieties: *P. divaricata* (wild blue phlox)—9 to 15 inches, spreading, blue flowers, fragrant in spring, Zones 4-9; 'Dirgo Ice'—8 to 12 inches, pale lavender flowers, very fragrant; 'Fuller's White'—8 to 12 inches, white flowers. *P. maculata* (spotted phlox, wild sweet William)—up to 3 feet with cylindrical flower heads in shades of pink to white from midsummer to fall, Zones 3-9; 'Miss Lingard'—6-inch trusses of pure white blossoms. *P. stolonifera* (creeping phlox)—up to 12 inches, spreading, evergreen leaves, dense clusters of flowers in shades of blue, pink, or white, spring bloom, excellent as a ground cover in partial shade, Zones 3-8; 'Blue Ridge'—8 inches, clear blue flowers; 'Bruce's White'—6 inches, white flowers. *P. subulata* (moss phlox, moss pink)—3 to 6 inches tall, spreads 2 feet, evergreen leaves, flowers in wide color range in early to mid spring, excellent ground cover for sunny, dry site, and very effective cascading over stones, Zones 3-9; 'Cushion Blue', 'Emerald Pink', and 'Snowflake' are among the many excellent varieties that offer brilliant spring colors.

Growing conditions and maintenance: Phlox have diverse cultural requirements. With care in selection, an appropriate

Phlox subulata 'Emerald Pink'

species can be found for nearly any site. Woodland phlox thrives in shady, moist, wooded areas, where it naturalizes freely. Spotted phlox prefers a sunny, well-drained site. It is well suited to a sunny border where it will stand erect without the need for staking. Both creeping phlox and moss phlox form lush mats of evergreen foliage and make wonderful ground covers. Creeping phlox will grow in moist sun or shade; partial shade is ideal. Moss phlox needs a drier site in full sun and is a perfect choice for a dry bank, rock garden, or stone wall. Promote dense growth and reblooming by cutting plants back after flowering.

Pieris
(PYE-er-is)
PIERIS

Pieris floribunda

Hardiness:	*Zones 5-8*
Plant type:	*shrub*
Height:	*2 to 12 feet*
Interest:	*foliage, flowers, buds*
Soil:	*moist, well-drained, acid*
Light:	*full sun to partial shade*

Pieris provides beauty all year long. It makes an outstanding specimen, foundation, border, or woodland shrub.

Selected species and varieties: *P. floribunda* (Japanese andromeda)—2 to 6 feet tall and wide, bushy, low habit, evergreen leaves 1 to 3 inches long, fragrant white flowers bloom in 2- to 4-inch upright clusters in midspring. *P. japonica*—9 to 12 feet tall, 6 to 8 feet wide, leaves emerge bronze-pink in spring, become dark green in summer, evergreen, 1½ to 3½ inches long, flowers are white, urn-shaped, in pendulous 3- to 6-inch clusters in early to mid spring, flower buds form in late summer in attractive, drooping chains; 'Dorothy Wyckoff'—compact form, red buds open to pale pink flowers; 'Flamingo'—deep rose red flowers; 'Valley Rose'—tall, open habit, pink flowers; 'White Cascade'—heavy flowering, white flowers, long-lasting.

Growing conditions and maintenance: Grow pieris in well-drained soil supplemented with organic matter. Provide protection from heavy winds.

Pinus
(PYE-nus)
LACE-BARK PINE

Pinus bungeana

Hardiness:	*Zones 4-8*
Plant type:	*tree*
Height:	*30 to 75 feet*
Interest:	*bark, foliage*
Soil:	*well-drained*
Light:	*full sun*

The bark of the lace-bark pine exfoliates in irregular plates to reveal attractive tones of brown, creamy white, and green. Though slow growing, it makes an outstanding specimen with year-round garden interest.

Selected species and varieties: *P. bungeana*—usually 30 to 50 feet tall but may reach 75 feet, 20 to 35 feet wide, rounded to pyramidal, picturesque habit, often with multiple trunks, older specimens become broad-spreading, needles are 2 to 4 inches long, stiff, medium to dark green, cones are 2 to 3 inches long, bark exfoliates at very young age, when branches are only 1 inch in diameter.

Growing conditions and maintenance: The lace-bark pine prefers a sunny site with well-drained soil. It is best placed in a spot where the bark can be viewed at close range. It is somewhat weak-wooded, and can be damaged by snow and ice loads. Remove snow before too much weight accumulates.

Pittosporum
(pit-o-SPO-rum)
JAPANESE PITTOSPORUM

Pittosporum tobira

Hardiness: *Zones 8-10*

Plant type: *shrub*

Height: *10 to 12 feet*

Interest: *leaves, flowers*

Soil: *well-drained*

Light: *full sun to full shade*

Japanese pittosporums are handsome evergreens for warm climates. They can be grown unpruned as an informal hedge, or can be sheared for a more formal look. They are attractively used as foundation plants, under trees, or in containers. Their flowers, although not very showy, are extremely fragrant in the late spring.

Selected species and varieties: *P. tobira*—10 to 12 feet tall, 15 to 20 feet wide with dense, impenetrable habit, leaves are 1½ to 4 inches long, leathery, dark green, flowers are creamy white, inconspicuous but fragrant, blooming in the spring.

Growing conditions and maintenance: Japanese pittosporums are durable and easy to transplant. They will adapt to almost any well-drained soil, including sandy, dry locations. They tolerate heat, wind, and salt spray, so are well suited to coastal conditions. Established plants will tolerate drought and withstand heavy pruning. Plants thrive in both full sun and dense shade.

Platycodon
(plat-i-KO-don)
BALLOON FLOWER

Platycodon grandiflorus 'Mariesii'

Hardiness: *Zones 4-9*

Plant type: *herbaceous perennial*

Height: *10 to 36 inches*

Interest: *flowers, buds*

Soil: *well-drained, acid*

Light: *full sun to partial shade*

Balloon flowers are long-lived perennials that bear blue, white, or pink flowers throughout the summer. The common name derives from the fat, round flower buds that pop open as they mature.

Selected species and varieties: *P. grandiflorus*—24 to 36 inches, leaves are blue-green, 1 to 3 inches long, in neat clumps, rounded flower buds look inflated and pop when squeezed, flowers are usually blue, saucer-shaped, 2 to 3 inches across, on erect stems; *P. g.* 'Mariesii'—18 inches tall, compact form, bright blue flowers; 'Apoyama'—10 inches tall, violet-blue flowers produced over a long period.

Growing conditions and maintenance: Plant balloon flowers in well-drained, slightly acid soil; they do not tolerate a soggy location. They are late to emerge in the spring, so mark their location in the garden to avoid injury or crowding. These are slow-growing perennials and can remain undisturbed for many years without division.

Plumbago
(plum-BAY-go)
CAPE PLUMBAGO

Plumbago auriculata

Hardiness: *Zones 9-11*

Plant type: *shrub*

Height: *6 to 8 feet*

Interest: *flowers, foliage*

Soil: *well-drained*

Light: *full sun to partial shade*

Cape plumbago is a large evergreen shrub that develops a mounded habit with long vinelike branches. Flowers are azure blue or white, and under ideal conditions they will appear year round.

Selected species and varieties: *P. auriculata*—6 to 8 feet tall, spreading 8 to 12 feet or more, leaves are 1 to 2 inches long, medium to light green, evergreen, flowers are 1 inch across in 3- to 4-inch clusters, blue or white, main blooming season is from early spring through fall.

Growing conditions and maintenance: Cape plumbago is a mounding shrub and can be maintained through pruning as a dense, low hedge or foundation plant. If trained it will climb a trellis or wall, and it is also well suited as a tall ground cover for large, well-drained slopes. Cape plumbago thrives in full sun but tolerates light shade in hot areas; it tolerates coastal conditions as well but is sensitive to frost. Prune oldest canes to the ground each year in early spring, and pinch new growth to encourage branching.

Polygonatum
(po-lig-o-NAY-tum)
SOLOMON'S-SEAL

Polygonatum biflorum

Hardiness: *Zones 3-9*

Plant type: *herbaceous perennial*

Height: *2 to 3 feet*

Interest: *flowers, foliage*

Soil: *moist, acid loam*

Light: *partial to full shade*

Small, nodding flowers dangle from the graceful, arching stems of Solomon's-seal. Pairs of broad leaves up to 4 inches long line the stems. Solomon's-seal combines well with spring-flowering bulbs or shade-loving shrubs, and the foliage can be used in arrangements.

Selected species and varieties: *P. multiflorum* (European Solomon's-seal)—handsome bright green leaves up to 6 inches long on stems up to 3 feet long. *P. odoratum thunbergii* 'Variegatum'—white flowers tipped with green and leaves edged in white.

Growing conditions and maintenance: Plant 1 foot apart in cool, moist, shady sites where soil contains ample organic matter. Propagate from seed or by division in spring.

Potentilla
(po-ten-TILL-a)
BUSH CINQUEFOIL

Potentilla fruticosa 'Primrose Beauty'

Hardiness: *Zones 2-7*

Plant type: *shrub*

Height: *1 to 4 feet*

Interest: *flowers, foliage*

Soil: *adaptable*

Light: *full sun to partial shade*

Bush cinquefoil is a low-growing shrub with neat foliage and a long flowering season. It has many landscape uses, serving as a low hedge, foundation planting, or edging; it can also be combined with other shrubs or perennials in a mixed border.

Selected species and varieties: *P. fruticosa*—1 to 4 feet tall, 2 to 4 feet wide, compound leaves, new leaves are gray-green, turning dark green, flowers are 1 inch across, bright yellow, from early summer to late fall; 'Abbotswood'—2 feet with white flowers and dark bluish green leaves; 'Coronation Triumph'—3 to 4 feet, gracefully arching habit, lemon yellow cuplike flowers; 'Primrose Beauty'—3 feet, primrose flowers with deeper colored centers; 'Tangerine'—2 to 4 feet, flowers are yellow flushed with orange-copper tones.

Growing conditions and maintenance: The bush cinquefoil thrives in moist, well-drained soil but tolerates poor, dry soil as well. It produces more flowers in full sun but grows well in partial shade. Prune a third of the oldest stems back to the ground in late winter.

Prunus
(PROO-nus)
CHERRY, CHERRY LAUREL

Prunus laurocerasus 'Otto Luyken'

Hardiness: *Zones 4-10*

Plant type: *shrub or small tree*

Height: *10 to 50 feet*

Interest: *foliage, flowers, bark*

Soil: *moist, well-drained*

Light: *full sun to moderate shade*

Cherry laurels are large evergreen shrubs with fragrant spring blossoms. They are useful for hedges, screens, and large foundation plantings. Flowering cherries are trees with year-round landscape interest. In spring, flowers cover the branches before the leaves emerge. The summer leaves are a lustrous dark green, and in some varieties they turn red or gold in fall. Winter exposes the shiny reddish bronze bark. The branches gnarl with age.

Selected species and varieties: *P. caroliniana* (Carolina cherry laurel)—20 to 30 feet tall, 15 to 25 feet wide, dense evergreen shrub with irregular outline, often pruned as a formal hedge, leaves are dark green, 2 to 3 inches long, flowers are small, white, fragrant, and appear in early spring; Zones 7-10. *P. laurocerasus* (common cherry laurel)—10 to 30 feet, wide-spreading evergreen shrub, dense, leaves are 2 to 6 inches long, glossy, medium to dark green, flowers are small, white, fragrant, blooming in 2- to 5-inch-long clusters in midspring, Zones 6-8; 'Otto Luyken'—3 to 4 feet tall, 6 to 8 feet wide; 'Schipkaensis'—4 to 5 feet tall, dark green, narrow leaves, hardy to Zone 5; 'Zabeliana'—3 feet tall, up to 12 feet wide, dark green leaves are narrow, willowlike. *P. sargentii* (Sargent cherry)—40 to 50 feet with equal spread, deciduous tree, leaves are 3 to 5 inches, emerging bronze in spring, turning dark green in summer and bronze or red in fall, bark is shiny, reddish brown, with horizontal markings (lenticels), flowers are single, pink, 1½ inches across, opening before leaves emerge in spring, excellent specimen tree; Zones 4-7. *P.* 'Hally Jolivette'—cross between *P. subhirtella* (Higan cherry) and *P. yedoensis* (Japanese flowering cherry), 15 to 20 feet, rounded, shrubby, deciduous tree, pink flower buds open to pale pinkish white double flowers 1¼ inches across in the late spring; Zones 5-7.

Growing conditions and maintenance: Cherry laurels and flowering cherries require a well-drained soil and benefit from the addition of generous amounts of organic matter. Cherry laurels thrive in

Prunus sargentii

both sun and shade. Common cherry laurel withstands wind and salt spray, making it useful as a windbreak. Carolina cherry laurel tends to discolor in winter if exposed to sun and heavy winds. Both cherry laurels take pruning well and can be maintained as a formal hedge or left unpruned as a screen. Avoid excess fertilization. The Sargent and 'Hally Jolivette' cherries perform best in full sun. Water during dry periods and provide a year-round mulch. Little pruning is necessary.

Pyracantha
(py-ra-KAN-tha)
SCARLET FIRETHORN

Pyracantha coccinea 'Mojave'

Hardiness:	*Zones 6-9*
Plant type:	*shrub*
Height:	*4 to 16 feet*
Interest:	*fruit, flowers, foliage*
Soil:	*well-drained*
Light:	*full sun*

The scarlet firethorn is a semi-evergreen shrub with white spring flowers and stunning orange-red berries that ripen in the fall and persist into winter. It can be used effectively as a hedge or barrier; its ½-inch spines along the stems make it impenetrable. It is also a good choice as an espalier specimen, trained against a wall.

Selected species and varieties: *P. coccinea* 'Apache'—4 to 6 feet, compact form, bright red fruit; 'Mojave'—6 to 10 feet, upright, densely branched, orange-red fruit in very heavy clusters; 'Navaho'—up to 6 feet, slightly greater spread, low-growing, mounded habit, orange-red fruit; 'Teton'—up to 16 feet tall, 9 feet wide, upright habit, yellow-orange fruit.

Growing conditions and maintenance: Plant scarlet firethorn in spring, choosing a well-drained site in full sun. Plants will grow in partial shade, but flower and fruit production will be reduced. Prune anytime to maintain desired size and shape.

Pyrus
(PY-rus)
CALLERY PEAR

Pyrus calleryana

Hardiness:	*Zones 5-8*
Plant type:	*tree*
Height:	*40 feet*
Interest:	*flowers, foliage*
Soil:	*well-drained*
Light:	*full sun*

Callery pears are showy, spring-flowering, deciduous trees with glossy green summer leaves that turn deep red to purple in the fall. The small, round, russet-colored fruit provides winter food for birds.

Selected species and varieties: *P. calleryana* 'Capital'—40 feet tall with 12-foot spread, distinctly columnar form with strongly ascending branching pattern, leaves are dark green in summer, red to red-purple in early fall, remaining on tree late, off-white flowers are profuse in early spring, useful as a tall screen or windbreak; 'Whitehouse'—40 feet tall, 18 feet wide, pyramidal form, leaves are long and pointed, glossy green, turning wine red in fall, white flowers in spring, useful where space is limited.

Growing conditions and maintenance: Plant callery pears in late winter or early spring while they are still dormant. They adapt to nearly any well-drained soil and tolerate dryness and pollution. Prune while dormant. 'Capital' may be susceptible to fire blight.

Raphiolepis
(raf-i-O-le-pis)
INDIAN HAWTHORN

Raphiolepis indica 'Springtime'

Hardiness: *Zones 8-10*

Plant type: *shrub*

Height: *3 to 6 feet*

Interest: *foliage, flowers*

Soil: *moist, well-drained*

Light: *full sun*

Indian hawthorn is a medium-size evergreen shrub that produces showy white or pink flowers in early spring. It is useful for massing or growing in containers, or is attractive as an unpruned hedge for southern gardens.

Selected species and varieties: *R. indica*—3 to 6 feet, equally wide, dense, rounded form, leaves are dark, leathery, evergreen, 2 to 3 inches long, flowers are white, pink, or rose red, blooming in early spring, followed by clusters of purple-black berries that persist through winter; 'Charisma'—3 to 4 feet, light pink double flowers; 'Snow White'—4 feet, white flowers; 'Springtime'—up to 6 feet, deep pink flowers, prolific bloom.

Growing conditions and maintenance: Indian hawthorn thrives in moist, well-drained soils but adapts to drier conditions, and established plants will withstand drought. Plants tolerate the salt spray of coastal conditions. They are well suited to growing in containers and rarely need pruning.

Rhododendron
(roh-doh-DEN-dron)
RHODODENDRON

Rhododendron catawbiense hybrid

Hardiness: *Zones 3-8*

Plant type: *shrub*

Height: *3 to 10 feet*

Interest: *flowers, foliage*

Soil: *moist, well-drained, acid*

Light: *full sun to partial shade*

The genus *Rhododendron* includes over 900 species of flowering plants that are commonly known as rhododendrons and azaleas. Although the distinguishing features between them are not always clear-cut, most true rhododendrons are evergreen, while most azaleas are deciduous. Also, rhododendron flowers are usually bell-shaped, whereas azaleas are funnel-shaped, and rhododendron leaves are often scaly, while azalea leaves never are. Numerous varieties of the different species afford gardeners choices in size, growth habit, hardiness, flower color, and season. Both azaleas and rhododendrons offer endless landscaping possibilities, from woodland gardens and mixed-shrub borders to specimen or foundation plants. They are effective both in small groupings and in large mass plantings.

Selected species and varieties: *R.* 'Boule de Neige'—5 feet tall, up to 8 feet wide, compact, rounded habit, leaves are dark, evergreen, flowers are white in large trusses; Zones 5-8. *R. calendulaceum* (flame azalea)—4 to 9 feet, with 10 to 15 foot spread, deciduous, upright habit, leaves are medium green in summer, turning yellow to red in fall, flowers are 2 inches across, scarlet, orange, or yellow, long-lasting, appear in late spring or early summer; Zones 5-7. *R. catawbiense* (Catawba rhododendron)—6 to 18 feet tall with slightly less spread, leaves are evergreen, large, dark, dense all the way to the ground, flowers are lilac-purple with green or yellow markings in 5- to 6-inch trusses, late spring bloom, hybrids are available with white, pink, red, lavender-blue, and bicolored flowers; Zones 4-8. *R. kaempferi*—up to 10 feet tall, 5 to 6 feet wide, leaves are dark, semi-evergreen to deciduous, turning reddish in fall, flowers are red, orange, salmon, pink, purple, violet, or white; Zones 5-8. *R. schlippenbachii* (royal azalea)—6 to 10 feet tall, equally wide, upright, rounded habit, leaves are deciduous, dark green in summer, turning red, orange, and yellow in fall, flowers are soft, rose

R. yakusimanum x R. 'Ibex'

pink, freckled on upper petals, fragrant, blooming in spring; Zones 4-7. *R. vaseyi* (pink-shell azalea)—5 to 10 feet tall with irregular, upright habit, leaves are deciduous, medium green in summer, turning red in fall, rose pink flowers bloom late spring to early summer, Zones 3-8; 'White Find'—fragrant white flowers with yellow-green blotch. *R. yakusimanum*—3 to 4 feet tall and 3 feet wide with dense, rounded habit, dark leaves, evergreen, flower buds are pink or rose-colored, opening to white flowers in spring, hybrids are available with flowers in shades of pink or red; Zones 5-8. *R. yedoense* var. *poukhanense* (Korean azalea)—3 to 6 feet tall with equal or greater spread, leaves are deciduous in the

North and nearly evergreen in milder zones, dark green in summer, turning orange, purple, or dark red in fall, reddish purple flowers in late spring; Zones 4-8.

Growing conditions and maintenance: Plant rhododendrons and azaleas in moist, well-drained, acid soil amended with generous amounts of organic matter. Do not plant in poorly drained soil, and avoid setting new plants too deep. They grow well in both sun and light

R. yakusimanum x R. sutchuenense

shade, though in warmer zones some shade is preferred. Pruning is almost never necessary. Plants do not tolerate alkaline or saline soils, and dry winter winds often cause leaf burn on evergreen types.

Romneya
(RAHM-nee-a)
CALIFORNIA TREE POPPY

Romneya coulteri

Hardiness:	*Zones 7-10*
Plant type:	*herbaceous perennial*
Height:	*4 to 8 feet*
Interest:	*flowers, foliage*
Soil:	*dry, infertile*
Light:	*full sun*

The California tree poppy produces fragrant 3- to 6-inch flowers with silky white petals surrounding a bright golden center. They bloom throughout the summer, and though each flower lasts only a few days, they make a handsome show in both the garden and indoor arrangements.

Selected species and varieties: *R. coulteri*—up to 8 feet tall, 3 feet wide, multiply branched stems, spreading by suckers from roots, leaves are gray-green and deeply cut, fragrant summer flowers are very large with 5 to 6 crinkled white petals that resemble crepe paper surrounding golden stamens, useful for naturalizing on dry banks, may become invasive in a border.

Growing conditions and maintenance: Plant California tree poppies in poor, dry soil in full sun where invasive roots will not cause a problem. They are most successfully grown in Zones 8 to 10 but can survive in Zone 7 with a heavy winter mulch. Cut them back nearly to the ground in late fall.

Rosa
(RO-za)
ROSE

Rosa virginiana

Hardiness:	*Zones 2-10*
Plant type:	*shrub*
Height:	*4 to 20 feet*
Interest:	*flowers, foliage, fruit*
Soil:	*well-drained, organic*
Light:	*full sun*

The following shrub roses bear lovely, fragrant blossoms, attractive foliage, and showy fruit with very little care.

Selected species and varieties: *R. alba* 'Incarnata' (cottage rose)—4 to 6 feet, double white flowers with pink blush in early summer, scarlet fruit in fall; Zones 4-10. *R. banksiae*—15 to 20 feet, climbing habit requires support, stems are nearly thornless, leaves are evergreen, white or yellow flowers bloom midspring to early summer; Zones 7-8. *R. rugosa* (rugosa rose)—4 to 6 feet tall and wide, leaves are lustrous and deep green in summer, yellow, bronze, or red in fall, flowers are purple to white, fruit is deep red in fall, Zones 2-10; 'Alba'—single white flowers. *R. virginiana* (Virginia rose)—4 to 6 feet tall, dark green summer leaves turn orange, red, and yellow in fall, single flowers are pink, bloom in early summer; Zones 3-8.

Growing conditions and maintenance: Plant roses in well-drained soil amended with organic matter. They require very little pruning. Rugosa and Virginia roses tolerate salt spray and sandy soils.

Rudbeckia
(rood-BEK-ee-a)
CONEFLOWER

Rudbeckia fulgida var. sullivantii 'Goldsturm'

Hardiness: *Zones 4-9*

Plant type: *herbaceous perennial*

Height: *2 to 7 feet*

Interest: *flowers*

Soil: *well-drained*

Light: *full sun to light shade*

Coneflowers bear prolific yellow flowers with a contrasting center over an exceptionally long season. They are an undemanding perennial and a rewarding addition to nearly any sunny border. They combine particularly well with ornamental grasses in an informal garden.

Selected species and varieties: *R. fulgida* var. *sullivantii* 'Goldsturm'—24 inches tall, compact, dark green leaves set off the flowers perfectly, deep yellow raylike flower petals surround black-brown centers, produced early summer through fall, extremely free-flowering, resistant to powdery mildew. *R. nitida* 'Herbstsonne'—2 to 7 feet tall, bright green leaves, flowers are 3 to 4 inches across and have drooping yellow rays with green centers, bloom from mid to late summer, excellent for the back of borders, often requires staking.

Growing conditions and maintenance: Coneflowers thrive in well-drained soil in full sun and tolerate heat, making them a good choice for southern gardens. They will grow in light shade but produce fewer flowers.

Salvia
(SAL-vee-a)
SAGE

Salvia greggii

Hardiness: *Zones 4-10*

Plant type: *herbaceous perennial*

Height: *2 to 4 feet*

Interest: *flowers, foliage*

Soil: *well-drained*

Light: *full sun*

Sage is a shrubby perennial that offers colorful summer and fall flowers and attractive, often fragrant, foliage. It has square stems and small, tubular flowers characteristic of the mint family. Its neat growth habits and long flowering season makes it a useful addition to the perennial border.

Selected species and varieties: *S. azurea* spp. *pitcheri* (Pitcher's sage)—3 to 4 feet tall, 4 feet wide, azure blue flowers from late summer through fall; Zones 5-9. *S. greggii* (autumn sage)—2 to 3 feet tall, fall flowers are red, purple-red, pink, or coral, may become a small shrub in the south; Zones 7-10. *S.* x *superba* (perennial salvia)—2 to 3 feet tall, 2 feet wide, blue to violet-blue flowers on 4- to 8-inch flower stems throughout summer; Zones 5-8.

Growing conditions and maintenance: Sage thrives in moist, well-drained soil but will adapt to light shade and drier conditions and can withstand drought. Excess moisture in winter usually causes plants to rot. Cut back old stems in late fall or winter.

Santolina
(san-to-LEE-na)
LAVENDER COTTON

Santolina chamaecyparissus

Hardiness: *Zones 6-8*

Plant type: *herbaceous perennial*

Height: *18 to 24 inches*

Interest: *foliage, flowers*

Soil: *well-drained to dry*

Light: *full sun*

Lavender cotton forms a broad, spreading clump of aromatic leaves. It makes an attractive edging to a bed or walkway, or can be used as a low-growing specimen in a rock garden. It can be sheared to a tight, low hedge.

Selected species and varieties: *S. chamaecyparissus*—up to 24 inches tall with equal or greater spread, forms a broad, cushionlike, evergreen mound, aromatic leaves are silvery gray-green and ½ to 1½ inches long, yellow flowers are button-shaped in summer and are often removed to maintain clipped hedge.

Growing conditions and maintenance: Lavender cotton is a tough plant, well suited to adverse conditions such as drought and salt spray. It prefers dry soils of low fertility and becomes unattractive and open in fertile soils. Avoid excess moisture, especially in winter. Prune after flowering to promote dense growth, or shear anytime for a formal, low hedge.

Sedum
(SEE-dum)
STONECROP

Sedum x 'Autumn Joy'

Hardiness: *Zones 3-10*

Plant type: *succulent perennial*

Height: *6 inches to 2 feet*

Interest: *foliage, flowers*

Soil: *well-drained*

Light: *full sun to light shade*

Stonecrops are valued both for their thick succulent leaves and for their dense clusters of star-shaped flowers. They add color and rich texture to a perennial border or rock garden from spring through fall.

Selected species and varieties: *S.* x 'Autumn Joy'—15 to 24 inches tall, attractive all year long, leaves emerge gray-green in spring, flower buds are rosy pink in midsummer, opening to bronze-red flowers in fall, turning golden brown in winter. *S.* x 'Ruby Glow'—8 inches, purple-gray leaves, red flowers in late summer and fall, excellent for front of border. *S.* x 'Vera Jameson'—12 inches, coppery purple leaves, pink flowers in fall. *S. sieboldii*—6 to 9 inches, somewhat trailing habit, blue-gray leaves, pink flowers in fall.

Growing conditions and maintenance: Stonecrops tolerate nearly any well-drained soil, including sterile, dry sites. They spread without becoming invasive and are usually content to be left undisturbed for many years without needing division.

Solidago
(sol-i-DAY-go)
GOLDENROD

Solidago sphacelata 'Golden Fleece'

Hardiness: *Zones 3-9*

Plant type: *herbaceous perennial*

Height: *1 to 3 feet*

Interest: *flowers*

Soil: *well-drained*

Light: *full sun to light shade*

Goldenrods are easy to grow and produce abundant late-season flowers over an extended period. The bold yellow flowers occur in dense, feathery clusters on erect stems. They are a cheerful addition to informal borders, or in fresh or dried indoor arrangements.

Selected species and varieties: A number of excellent hybrids represent improvements to the wild goldenrods; 'Goldenmosa'—30 to 36 inches tall with large dark yellow flowers from late summer through fall; 'Golden Fleece'—12 to 24 inches tall, dwarf, spreading habit, dark green leaves, arching and multiply branched stems bear bright yellow flowers from late summer to early fall, good choice for ground cover.

Growing conditions and maintenance: Goldenrods thrive in any well-drained soil and look their best when fertility is low to average. A fertile site leads to rank, invasive growth. Tall varieties often require staking. Contrary to popular belief, goldenrod does not cause hay fever.

Spigelia
(spy-JEE-li-a)
PINKROOT, INDIAN PINK

Spigelia marilandica

Hardiness: *Zones 5-9*

Plant type: *herbaceous perennial*

Height: *1 to 2 feet*

Interest: *flowers*

Soil: *moist, well-drained, acid*

Light: *partial shade*

Pinkroot bears interesting trumpet-shaped flowers along one side of an arching stem. The 2-inch flowers are red with yellow throats, and all face upward, creating an unusual and pleasing effect. This is a nice selection for the front of a shady border or along a garden path, where its flower display can be viewed at close range.

Selected species and varieties: *S. marilandica*—1 to 2 feet tall, 18 inches wide, erect stems, 3- to 4-inch-long leaves, flowers are pinkish red with yellow throat and trumpet-shaped in elongated clusters at ends of stems, blooming late spring to early summer.

Growing conditions and maintenance: Plant pinkroot in a well-drained, slightly acid soil amended with organic matter. It thrives in partial shade, especially in warmer climates, but tolerates full sun if adequate moisture is supplied. It does not compete well with surface tree roots. Division of the clumps is an easy way to increase plants.

Spiraea
(spy-REE-a)
SPIREA

Spiraea x bumalda 'Anthony Waterer'

Hardiness: *Zones 3-8*

Plant type: *shrub*

Height: *3 to 5 feet*

Interest: *flowers, foliage*

Soil: *well-drained*

Light: *full sun*

Spireas are easy-to-grow deciduous shrubs that produce an abundance of dainty flowers in spring or summer. Spring-blooming spireas bear flowers in clusters along the entire length of the stems; summer-blooming types bear their flower clusters at the ends of stems.

Selected species and varieties: S. x *bumalda* 'Anthony Waterer'—2 to 4 feet tall, 4 to 5 feet wide, leaves emerge bronze in spring and turn blue-green in summer, carmine-pink flowers bloom in 4- to 6-inch clusters in summer. S. x *cinerea* 'Grefsheim'—4 to 5 feet tall and wide, arching stems, soft green leaves are 1 inch long, white flowers bloom along stem in spring. S. *nipponica* 'Snowmound'—3 to 5 feet tall and wide, dark blue-green leaves, white flowers bloom along stem in late spring.

Growing conditions and maintenance: Spireas perform best in full sun; they tolerate partial shade but produce fewer flowers. They adapt to nearly any well-drained soil. Remove faded flowers of 'Anthony Waterer' spirea to encourage a second bloom.

Stachys
(STA-kis)
LAMB'S EARS

Stachys 'Helene Von Stein'

Hardiness: *Zones 4-9*

Plant type: *herbaceous perennial*

Height: *6 to 18 inches*

Interest: *foliage*

Soil: *well-drained*

Light: *full sun to light shade*

Lamb's ears is a low-growing, spreading perennial that adds soft color and texture to the front of a perennial border, alongside a path, or as a ground cover. Its gray-green leaves are covered with white hairs, giving them the appearance and feel of velvet. Nonflowering varieties eliminate the need for removing flowers that are often considered unattractive.

Selected species and varieties: S. *byzantina* 'Silver Carpet'—12 to 15 inches tall with 18- to 24-inch spread, leaves and stems densely covered with white hairs, leaves up to 4 inches long, no flowers; 'Helene Von Stein'—larger leaves, few flowers, tolerates hot, humid weather.

Growing conditions and maintenance: Plant lamb's ears in well-drained soil that is not too fertile. Excess moisture encourages leaf rot. For use as a ground cover, space plants 12 to 18 inches apart. Remove old leaves before new growth begins in spring.

Stephanandra
(stef-a-NAN-dra)
LACE SHRUB

Stephanandra incisa 'Crispa'

Hardiness: *Zones 3-8*

Plant type: *shrub*

Height: *1½ to 3 feet*

Interest: *foliage*

Soil: *moist, well-drained, acid*

Light: *full sun to light shade*

Lace shrub is a tidy plant with a gracefully mounding habit. It may be grown on banks to prevent erosion or may be used as a low hedge or tall ground cover. Its dense foliage and low habit make it well suited to growing under low windows or among tall, leggy shrubs in a mixed border.

Selected species and varieties: S. *incisa* 'Crispa'—1½ to 3 feet tall, 4 feet wide, spreads by arching branches rooting readily when they touch the ground, leaves are 1 to 2 inches long, deeply lobed, bright green, turning reddish purple or red-orange in the fall, inconspicuous pale yellow flowers appear in early summer.

Growing conditions and maintenance: Plant lace shrub in moist, acid soil in full sun or light shade. Add generous amounts of organic matter to the soil prior to planting to help retain moisture. Plants require little pruning other than removing winter-damaged tips in the early spring.

Syringa
(si-RING-ga)
LILAC

Syringa patula 'Miss Kim'

Hardiness: *Zones 3-8*

Plant type: *shrub*

Height: *3 to 6 feet*

Interest: *flowers, foliage*

Soil: *moist, well-drained*

Light: *full sun*

Lilacs are old-fashioned, deciduous shrubs that produce fragrant, late-spring flowers in dense grapelike clusters. They make attractive landscape specimens and informal hedges, and are well suited to use in a mixed-shrub border.

Selected species and varieties: *S. microphylla* 'Superba'—6 feet tall and 12 feet wide with dense, wide-spreading habit, medium green leaves 1 to 2½ inches long, deep pink flowers, prolific; Zones 4-7. *S. patula* 'Miss Kim'—3 feet tall and wide (but may grow somewhat larger under ideal conditions), dark green leaves 2 to 5 inches long, flowers in 3-inch-long clusters are purple in bud and icy blue when open; Zones 3-8.

Growing conditions and maintenance: Plant lilacs in well-drained soil amended with organic matter. Fertilize every other year. Prune the oldest stems with reduced flower production back to the ground immediately after flowering, and remove faded flowers as well.

Taxus
(TAKS-us)
YEW

Taxus x media 'Hicksii'

Hardiness: *Zones 4-7*

Plant type: *shrub*

Height: *2 to 20 feet*

Interest: *foliage, fruit*

Soil: *fertile, moist, well-drained*

Light: *full sun to full shade*

Yews are evergreen shrubs with flat, needlelike leaves. The deep green glossy foliage provides a stunning contrast with other, brightly colored, plants. Yews are effective as foundation plants, hedges, and specimens. Seeds, leaves, and bark are poisonous.

Selected species and varieties: *T. baccata* 'Repandens'—2 to 4 feet tall, 12 to 15 feet across, dwarf, wide-spreading habit, extremely dark green leaves, red fruit; Zones 5-7. *T. cuspidata* 'Densa'—3 to 4 feet high, 6 to 8 feet wide, dense habit, dark green leaves, abundant fruit; 'Thayerae'—up to 8 feet tall, 16 feet wide, flat-topped habit. *T. x media* 'Densiformis'—3 to 4 feet tall, 4 to 6 feet wide, dense, bright green leaves; 'Hicksii'—20 feet tall, ascending branches, columnar habit, dark green leaves.

Growing conditions and maintenance: Excellent drainage is essential for growing yews. They perform well in sun or shade and benefit from protection from drying winds. Yews take pruning and shearing well.

Vaccinium
(vak-SIN-i-um)
BLUEBERRY

Vaccinium corymbosum

Hardiness: *Zones 2-8*

Plant type: *shrub*

Height: *6 inches to 12 feet*

Interest: *leaves, flowers, fruit*

Soil: *moist, well-drained, acid*

Light: *full sun to partial shade*

The blue-green summer leaves of blueberries become a riot of color in fall. Delicate spring flowers and edible, delicious berries add to the landscape value of this native shrub.

Selected species and varieties: *V. corymbosum* (highbush blueberry)—6 to 12 feet tall, 8 to 12 feet wide, multiple-stem shrub with rounded, upright habit, leaves are 1 to 3½ inches long, blue-green in summer, turning red, orange, yellow, and bronze in fall, flowers are white, urn-shaped, ½ inch long, fruit is blue-black, ¼ to ½ inch across; Zones 3-8. *V. angustifolium* (lowbush blueberry)—6 inches to 2 feet tall, 2 feet wide, low spreading habit, leaves are ⅓ to ¾ inch long, blue-green in summer, turning red to bronze in fall, flowers are white with red tinge, delicious fruit is blue-black and ¼ to ½ inch across; Zones 2-6.

Growing conditions and maintenance: Plant blueberries in moist, well-drained soil with a pH of 4.5 to 5.5. Add generous amounts of organic matter prior to planting. Mulch to preserve moisture. Prune after fruiting.

Veronica
(ve-RON-i-ka)
SPEEDWELL

Veronica 'Sunny Border Blue'

Hardiness: *Zones 4-8*

Plant type: *herbaceous perennial*

Height: *10 to 48 inches*

Interest: *flowers*

Soil: *well-drained*

Light: *full sun to partial shade*

The long-lasting flowers of veronica add intense color and a vertical accent to a perennial border.

Selected species and varieties: *V. incana*—white leaves are woolly and form a 6-inch mat, flowers are lilac-blue in early summer on erect, 12- to 18-inch stems. *V. longifolia*—2 to 4 feet, dense lilac-blue flowers bloom for 6 to 8 weeks, midsummer to fall. *V. spicata*—10 to 36 inches tall, blue flowers in late spring to midsummer. *V. teucrium* 'Crater Lake Blue'—12 to 15 inches, flowers are bright blue in loose, terminal clusters, late spring to early summer. Veronica hybrids: 'Blue Charm'—24 inches tall, lavender-blue flowers throughout summer; 'Minuet'—15 inches, pink flowers in late spring and early summer; 'Sunny Border Blue'—18 to 24 inches, leaves are lush, dark green, dark blue flowers bloom summer to fall.

Growing conditions and maintenance: Plant speedwell in well-drained soil. It thrives in full sun and will adapt to partial shade but will flower less. Taller types may need support. Deadhead for extended blooming season.

Viburnum
(vy-BUR-num)
VIBURNUM

Viburnum plicatum 'Shasta'

Hardiness: *Zones 4-8*

Plant type: *shrub*

Height: *4 to 10 feet*

Interest: *flowers, foliage, fruit*

Soil: *moist, well-drained*

Light: *full sun to partial shade*

Viburnums are highly ornamental shrubs that provide landscape interest in several seasons. Many produce showy, often fragrant, spring flowers, colorful fall fruit that can persist well into winter, and leaves that are deep green in summer and frequently turn red in the fall.

Selected species and varieties: *V. carlesii* (Koreanspice viburnum)—4 to 8 feet tall and nearly as wide, deciduous, rounded, dense, upright habit, leaves are 1 to 4 inches long, dull, dark green, often turning dark red in fall, flower buds are deep pink, opening to white, extremely fragrant, spring-blooming flowers grouped in 2- to 3-inch clusters, excellent choice for planting near entrance or walkway where fragrance can be appreciated; Zones 4-8. *V.* x *carlcephalum* (fragrant viburnum)—6 to 10 feet high and wide, deciduous, rounded, open habit, leaves are up to 4 inches long, dark green, turning reddish purple in fall, flower buds are pink, opening to fragrant white flowers in 5-inch clusters in late spring; Zones 5-8. *V. dilatatum* (linden viburnum)—8 to 10 feet tall, 6 to 10 feet wide, upright, deciduous, spreading habit, leaves 2 to 5

inches long, coarsely toothed, dark green, lustrous, white flowers in flattened 3- to 5-inch clusters, covering entire plant, in late spring, fruit is bright red or scarlet, produced in heavy clusters, effective in fall and early winter, best used in groupings such as a screen or shrub border; Zones 5-7. *V.* var. *plicatum tomentosum* (double file viburnum)—8 to 10 feet tall with slightly greater spread, broad, rounded form with horizontal branches, leaves are 2 to 4 inches long, toothed, dark green, turning reddish purple in fall, flowers are white, in 2- to 6-inch flattened clusters, held above the foliage on short stems, accentuating horizontal habit, bright red fruit in late summer is usually eaten quickly by birds, makes a superb specimen, Zones 5-8; 'Shasta'—compact variety, 6 feet tall, 12 feet wide, creamy white flowers. *V.* x 'Eskimo'—4 feet tall, 5 feet wide, compact, uniform habit, leaves are glossy, dark, semi-evergreen, flower buds are pale pink, opening to creamy white flowers in 3-inch snowball-shaped clusters in

Viburnum carlesii

spring, dull red fruit turns black in late summer, useful as specimen or low hedge; Zones 6-8.

Growing conditions and maintenance: Viburnums transplant easily and thrive in moist, well-drained soil supplemented with organic matter. They adapt to both full sun and partial shade. When necessary, prune viburnums immediately after flowering.

Vinca
(VING-ka)
PERIWINKLE, MYRTLE

Vinca minor

Hardiness: *Zones 3-9*

Plant type: *evergreen ground cover*

Height: *3 to 6 inches*

Interest: *foliage, flowers*

Soil: *moist, well-drained*

Light: *full sun to full shade*

Periwinkle is a wide-spreading evergreen ground cover that provides a dense carpet of leaves in a relatively short time. Its runners extend in all directions along the ground, rooting where they contact soil. In spring, lilac-blue flowers appear in profusion and continue blooming sporadically into the summer.

Selected species and varieties: *V. minor*—3 to 6 inches tall, spreading indefinitely, fast growing, mat-forming habit, leaves emerge yellow-green and mature to dark, glossy green, ½ to 1½ inches long, flowers are lilac-blue, 1 inch across, blooming mainly in the spring, effective ground cover under trees or in front of shrubs.

Growing conditions and maintenance: Periwinkle spreads quickly in well-drained moist soil amended with organic matter. In warmer climates, it performs better in light to deep shade. Space plants to be used as a ground cover 12 inches apart. Shear once a year after the main flowering season to promote dense growth.

Yucca
(YUK-a)
YUCCA

Yucca filamentosa 'Golden Sword'

Hardiness: *Zones 5-10*

Plant type: *shrub*

Height: *2 to 12 feet*

Interest: *foliage, flowers*

Soil: *light, well-drained*

Light: *full sun*

Yucca develops a rosette of sword-shaped evergreen leaves that provide a striking accent to rock and perennial gardens or among shrubs. In summer, stiff stems arise from the center of the rosette, bearing white, nodding flowers.

Selected species and varieties: *Y. filamentosa* (yucca, Adam's-needle)—2- to 3-foot-tall rosette of leaves, 3- to 12-foot-tall flower scape, leaves are 2½ feet long with sharp terminal spine, threads curl off margins, flowers are creamy white, 1 to 2 inches long, in erect clusters, Zones 5-9; 'Bright Edge'—leaves have gold margins; 'Golden Sword'—variegated leaves with yellow center and green margin. *Y. glauca* (soapweed)—similar habit as *Y. filamentosa* but more delicate, leaves have white margins, flowers are greenish white on 3- to 4½-foot stems, good choice for rock gardens; Zones 4-8.

Growing conditions and maintenance: Yuccas thrive in full sun in soil that is well drained to dry. They are highly tolerant of drought.

Zantedeschia
(zan-tee-DES-ki-a)
CALLA LILY, ARUM LILY

Zantedeschia aethiopica

Hardiness: *Zones 9-10*

Plant type: *herbaceous perennial*

Height: *24 to 36 inches*

Interest: *flowers, foliage*

Soil: *moist, organic*

Light: *full sun to partial shade*

Calla lilies produce bold, arrow-shaped leaves and flowers composed of a gently flaring, white spathe surrounding a central golden spadix. They grow from tender rhizomes and survive winters only in mild climates, unless they are dug up in the fall for indoor storage. They are well suited to growing at the edge of a pond or stream, where the soil is constantly moist. They can also be planted in a moist perennial border or in a container.

Selected species and varieties: *Z. aethiopica* 'Crowborough'—24 to 36 inches tall, 24 inches wide, leaves arise from base and form a dense, erect cluster, white flowers are 6 to 10 inches on leafless stalk, spathe wraps around fragrant yellow spadix, blooming late spring to early summer.

Growing conditions and maintenance: Plant calla lily rhizomes 4 inches deep in soil that is constantly moist. They thrive in bogs and near water. To maintain adequate moisture in garden soil, add generous amounts of organic matter prior to planting.

Acknowledgments

The editors wish to thank the following individuals and institutions for their valuable assistance in the preparation of this volume:

Ann Armstrong, Charlotte, N.C.; Dan Banks, Phoenix, Ariz.; Elizabeth Barclay, Santa Barbara, Calif.; Barbara Bower, Crenshaw & Douget Turfgrass, Austin, Tex.; C. Colston Burrell, Minneapolis, Minn.; Margery Daughtrey, Long Island Horticultural Research Laboratory, Riverhead, N.Y.; Mr. and Mrs. Wilbur Davis, Austin, Tex.; Tom Delaney, Professional Lawn Care Association of America, Marietta, Ga.; Margaret Fabrizio, Ithaca, N.Y.; Douglas Fender, Turfgrass Producers International, Rolling Meadows, Ill.; Stanton Gill, Regional Specialist, Nursery and Greenhouse Management, University of Maryland Cooperative Extension Research and Education Center, Ellicott City; Eric and Jacqueline Gratz, Baltimore, Md.; Gale Haggard, Plants of the Southwest, Santa Fe, N.M.; Don Hylton, Richmond, Va.; Bob Lyons, Horticultural Department, Virginia Polytechnic Institute and State University, Blacksburg, Va.; Marnie Mahoney, Del Mar, Calif.; Merrifield Garden Center, Merrifield, Va.; Kevin Morris, Director, National Turfgrass Evaluation Program, Beltsville, Md.; Dick Peterson, Austin, Tex.; Daryl Puterbaugh, New York, N.Y.; Richard Secor, Rainmatic Corporation, Omaha, Neb.; John Stevens, Alexandria, Va.; André Viette, Fishersville, Va.; Pauline Vollmer, Baltimore, Md.; Will H. Walker, Austin, Tex.; Weedblock/Easy Gardener, Waco, Tex.; Mr. and Mrs. Allan R. Youngs, Atlanta, Ga.

Picture Credits

The sources for the illustrations that appear in this volume are listed below. Credits from left to right are separated by semicolons, from top to bottom by dashes.

Cover: © Roger Foley/designed by Oehme, van Sweden and Associates, Inc. Backcover insets: Ken Druse/The Natural Garden—art by Stephen R. Wagner—Jerry Pavia. End papers: © Karen Bussolini 1995. 2, 3: © Roger Foley/designed by Oehme, van Sweden and Associates, Inc. 4: Susanna Napierala-Cox; courtesy Robert S. Hebb. 6, 7: Steven Still. 8: © Gay Bumgarner/Tony Stone Images, New York City. 9: Roger Foley. 10, 11: Suzanne O'Connell; Jerry Pavia. 12: Map by John Drummond, Time-Life Books. 15, 16: Art by Andrew Lewis/ARCOBALENO. 17: Jerry Pavia. 18: Roger Foley. 19: Map by John Drummond, Time-Life Books. 20: Jerry Pavia. 21: Mary-Gray Hunter/designed by Dan B. Franklin, Landscape Architect, ASLA, Atlanta, Ga., courtesy Mr. and Mrs. Allan R. Youngs. 23: © Lynne Harrison—© Cosmo Condina/Tony Stone Images, New York City. 24: Jerry Pavia/designed by Johnathan Plant, Los Angeles. 25: Art by Andrew Lewis/ARCOBALENO. 27: Cynthia Woodyard—art by Stephen R. Wagner. 28: Jerry Pavia. 29: Charles Mann. 30, 31: Cynthia Woodyard. 33: © Michael Selig/designed by Oehme, van Sweden and Associates, Inc./courtesy Baltimore garden of Eric and Jacqueline Gratz. 34: Dency Kane. 35: Cynthia Woodyard. 36: Art by Nicholas Fasciano. 37: Map by John Drummond, Time-Life Books. 38-41: Ken Druse/The Natural Garden. 42: © Mark Lovejoy. 43: Dency Kane. 44: Art by Stephen R. Wagner. 45: Art by Stephen R. Wagner—Thomas E. Eltzroth. 46, 47: © Virginia P. Weinland/Photo Researchers—art by Andrew Lewis/ARCOBALENO. 48, 49: Cynthia Woodyard. 50, 51: Charles Mann. 52, 53: Dency Kane/Landscape by Atlantic Nurseries, Dix Hills, N.Y.; Dency Kane/designed by Marla Gagnum, East Hampton, N.Y. 54, 55: Jerry Pavia/designed by Beautrice Grow. 56, 57: Jerry Pavia/designed by Philip Marks. 58, 59: © Roger Foley/designed by Osamu Shimizu; Roger Foley. 60: Cynthia Woodyard (2)—Charles Mann (2). 61: Dency Kane/Landscape by Atlantic Nurseries, Dix Hills, N.Y. (2)—Dency Kane/designed by Marla Gagnum, East Hampton, N.Y. (2). 62: Jerry Pavia/designed by Beautrice Grow (2)—Jerry Pavia/designed by Philip Marks (2). 63: © Roger Foley/designed by Osamu Shimizu (2)—Roger Foley (2). 64, 65: © Michael Selig/designed by Oehme, van Sweden and Associates, Inc. 67: Art by Stephen R. Wagner. 68: © Richard Shiell—art by Stephen R. Wagner. 69: Art by Stephen R. Wagner. 70: © Roger Foley/designed by Osamu Shimizu. 71-73: Art by Stephen R. Wagner. 74: Mark Lovejoy; © Christine M. Douglas/Photo Researchers. 75, 76: Art by Stephen R. Wagner. 77: Alison Shaw. 78, 79: Art by Stephen R. Wagner, except for landscape design plan, art by Andrew Lewis/ARCOBALENO. 81: © Gary Irving/Tony Stone Images, New York City. 82: Art by Nicholas Fasciano. 83, 84: Art by Stephen R. Wagner. 85: © Saxon Holt—art by Stephen R. Wagner. 86, 87: Art by Stephen R. Wagner. 94: Art by Nicholas Fasciano. 95: Art by Nicholas Fasciano—art by Fred Holz (2). 96-99: Art by Nicholas Fasciano. 100: Art by Fred Holz—art by Nicholas Fasciano (2). 101: Art by Nicholas Fasciano (2)—art by Robert E. Hynes. 108: Map by John Drummond, Time-Life Books. 110: © Richard Shiell; Michael Dirr. 111: Michael Dirr; © Richard Shiell (2). 112: Joanne Pavia; Dency Kane; Thomas E. Eltzroth. 113: Ken Druse/The Natural Garden; Jerry Pavia; Steven Still. 114: Jerry Pavia; © Richard Shiell; Jerry Pavia. 115: Michael Dirr; Thomas E. Eltzroth; Michael Dirr. 116: Jerry Pavia; Steven Still; Jerry Pavia. 117: © R. Todd Davis; © Richard Shiell; Jerry Pavia. 118: Steven Still (2); © Saxon Holt. 119: Steven Still; Michael Dirr; Jerry Pavia. 120: Jerry Pavia; © Richard Shiell; Jerry Pavia. 121: Thomas E. Eltzroth (2); Jerry Pavia. 122: © Richard Shiell; Jerry Pavia (2). 123: Steven Still; Thomas E. Eltzroth; Steven Still. 124: Jerry Pavia (2); © R. Todd Davis. 125: Jerry Pavia; Michael Dirr; © Richard Shiell. 126: Jerry Pavia; © Richard Shiell (2). 127: Joanne Pavia; Jerry Pavia; Joanne Pavia. 128: © R. Todd Davis; Steven Still; Joanne Pavia. 129: Jerry Pavia; © Richard Shiell; Jerry Pavia. 130: Joanne

Bibliography

Books:

All about Landscaping. San Ramon, Calif.: Ortho Books, 1988.

Armitage, Allan M. *Herbaceous Perennial Plants.* Athens, Ga.: Varsity Press, 1989.

Arms, Karen. *Environmental Gardening.* Savannah, Ga.: Halfmoon Publishing, 1992.

Basic Gardening Illustrated (Sunset Books). Menlo Park, Calif.: Lane Publishing, 1981.

Bormann, F. Herbert, Diana Balmori, and Gordon T. Geballe. *Redesigning the American Lawn.* New Haven, Ct.: Yale University Press, 1993.

Carleton, R. Milton. *The Small Garden Book.* New York: Macmillan, 1971.

Christopher, Thomas. *Water-Wise Gardening.* New York: Simon and Schuster, 1994.

Clausen, Ruth Rogers, and Nicolas H. Ekstrom. *Perennials for American Gardens.* New York: Random House, 1989.

Cox, Jeff. *Landscaping with Nature.* Emmaus, Pa.: Rodale Press, 1991.

Cresson, Charles O. *Ornamental Trees* (Burpee American Gardening series). New York: Prentice Hall Gardening, 1993.

DeFreitas, Stan. *The Water-Thrifty Garden.* Dallas: Taylor Publishing, 1993.

Dirr, Michael A. *Manual of Woody Landscape Plants.* Champaign, Ill.: Stipes Publishing, 1990.

Druse, Ken. *Flowering Shrubs* (Burpee American Gardening series). New York: Prentice Hall Gardening, 1992.

Easy-Care Gardening (Sunset Books). Menlo Park, Calif.: Lane Publishing, 1988.

Ellefson, Connie Lockhart, Thomas L. Stephens, and Doug Welsh. *Xeriscape Gardening.* New York: Macmillan, 1992.

Ellis, Barbara, and Fern Marshall Bradley (Eds.). *The Organic Gardener's Handbook of Natural Insect and Disease Control.* Emmaus, Pa.: Rodale Press, 1992.

Flint, Harrison L. *Landscape Plants for Eastern North America.* New York: John Wiley and Sons, 1983.

Garden Design Ideas (The Best of *Fine Gardening* series). Newtown, Ct.: Taunton Press, 1994.

The Garden That Cares for Itself. San Ramon, Calif.: Ortho Books, 1990.

Garden Pests and Diseases. Menlo Park, Calif.: Sunset Books, 1993.

Gilmer, Maureen, and the Editors of Consumer Reports Books. *Easy Lawn and Garden Care.* Yonkers, N.Y.: Consumers Union, 1994.

Harper, Peter, with Chris Madsen and Jeremy Light. *The Natural Garden Book.* New York: Simon and Schuster, 1994.

Hastings, Don. *Gardening in the South with Don Hastings.* Dallas: Taylor Publishing, 1987.

Hebb, Robert S. *Low Maintenance Perennials.* New York: Quadrangle/New York Times Book Company, 1975.

How to Build Walks, Walls, and Patio Floors (Sunset Books). Menlo Park, Calif.: Lane Books, 1973.

How to Select, Use, and Maintain Garden Equipment. San Francisco: Ortho Books, 1981.

Hudak, Joseph. *Shrubs in the Landscape.* New York: McGraw-Hill, 1984.

Improving Your Garden Soil. San Ramon, Calif.: Ortho Books, 1992.

Jenkins, Virginia Scott. *The Lawn.* Washington, D.C.: Smithsonian Institution Press, 1994.

Johnson, Warren, and Howard Lyon. *Insects That Feed on Trees and Shrubs.* Ithaca, N.Y.: Cornell University Press, 1976.

Knopf, Jim. *The Xeriscape Flower Gardener.* Boulder, Colo.: Johnson Publishing, 1991.

Kramer, Jack. *Gardening without Stress and Strain.* New York: Charles Scribner's Sons, 1973.

Lacey, Stephen. *Lawns and Ground Cover* (National Trust Guide series). North Pomfret, Vt.: Trafalgar Square Publishing, 1991.

Liberty Hyde Bailey Hortorium. *Hortus Third.* New York: Macmillan, 1976.

Loewer, Peter:

Tough Plants for Tough Places. Emmaus, Pa.: Rodale Press, 1992.

The Wild Gardener. Harrisburg, Pa.: Stackpole Books, 1991.

Lovejoy, Ann. *The American Mixed Border.* New York: Macmillan, 1993.

MacCaskey, Michael. *Lawns and Ground Covers.* Tucson, Ariz.: Fisher Publishing, 1982.

McHoy, Peter. *Pruning.* New York: Abbeville Press, 1993.

Mossman, Tam. *Gardens That Care for Themselves.* Garden City, N.Y.: Doubleday, 1978.

Neumann, Erik A. *Landscape Plants for the Twenty-First Century.* Washington, D.C.: Friends of the National Arboretum, 1992.

Ogden, Scott. *Gardening Success with Difficult Soils.* Dallas: Taylor Publishing, 1992.

O'Keefe, John M. *Water-Conserving Gardens and Landscapes.* Pownal, Vt.: Storey

163

Communications, 1992.

Ortho Home Garden Problem Solver. San Ramon, Calif.: Ortho Books, 1993.

Perennials (Vol. 1 of *Index Hortensis*, compiled and edited by Piers Trehane). Wimborne, Dorset, U.K.: Quarterjack Publishing, 1989.

Perry, Bob. *Landscape Plants for Western Regions.* Claremont, Calif.: Land Design Publishing, 1992.

Reader's Digest Book of Skills and Tools. Pleasantville, N.Y.: Reader's Digest Association, 1983.

Reader's Digest Practical Guide to Home Landscaping. Pleasantville, N.Y.: Reader's Digest Association, 1986.

Roach, Margaret. *Groundcovers* (Burpee American Gardening series). New York: Prentice Hall Gardening, 1993.

Rose, Graham. *The Low Maintenance Garden.* New York: Viking Press, 1983.

Schuler, Stanley. *Gardening with Ease.* New York: Macmillan, 1970.

Sinclair, Wayne, Warren Johnson, and Howard Lyon. *Diseases of Trees and Shrubs.* Ithaca, N.Y.: Cornell University Press, 1987.

Sombke, Laurence. *Beautiful Easy Lawns and Landscapes.* Old Saybrook, Ct.: Globe Pequot Press, 1994.

Springer, Lauren. *Waterwise Gardening* (Burpee American Gardening series). New York: Prentice Hall Gardening, 1994.

Still, Steven M. *Manual of Herbaceous Ornamental Plants* (4th ed.). Champaign, Ill.: Stipes Publishing, 1994.

Successful Organic Gardening: Trees, Shrubs, and Vines. Emmaus, Pa.: Rodale Press, 1993.

Taylor, Patricia A. *Easy Care Shade Flowers.* New York: Simon and Schuster, 1993.

Taylor's Guide to Gardening in the South. Boston: Houghton Mifflin, 1992.

Taylor's Guide to Gardening in the Southwest. Boston: Houghton Mifflin, 1992.

Taylor's Guide to Water-Saving Gardening. Boston: Houghton Mifflin, 1990.

Thomas, Graham Stuart. *Plants for Ground-Cover.* Portland, Ore.: Sagapress/Timber Press, 1992.

Wasowski, Sally, with Andy Wasowski. *Gardening with Native Plants of the South.* Dallas: Taylor Publishing, 1994.

Weather-Wise Gardening. San Francisco: Ortho Books, 1974.

The Western Garden Book (Sunset Books). Menlo Park, Calif.: Lane Publishing, 1990.

Whitner, Jan Kowalczewski. *Stonescaping* (Garden Way Publishing). Pownal, Vt.: Storey Communications, 1992.

Williams, Niña, and Rebecca R. Sawyer. *Country Living: Country Gardens.* New York: Hearst Books (William Morrow), 1993.

Wyman, Donald. *The Saturday Morning Gardener.* New York: Collier Books (Macmillan), 1974.

Yepsen, Robert. *The Encyclopedia of Natural Insect and Disease Control.* Emmaus, Pa.: Rodale Press, 1984.

Zucker, Isabel. *Flowering Shrubs and Small Trees.* Revised and expanded by Derek Fell. New York: Grove Weidenfeld, 1990.

Periodicals:

Bir, Richard E. "Soil Drainage: What's Soggy, What's Not, and What to Do about It." *Fine Gardening,* July/August 1993.

Carney, Nancy. "How to Shop for Shrubs and Trees." *Fine Gardening,* May/June 1993.

Galbreath, Bob. "Water Wisdom: Watering Slopes." *Southern California Gardener,* March/April 1994.

"Getting the Best of Groundcovers." *Avant Gardener,* October 1994.

Gillis, Cynthia. "Making a Moss Garden." *Fine Gardening,* September/October 1991.

Hallgren, Lee. "The Kinds of Sun and Shade." *Fine Gardening,* May/June 1993.

"Raise Your Garden to New Heights." *Southern Living Garden Guide,* Spring/ Summer 1992.

Rosenblum, Chip, and Gail Rosenblum. "Island Beds in a Brick Sea." *Fine Gardening,* November/December 1989.

Shimizu, Holly, and Osamu Shimizu. "Designing a Hillside Garden." *Fine Gardening,* March/April 1991.

Sulgrove, Sabina Mueller. "Promising Landscape Ivies from the American Ivy Society." *American Nurseryman,* September 1, 1987.

Other Sources:

Jones, Gerald E. "Xeriscape." Booklet. San Antonio: Texas Agricultural Extension Service, 1991.

"Pruning Techniques." *Plants and Gardens, Brooklyn Botanic Garden Record,* 1994.

Roberts, Eliot C., and Beverly C. Roberts. "Lawn and Sports Turf Benefits." Booklet. Pleasant Hill, Tenn.: Lawn Institute, n.d.

"Trees: A Gardener's Guide." *Plants and Gardens, Brooklyn Botanic Garden Record,* 1992.

"Water-Conserving Plants and Landscapes for the Bay Area." Oakland, Calif.: East Bay Municipal Utility District, 1990.

"Xeriscape Landscaping in the Austin Area." Booklet. Austin, Tex.: Xeriscape Garden Club of the Austin Area, Environmental and Conservation Services, June 1993.

Index